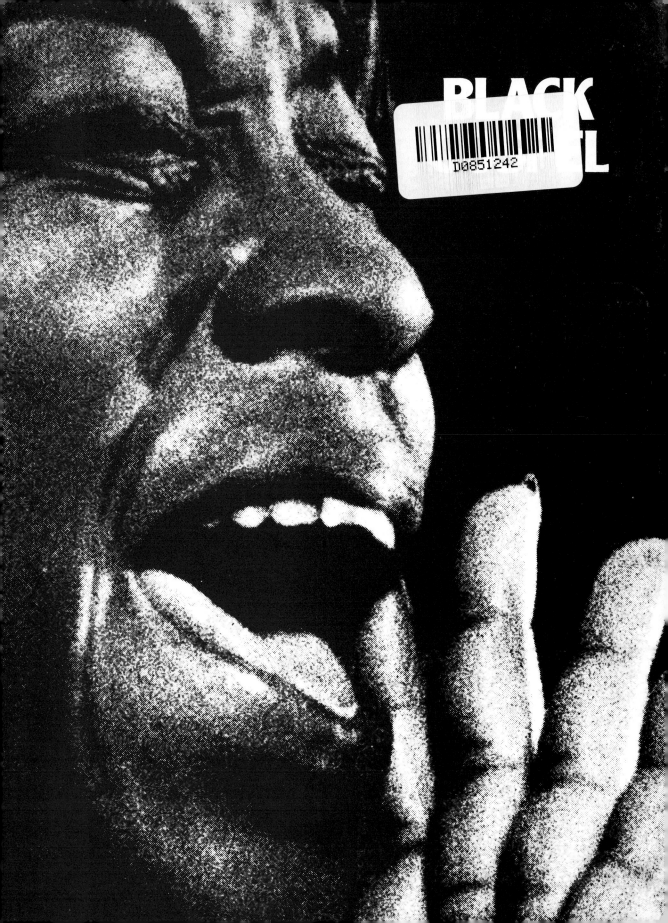

BLACK

L

*The Patterson Singers*

Lippman + Rau

# BLACK GOSPEL

## An Illustrated History of the Gospel Sound

## Viv Broughton

**BLANDFORD PRESS**
Poole · Dorset

First published in the U.K. in 1985 by
Blandford Press,
Link House, West Street, Poole,
Dorset, BH15 1LL

Distributed in the United States by
Sterling Publishing Co., Inc.,
2 Park Avenue, New York, N.Y. 10016

**British Library Cataloguing in Publication Data**

Broughton, Viv
    Black gospel: an illustrated history
    of the gospel sound.
    1. Gospel music——History
    I. Title
    783.7'09          ML3187

ISBN 0 7137 1530 8 (Hardback)
ISBN 0 7137 1540 5 (Paperback)

Designed by Viv Broughton and Blackrose Press,
London, EC1.
Typeset by Newstech, London EC1.
Printed in Great Britain by R.J. Acford
Chichester, Sussex.

To the following people who spared their time to help me
research this book, I will be eternally grateful:

Lyn Abbot, Simon Albery, Maggie Allen, Tim Anderson
Chris Barber, Madeline Bell, Milton Biggham, Simon
Black, David Bruce, Shirley Caesar, Marlene Cato,
George Chandler, The Clark Family, James Cleveland,
Tony Cummings, Jessy Dixon, George Escoffery, Juliet
Fletcher, Rupert Francis, L D Frazier, Patrick Friday,
Ray Funk, Al Green, Simon Hammond, Gloria
Hawkins, Tony Heilbut, David Horn, Maxine Jarret,
Ken Johnson, Paul Johnson, Terry Jervis, Anne Knox,
Bob Laughton, Justin Lewis, Horst Lippman, Movery
Livingstone, Gentry McCreary, Earl Malone, Bazil and
Andrea Meade, Fred Mendehlson, Opall Nations, Mau-
reen Quinlan, Jean Reynolds, Clive Richardson, Steve
Roud, Moses Sephula, Anna Smallwood, Frank Stewart,
Paulette Vassell, Mike Vernon, Doug Wallace, Dionne
Warwick, Ralph Weekes.

I'd also like to thank Stuart Booth at Blandford Press
for taking the risk and Val McCalla at *The Voice* for
creating the circumstances. Most of all though I'm in-
debted to Nikki Collins, who prodded me to start, scol-
ded me to finish and generally advised and assisted
beyond the call of duty.

I must also acknowledge the invaluable source material
gleaned from the following books and publications: *The
Gospel Sound* by Tony Heilbut (Simon & Schuster 1971);
*The Story of The Jubilee Singers and Their Songs* (Hodder &
Stoughton 1876); *The Devil's Music* by Giles Oakley
(Ariel Books 1976); *The Country Blues* by Samuel Char-
ters (Da Capo 1959); *Gospel Records 1937-1971* by Ce-
dric Hayes (Karl Emil Knudsen 1973); *Where Do We Go
From Here?* by Ira Brooks (I.V. Brooks 1982); *The Progress
Of Gospel Music* by Dr Joan Hillsman (Vantage Press
1983); *Sinful Tunes & Spirituals* by Dena J. Epstein (Uni-
versity of Illinois Press 1977); *The Music of Black Ameri-
cans* by Eileen Southern (W.W. Norton 1971); *Recording
The Blues* by R M W Dixon and J Godrich (Studio Vista
1971); *Folk Song of The American Negro* by John Wesley
Work (Negro Universities Press 1915); *Charles Albert
Tindley* by Horace Clarence Boyer (Black Perspective In
Music 1983); *Black Religions In The New World* by George
Eaton Simpson (Columbia University Press 1978); and
sundry references from *Gospelrama News, Contemporary
Christian Music, Buzz, Black Music, Gospel News Journal,
Exodus, Gospel Review, Ebony, Jet, Time, Blues Unlimited,
The Savoy Sound* and *Ethnomusicology Journal*.

In addition, I've borrowed freely from material published by Doug Seroff, Paul Oliver and Adam Finn, who all
deserve special credit for their work.

To
My Mum and Dad,
Nikki &
Daniel and Matthew

# Contents

'There is no music like that music, no drama like the drama of the saints rejoicing, the sinners moaning, the tambourines racing, and all those voices coming together and crying holy unto the Lord. There is still, for me, no pathos quite like the pathos of those multi-coloured, worn, somehow triumphant and transfigured faces, speaking from the depths of a visible, tangible, continuing despair of the goodness of the Lord. I have never seen anything to equal the fire and excitement that sometimes, without warning, fills a church, causing the church, as Leadbelly and so many others have testified, to "rock". Nothing that has happened to me since, equals the power and the glory that I sometimes felt when, in the middle of a sermon, I knew that I was somehow, by some miracle, really carrying, as they said, 'the Word' – when the church and I were one. Their pain and their joy were mine, and mine were theirs – they surrendered their pain and joy to me, I surrendered mine to them – and their cries of "Amen!" and "Hallelujah" and "Yes Lord!" and "Praise His name!" and "Preach it, brother!" sustained and whipped on by solos until we all became equal, wringing wet, singing and dancing, in anguish and rejoicing, at the foot of the altar'.

James Baldwin
(*The Fire Next Time*)

Errol Bent

# Introduction

Gospel digs deeper than other music. Those who make it so – and those who have made it so in the past – form an uncompromising band of saints who have spent decades in contention with all manner of demons. Where most performers sing out of their own artistic resources and for their own reward, any gospel singer worth half an amen will begin and end on an entirely different plane.

It's a disturbing kind of joy they dispense. It can hardly be tagged as entertainment, though it's often more entertaining than blues or soul or jazz or R 'n' B or any of the other music with which it overlaps. Gospel is altogether more extreme in its depths and in its heights ... always at its best when at its most emotive and cathartic. This is after all, a religious expression about life and death, invariably made under extreme circumstances. Few performers have had it quite so tough as gospel singers and it shows in the way they commit themselves within a song: diamond hard voices from low down on the human scale, rising up against all the odds to transcend the evil days and proclaim a special kind of victory.

A victory in the first instance over physical servitude. Bernice Reagon throws the early spirituals into sharp focus – 'Into our songs we worked the full range and intensity of our legacy in this land that made us slaves. Into our singing, we forged the sounds of a people of resolute spirit and fortitude in this land that debated our worth as human beings.'

The Christian vision of deliverance from spiritual and social shackles has always held out the greatest hope to those with least to lose and the gospel song is essentially a song of deliverance. The real, breathtaking power of gospel singing cannot be understood as anything less than the ecstatic shout of a soul set free at last.

It's not necessarily a pleasurable experience for the uninitiated. Even a childhood steeped in the rites of the gospel church won't always prepare you for the upset created by a certain song or a certain singer at an uncertain moment. For an outsider coming upon the dramatic fervour of gospel unprepared, the disturbance can be utterly overwhelming. Repellent even. 'There's something about the gospel blues, said Sister Rosetta Tharpe to author Tony Heilbut, 'That's so deep the world can't stand it.'

Which goes some way to explain, though not excuse, the extraordinary neglect that gospel music has suffered from the world at large. Even though strains of the gospel sound are heard throughout the whole of popular music, even though 'negro spirituals' (in multi-diluted form) are known by school children everywhere, even though virtually every major black American singer since the 1950s has graduated from gospel, almost nothing is generally known about gospel music itself. A measure of the neglect is that this is the first

Lippman + Rau

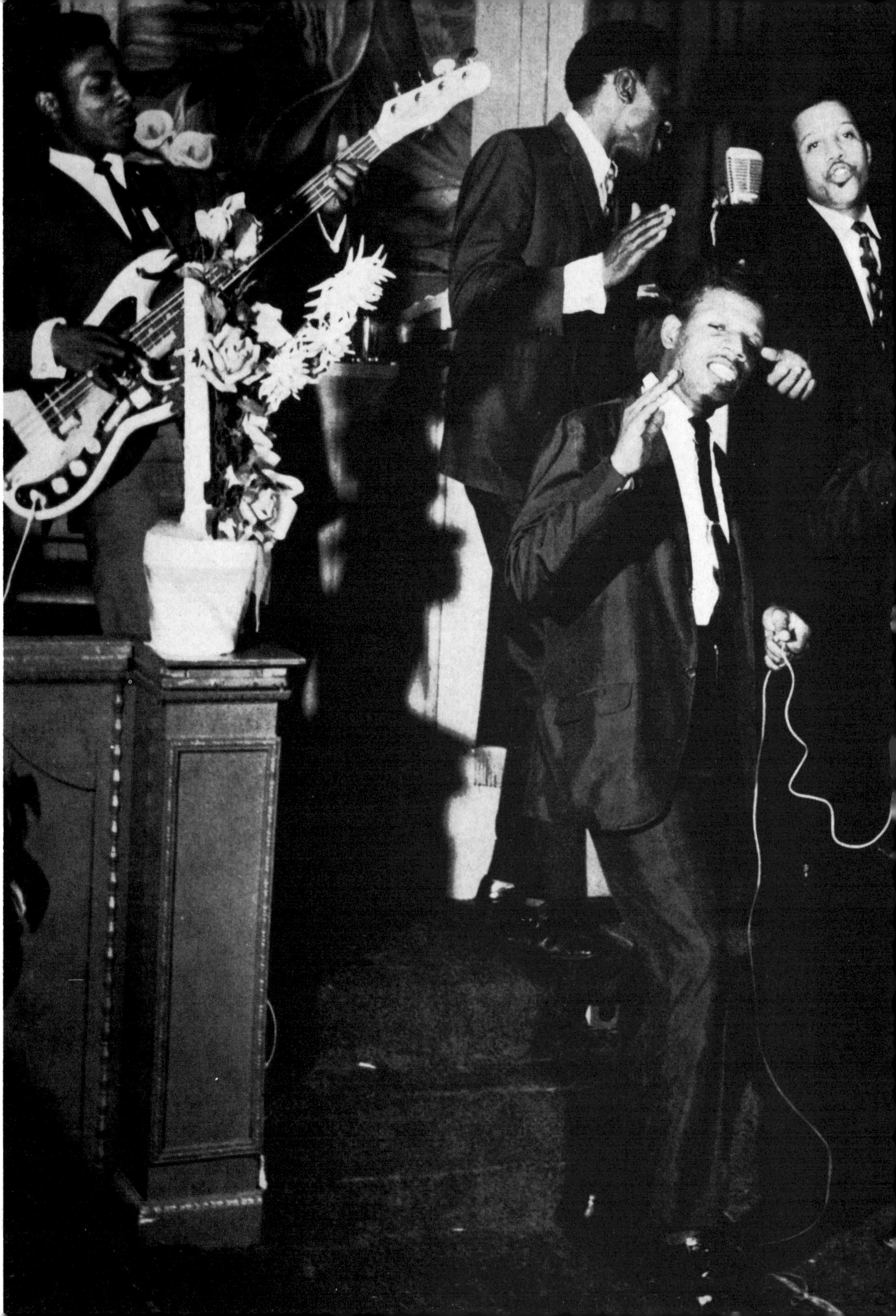

book on the subject ever to have been published in Britain.

The book isn't the whole story by any means. The full glorious history of spiritual and gospel music is so vast and complex and even now still so hidden, that I can only hope to introduce the major figures and events that shaped this most remarkable of Christian cultures. It isn't the definitive historical record any more than it is a musicological assessment of gospel; rather, it is offered as one doorway between the music and the world ...opening in on the band of saints who made (and are still making) some of the most extraordinary vocal music, and opening out so that their good news may be more widely heard.

I'd like to hope that the world would begin to listen to black gospel. Not for its excitement, not for entertainment, not as an anachronism, not as a precursor of other music, not as a collector's obsession, not as a primitive art form, not as a folk music (though it may be all of these); not even necessarily for the lyrics of the songs, for they are frequently banal in isolation. Gospel deserves to be heard for the depth of its prophecy out of the mouths of its prophets ... great wisdoms and jubilations, pulsing through the music quite apart from what is actually being articulated.

It goes right back to St Augustine in his *Commentary on the Psalms:* 'We acknowledge our inability to express in words what our heart is singing... whenever people singing at the harvest, in the vineyards, or elsewhere in the ardour of their work are so gladdened by the words of their song that their joy becomes too great to express in words, they leave the syllables be and burst into exultation... And who beseems this jubilation more than the unutterable God? And when you cannot utter it, and yet must not withold it, what remains for you to do but jubilate and let your heart exult wordlessly by breaking down all barriers in the immeasurable fullness of your joy...'

It can hardly therefore, be contained in a book. It's important that the story begins to be told, but even more important that we begin to listen to what cannot be said.

Viv Broughton
*London, October 1984*

*The Mighty Clouds of Harmony*

# 1

# TOUCH NOT MY ANOINTED

## Slavery, Spirituals and the Great Jubilee

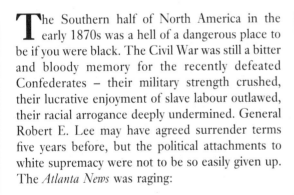

I AM I NOT A MAN AND A BROTHER?

The Southern half of North America in the early 1870s was a hell of a dangerous place to be if you were black. The Civil War was still a bitter and bloody memory for the recently defeated Confederates – their military strength crushed, their lucrative enjoyment of slave labour outlawed, their racial arrogance deeply undermined. General Robert E. Lee may have agreed surrender terms five years before, but the political attachments to white supremacy were not to be so easily given up. The *Atlanta News* was raging:

'All pride is to be crushed within us. We are to be the slave; the Negro is to be the master. . . We have submitted long enough to indignities, and it is time to meet brute force with brute force. Every Southern state should swarm with White Leagues, and we should stand ready to act . . . our hate must be unquenchable, our war interminable and merciless.'

The Ku Klux Klan was only the largest of several secret societies offering the means and opportunity for revenge on the newly liberated black popula-tion. In many ways, the entire power structure of the South was now emotionally ranged against the ex-slaves, with both legislature and judiciary conni-ving in the terror and abuse being meted out indis-criminately. The Klan was on the rampage in every county – robbing, lynching, raping, whipping and burning with impunity and without provocation. With no defence available, neither physical nor legal, black citizens were forced to petition Congress for emergency measures:

'We would respectfully state that life, liberty and property are unprotected among the colo-red race. . . Organised bands of desperate and lawless men, mainly composed of soldiers of the late Rebel armies, armed, disciplined and disguised, and bound by oath and secret obli-gations, have by force, terror and violence sub-verted all civil society among colored people, thus utterly rendering insecure the safety of persons and property, overthrowing all those rights which are the primary basis and objects of the government. . . The legislature has ad-journed; they refused to enact any laws to suppress Ku Klux disorder. We regard them now as being licensed to continue their dark and bloody deeds under the cover of the dark night. . . We appeal to you as law-abiding citizens to enact some laws that will protect us and that will enable us to exercise the rights of citizens.'

In May 1870 and again a year later, Congress responded by passing the Ku Klux Klan Acts in an attempt to control the secret societies. Thousands of members were indicted, resulting in 1250 convictions. Nevertheless, though it served to curb the worst excesses of the South, it did little to transform the all-consuming hatred harboured by defeated whites towards emergent blacks. The South was to remain for decades a volatile and dangerous territory for the black race.

At this time and in these circumstances, the very first public performances of Afro-American church music took place. On October 6th 1871, eleven singers left the Tennessee town of Nashville, travelling by train on what was to be a historic and epic journey. They were students – six women and five men – from Fisk University, one of several chartered institutions established by the American Missionary Society 'to give the freedmen a high and Christian education.' With them were the school treasurer, Mr George L. White, a 'skilled young Negro pianist' Ella Shepherd, and a teacher (Miss Wells) from a missionary school in Athens, Alabama, to chaperone the women students. To set out on such a journey was an act of the very greatest faith. Though they had already presented concerts to local audiences (even collectng a favourable notice or two in the press), the wider American public had heard nothing of black music except minstrel novelties, and the little group had virtually no money with them other than the fare to their first stop – Cincinatti, Ohio.

George White had come up with the idea of a concert tour out of desperation over funds for the Fisk College, which had been in continuous financial difficulties since it opened its doors in 1866. In fact, White had put his own money and property forward as security, in the hope that the Fisk Jubilee Singers as they were later known, would be able to raise sufficient from their performances to continue the tour and send any surplus back for the Fisk building programme. They travelled northwards on the off-chance that the more enlightened of the white church ministers would support them, let them sing in the churches and take up collections. They had expected to be away for just a few months but their fame was spreading and the invitations came thicker and faster. In Boston, one newspaper critic wrote that their songs were 'rendered with a power and pathos never surpassed'.

The following year, they arrived back in Boston to take part in the huge World Peace Jubilee of 1872. It was expected to be something of a highlight, but in fact they would have been simply hidden away as part of the massive Festival chorus, had it not been for a remarkable incident. During the singing of the *Battle Hymn of the Republic*, it became clear that a fiasco was imminent – the orchestra had begun on too high a pitch and the opening verses were a 'painful failure'. In dramatic manner, the Jubilee Singers stepped into the breech: 'Every word . . . rang through the great Coliseum as if sounded out of a trumpet. The great audience was carried away with a whirlwind of delight. . . Men threw their hats in the air and the Coliseum rang with cheers and shouts of "The Jubilees! The Jubilees forever!"'

The reputation of the Fisk Jubilee Singers was now firmly established, and on an international stage. They began to travel abroad, singing to commoners and royalty in Europe. They visited Britain five times, invited by Lord Shaftesbury, appearing at such unlikely places as Woodford Congregational Church in Essex and Dunoon in Scotland. They performed for Gladstone and for Queen Victoria, who is reported to have wept with joy when she heard them sing. In tribute to them, she had their portrait commissioned, which now hangs in the New York Public Library.

It is said that all this fulfilled a remarkable prophecy. John Wesley Work, one of the first music instructors at Fisk University, recounted in 1915, the following story:

'A master of a Tennessee plantation had sold a mother from her babe, and the day for the separation was fast approaching when the mother was to be taken "down South". Now, the condition of the slave in Tennessee was better than in any other state, with the possible exception of Virginia. To be sold "South" was, to the slave, to make the journey from which no traveller ever returned. So it was not strange that the mother would sooner take her life and that of her babe, than to go down into Mississippi, which, to her, was going to her grave. Bent upon throwing herself and her child over the steep banks of the Cumberland River, she was stumbling along the dusty road, her infant clasped close to her breast, muttering in frenzy her dire determination, "Before I'd be a slave, I'd be buried in my grave!" An old "mammy", seeing the terrible expression on her face, and hearing these words, read her intentions. In love she laid her dear old hand upon the shoulder of the distressed mother and said, "Don't you do it, honey; wait, let de chariot of de Lord swing low, and let me take one of de Lord's scrolls an' read it to you." Then, making a motion as reaching for something and unrolling it, she read, "God's got a great work for dis baby to do; she's goin' to stand befo' kings and queens. Don't you do it, honey." The mother was so impressed with the words of the old "mammy" she gave up her fell design and allowed herself to be taken off down into Mississippi, leaving her baby behind.'

The baby girl was Ella Shepherd, who later entered Fisk University and fulfilled the prophecy by becoming the original pianist of the Fisk Singers. The story also has a lovely post-script because, after the long tour was over, Ella set out alone southwards to try and find her mother. An almost hopeless task, but eventually she did find her and brought her back to live in peace and comfort through her old age. Mrs Sarah Hannah Shepherd died in her sleep in the summer of 1912.

The epic tour of the Fisk Singers lasted an amazing seven years and raised the huge sum of $150,000, which was used to build a magnificent new Jubilee Hall at Fisk University, on the site of the former slave-pen. It was affectionately known as 'Frozen Music'.

For all their great international success though, the Fisk Jubilee Singers were something of an anomaly, eccentric to the norm of black music at the time. The audiences they sang to were white, and the spirituals they sang were tailored accordingly. The Fisks were the first, but certainly not the last, black American artists who dressed up the image and dressed down the music in order to crossover to the white market. As they themselves were quick to reassure the genteel church-goers who flocked to hear them, they had 'purged the songs of all ungainly africanism'.

Even so, leading abolitionist and patron of the Fisks, Henry Ward Beecher, was warning friends in England that 'you will hear from them the wild slave songs, some of which seem like the inarticulate wails of breaking hearts made dumb by slavery'. No doubt Victorian Britain appreciated the melodrama, but listening to the scratchy (later) recordings that remain of the Fisk Jubilee Singers, it is clear that, shrewd and skilful as they may have been in parting white audiences from their cash, the 'negro spirituals' themselves had already been anglicised out of all recognition. Unfortunately, the popularised conception endures even to this day. Ask most people what they think a 'negro spiritual' sounds like and they attempt to describe something much like the expurgated songs of the Fisk Singers. There can be no doubting the fantastic courage, faith and endurance of the little band of pioneer fund-raisers from Nashville, but the real spirituals were a different music entirely.

*An attempt in 1876 to notate one of the Fisk spirituals.*
Overleaf: *The Fisk Jubilee Singers (Ella Sheppard seated at harmonium)*

The true roots of black gospel and spirituals can be traced to the extraordinary collision of cultures that took place at the beginning of the 18th century, as bonded African slave met the first flood of English church hymns on American soil. From as early as 1619, when the very first abducted African set foot in the (then) English colonies at Jamestown, Virginia, the Christian church was anxious for the souls of the new arrivals in their midst. It will be to the eternal shame of the church that equal anxiety was not aroused for the physical liberation of their captured children of God, but in comparison to the masters' treatment of slaves as mere livestock, the influence of the church may be regarded as relatively humane.

Not until the beginning of the 18th century did the evangelising of negro slaves proceed in earnest. The Society for the Propagation of the Gospel was set up in London to supply and maintain missions in the Americas. At first there was great opposition, not just from slaves themselves who were suspicious of the white man's religion, but also from the masters, uneasy about any gatherings of slaves which might serve as a cloak for organised revolt. Laws were passed to control the work of missionaries, like this one passed in North Carolina in 1715:

**'That if any master or owner of Negroes or slaves, or any other person or persons whatsoever in the government, shall permit or suffer any Negro or Negroes to build on their, or either of their lands, or any part thereof, any house under pretense of a meeting-house upon account of worship, or upon any pretense whatsoever, and shall not suppress and hinder them, he, she, or they so offending, shall, for every default, forfeit and pay fifty pounds, one-half toward defraying the contingent charges of the government, the other to him or them that shall sue for the same.'**

In Maryland, a law was enacted in 1723 'to suppress tumultuous meetings of slaves on Sabbath and other holy days' and in Georgia, the constables were commanded to disperse any assembly or meeting of slaves 'which may disturb the peace or endanger the safety of His Majesty's subjects; and every slave which may be found at such a meeting may . . . immediately be corrected, without trial, by receiving on the bare back twenty-five stripes, with a whip, switch or cowskin.'

Despite the laws and despite the violence, tribesmen and women from the Fon, the Yoruba, the Ibo, the Fanti, the Ashanti, the Mandingo and the Jolof, sustained themselves in their terrible exile with the only things, apart from life itself, which hadn't already been taken from them: the cultures and religions of their people. Precious West African traditions of chant, ritual, polyrhythm and dance are known to have survived attempts by the first masters to wipe them out. Some even survived into the twentieth century, like the 'ring shout' – a shuffling circular dance ritual that later became a feature of black Christian services. The heritage of the motherland was not to be so simply displaced by the alien God of Europe and the old faiths and customs remained strong for almost a century. Though there are records of slave baptism into the Christian church going back as far as 1641, the progress of religious instruction was slow.

When the Bishop of London inquired in 1724, 'Are there any Infidels, bond or free, within your Parish; and what means are used for their conversion?', he met a disappointing response: 'Our Negroe Slaves imported daily, are altogether ignorant of God and Religion, and in truth have so little Docility in them that they scarce ever become capable of Instruction; but . . . I have examined and improved Several Negroes, Natives of Virginia . . .' (From James City Parish).

However, tribal memories were beginning to fade, giving way to the new realities of six days hard labour and rest on the Sabbath. Even the gross hypocrisy of Christian slave owners didn't usually extend to the violation of the fourth commandment and, using all their acquired skills of survival, black slaves gradually embraced the only forms of worship and ritual permitted to them. One early catechism demonstrates the attempt to use religious instruction as a method of social control:

'Q   "What did God Make you for?"
A   "To make a crop."
Q   "What is the meaning of 'Thou shalt not commit adultery'?"
A   "To serve our heavenly Father, and our

earthly master, obey our overseer, and not steal anything.'"

It didn't fool everyone and the objective was often subverted. As one ex-slave put it,

**'When I starts preaching I couldn't read or write and had to preach what Master told me, and he say tell them niggers iffen they obeys the Master they goes to Heaven; but I knowed there's something better for them, but daren't tell 'cept on the sly. That I done lots. I tells 'em iffen they keeps praying, the Lord will set 'em free.'**

Church music up to this point was confined to the singing of psalms in a 'grave and serious' manner – that is, at a snail's pace and devoid of instrumentation. Though preferable in entertainment value to the interminable pulpit preachers, it was hardly a fair substitute for the exuberances of Africa. Even white church-goers were becoming dissatisfied with the dreary psalms as a suitable means of praising God.

The new religious movement that swept through the colonies in the 1730s was known as the 'Great Awakening' and chief among its features was the use of new hymns in place of scriptural psalms. It may not seem such a tremendous development to us today, but it was profoundly significant to the patterns of worship – and therefore, music – at the time. Both black and white were caught up in great waves of fervour over the new hymnody. Slaves especially, seized upon the stirring, lively tunes of a certain Non-conformist English minister – Dr Isaac Watts.

Dr Watts was an unlikely and unwitting catalyst for black American music – his name isn't normally linked to the illustrious voices of gospel and soul! There's no doubt at all though, that he must be considered the single most important composer in the early history of spiritual song in America. Born in Southampton on July 17th 1674, Isaac Watts spurned the offer of a university education and ordination in the Church of England, entering a Non-conformist academy in the then London ham-

let of Stoke Newington in 1690. He joined the independent congregation at the Girdlers' Hall which still stands near Moorgate in the City, returning briefly to Southampton, where he wrote the bulk of his most influential work *Hymns and Spiritual Songs*, first published in 1707. Two years later he was back in Stoke Newington and it is a quirk of history that the London Community Gospel Choir emerged in the early 1980s from that very same part of London as Dr Watts, thus completing an enormous spiritual and musical circle. He died in 1748 and was buried in the Puritan resting-place at Bunhill Fields, but a monument to him still exists in Westminster Abbey. His legacy is a mass of more than four hundred hymns, psalms and spirituals that can still be heard throughout the black churches of Britain and America.

Quite why the hymns of a Non-conformist Englishman should have so captured the imagination of negro slaves in America, is a bit of a mystery, but capture it they did. Many letters from colonial missionaries testify to their immense popularity. A Rev Mr Wright reports to England soon after the publication of *Hymns and Spiritual Songs* (in Boston 1739),

**'My landlord tells me, when he waited on the colonel at his country seat two or three days, they heard the Slaves at worship in their lodge, singing Psalms and Hymns in the evening and again in the morning, long before break of day. They are excellent singers, and long to get some of Dr Watts' Psalms and Hymns, which I encouraged them to hope for.'** Some years later another minister, the Reverend Mr Todd, wrote regretting he had been **'obliged to turn sundry empty away who have come to me for Watts' *Psalms and Hymns.'***

The conventional wisdom has it that Watts' hymns caught on so forcefully with slave congregations because they offered lively tunes and engaging poetry at the precise point they were desired most. I prefer to think that, in addition to this, they brought comfort and strength to an oppressed people; that Dr Watts (and some of the other great 18th century hymnwriters) was able to capture so completely the essence of the Christian vision of blessedness for

the poor, rest for the weary and deliverance for the captive, that he altogether transcends the cultural divide. Whatever, we do know that the so-called 'Era of Watts' had begun and there was no stopping it.

Other English hymnwriters followed in Watts' footsteps: John Wesley, who had founded the Methodist Church with his brother Charles, published *A Collection of Psalms and Hymns* – half of them by Isaac Watts. John Newton, born in London in 1732, was to write one of the most famous and enduring spirituals – *Amazing Grace* – often credited wrongly to Watts. There is an especial irony in this, since Newton had himself spent fifteen months 'in abject degradation under a slave-dealer in Africa' before escaping and commanding his own slave ship for six years! All prior to a dramatic Christian conversion and the authorship of his most universal spiritual song – it's certainly curious to think, as you listen to Sam Cooke or Aretha Franklin singing *Amazing Grace*, that this great hymn of solace for a race in captivity was penned by a former slave ship captain.

By the time of the American Revolution in 1775, black people comprised nearly a quarter of colonial society, though performing a rather greater proportion of the physical labour that sustained it. It was still, for the most part, a cruelly debilitating existence – but there were signs that the beginning of the end of slavery was near. The first of many anti-slavery societies was set up by the Quakers in Philadelphia. In England, slavery had been abolished three years before and the British Army was quick to exploit the slight moral advantage, undermining the American independence movement from within by offering freedom to any slaves who enlisted. Hundreds responded, but many more stayed loyal and joined the colonists' struggle for independence – more than five thousand fought the seven year war, not for their own freedom and self-government but for that of their masters.

Many slaves though, sensed that momentous changes were in the air – changes that would, or could, improve their wretched lot. As has so often happened in history, the Christian church – almost despite itself – became the focus of political evolution. The Sabbath was still the only day of rest for slaves and the churches were by now drawing large black congregations. The Methodists especially, had recruited a large black membership, but the Baptists too were rapidly overtaking the main Church of England in mission activities. Notwithstanding the complicity of ministers and clergy in the system of slavery, the various biblical messages of hope and liberation could not forever be obscured, eventually transcending the misdeeds and shortcomings of the missionaries. The black church was soon to be born.

The first black man to be granted a licence to preach was one George Leile, a slave belonging to a Baptist deacon in Kiokee, Georgia. Around 1780 he helped set up the African Baptist Church in Savannah – the first negro congregation in America. Thereafter, and throughout Afro-American history, the Baptist church formed a vanguard of leadership for black people, Rev Martin Luther King Jr being only one of its many great sons.

Perhaps the most significant figure of the time though, both in terms of black independence and black music, was Richard Allen. Born a slave in Philadelphia in 1760 but taking advantage of the liberalising of the law in the North, he purchased his freedom at the age of seventeen. He became an itinerant Methodist preacher, eventually being assigned to the Old St George's Methodist Episcopal Church in Philadelphia – at that time the capital city of the new United States.

He began to draw large congregations – both black and white – but as the numbers of black worshippers increased, so did the resentment of the white parishioners, who wanted them 'removed from their original seats and placed around the wall'. During one particular service in 1787, an act of racism occurred which was to trigger the whole independent black church movement and, as we shall see, hasten the development of black spiritual song. A group of black church members, including associate minister Absalom Jones and Allen himself, were set upon by white deacons who pulled them from their knees while praying. Such an extreme outrage by his fellow 'brothers in the Lord'

*Rev Richard Allen, founder of the African Methodist Episcopal Church*

*Dr Isaac Watts* (opposite, top) *and Rev John Newton*

decided Richard Allen for separatism: '. . . we all went out of the church in a body, and they were no more plagued with us in the church.'

Richard Allen and Absalom Jones jointly set up the Free African Society. But within seven years, the two pioneer clergymen had diverged: Jones to found the African Episcopal Church, which quickly affiliated to the main white Episcopal denomination; Allen to found the ultimately more influential African Methodist Episcopal Church entirely separate from the white Methodist Church. He did not however renounce Methodism itself: 'I was confident that no religious sect or denomination would suit the capacity of the colored people so well as the Methodists, for the plain simple gospel suits best for any people, for the unlearned can understand and the learned are sure to understand.'

Allen's church – Mother Bethel as it was called – was inaugurated in 1794, electing him the first black bishop of America twenty two years later, to oversee the many branches and members. The AME today is one of the largest of the Afro-American denominations.

The significance of Richard Allen for us however, lies with his celebrated hymnal, published in 1801 and titled *A Collection of Spiritual Songs and Hymns Selected From Various Authors by Richard Allen, African Minister*. It is the clearest evidence we have today of the songs that enjoyed greatest popularity among black congregations at the start of the 19th century, confirming the ascendancy of Dr Watts' compositions together with Wesleyan and Baptist hymns and several written by Allen himself. The most popular hymn of all with black people throughout this period, was the Watts' composition *When I Can Read My Title Clear* (No. 26 in Allen's Collection). This collection also provides us with one of the most important sources of black church music as it metamorphosed into 'negro spirituals'.

The African Methodists came under fierce verbal attack from other Methodists, not least for their 'noisy' styles of worship. One prominent critic wrote caustically, 'We have too, a growing evil in the practice of singing in our places of worship, *merry* airs, adapted from old *songs*, to hymns of our composing: often miserable as poetry and senseless as matter. . . Most frequently composed and first sung by the illiterate *blacks* of the society.'

*Absalom Jones* (below) *founded the much caricatured African Episcopal Church (R)*

What was happening of course was that an indigenous folk music of praise, worship and lament was in the process of being born. It could not be truly identified any more as being strictly in the English hymn tradition – hence the consternation of the white church critics. Nor could it be acknowledged as wholly African, though it drew upon the many conventions and styles of mother Africa. These new hymns were still in large part those of Dr Watts, adapted for the practical use of a community with a healthy disrespect for purism, who added their own choruses, verses, stanzas or refrains and, increasingly, joined them to the old African pentatonic (5-note) scale, sometimes adding the 'flatted seventh' – that peculiarly Afro-American note of melancholy which also characterises the secular blues.

Eventually, the original tune was almost unrecognisable and, with the lyrics now a folk in-

terpretation with a rough sense of the original, it can be seen that entirely new songs emerged. The connections can still be easily spotted though. Take the old spiritual rendered most perfectly by the Harmonising Four (in the next century) as:

> My Lord, what a morning,
> My Lord, what a morning,
> My Lord, what a morning,
> When the stars begin to fall.

> You will hear the trumpet sound
> To wake the nations underground,
> Looking to my God's right hand,
> When the stars begin to fall.

This can be directly traced to verses of Hymn No. 10 in Allen's first Hymnal:

> Behold the awful trumpet sounds,
> The sleeping dead to raise,
> And calls the nations underground:
> O how the saints will praise!

> The falling stars their orbits leave,
> The sun in darkness hide:
> The elements asunder cleave,
> The moon turn'd into blood!

> Behold the universal world
> In consternation stand,
> The wicked unto Hell are turn'd
> The Saints at God's right hand.

John Wesley Work, one of the earliest black historians, confirms the process of adaptation: 'In truth, the uninitiated would not recognise the best known hymn sung thus, unless he could catch a familiar word every now and then. An example of variation may be found in such songs as *I've Been Redeemed*. The chorus is Negro, but the stanzas of *There Is A Fountain Filled With Blood* are used.'

There are dozens of similar songs traceable directly to the old hymns of Dr Watts and his contemporaries, providing the route whereby many of the new spirituals emerged. In the cities at least, an indigenous black music was being forged for the first time in the New World, reflecting all the pre-occupations of slavery and deliverance.

Further South in the rural heartlands of North America, a similar thing was happening around the phenomenon of the 'camp meetings', which captured the imagination of frontier communities during a massive revival movement spanning fifty years from around 1780. The revival was known as the 'Second Awakening' and it fired the religious zeal of the common people of all the Protestant denominations, both black and white. Led by the evangelical pioneers of Methodism, seized upon by the Baptists and other Non-conformist sects, the Second Awakening placed religious experience before theological doctrine and introduced pentecostal fire to the masses. Extended and extempore prayers, dramatic conversions, glossolalia (the gift of tongues), shouting in the Spirit, ecstatic baptism, mass baptism and spiritual healing all began to be common, corresponding to a new urgency and populism in church music. The Anglican practice of 'lining out' dreary psalms was being superceded by soul stirring hymns and songs, more closely expressing the simple faith and immediate concerns of the people. In Britain, Methodism was sowing the seeds of socialist reform; in America, it produced a different kind of popular activism.

In July 1800, thousands of people flocked to a historic first camp meeting organised by a Presbyterian minister, Reverend James McGready, but involving a number of different churches. It was set up in the middle of a forest in Logan County, Kentucky . . . a week-long mass rally of worshippers in tents of every shape and size. At night, so many fires were lit around the camp that it appeared almost as if the entire forest was aflame. The experiment was instantly a huge success and the novelty spread (appropriately) like wildfire throughout Kentucky and then in all directions across the country.

These vast gatherings in the open air – anything up to twenty thousand people at a time – were quite without precedent and defy rational explanation. The main tent was usually a circus style big-top (known as the tabernacle) where fiery itinerant evangelists held sway, preaching for up to four hours at a stretch. Interspersed between the sermons were marathon sessions of congregational singing – hour after hour of evangelistic hymns and choruses. Once again, the name of Dr Watts appears, his compositions enjoying enormous popularity with camp audiences.

Perhaps they sound like exhausting occasions to us today, but there was a distinct holiday atmosphere in the camp meetings, especially for slaves attuned to the endless routine of back-breaking work in rice and cotton plantations. The camp offered festive relief, a chance to sing and shout, a chance to do more than fetch and carry. Hardly surprising then that slaves flocked to the camps, sometimes outnumbering the whites and usually dominating the singing. Though camp meetings were almost always inter-racial, strict segregation prevailed in the seating or standing arrangements

*A stylised representation of an integrated country church*

and this served to set up intense rivalries in singing power. One visitor to a camp in Georgia remembered the spontaneous 'choirs' that formed: 'Most likely the sound proceeded from the black portion of the assembly, as their number was three times that of the whites, and their voices are naturally beautiful and pure.'

At another camp meeting in Pennsylvania, black singers among the 7000 strong crowd prompted an observer to comment, 'Their shouts and singing were so very boisterous that the singing of the white congregation was often completely drowned in the echoes and reverberations of the colored people's tumultuous strains!' Nor was it at all unusual for the black camp members to carry on singing long after their white counterparts had retired to bed. 'At about half-past five the next morn ... the hymns of the Negroes were still be heard on all sides.'

Interestingly, there is also much evidence that some of the rituals of Africa re-emerged at the camp meetings. Surreptitiously of course and suitably Christianised, but quite definitely African in origin. Like the shouts and the ring-shouts – circles of chanting singers, half-dancing, half-marching, stamping out the beats on each word of a drawn out chorus, sometimes complementing the rhythm with hand claps or thigh claps. The final morning of camp meetings often featured the 'weird spectacle' of an enormous ring-shout completely encircling the whole camp. All the black campers, having sung and worshipped throughout the previous night, now shuffled, chanted, danced and shouted in a spectacular sunrise farewell march.

The camp meetings produced spirituals in much the same way that the new black churches in the cities produced spirituals – as an uneven synthesis of African chant and English hymn. In fact, some of the choruses which formed the basis of several spirituals and which were most popular with the camp audiences (white as well as black), first appear in that hymnal of Richard Allen and the African Methodists. Copies of the hymnal itself though were scarce – copies of any hymnal were scarce – so that the hymns were passed from person to person by memory. Inevitably, some parts of hymns were lost or mixed up with other hymns, some were re-expressed in colloquialisms, some were lost completely. The most memorable therefore, and the most apposite versions, formed the raw material of many black religious songs.

Other spirituals were born directly of the camp experience itself, like the one that appears in Work's collection:

> Going to moan and never tire
> Moan and never tire
> Moan and never tire
> There's a great camp meeting in the promise land

This spiritual, composed in secret by a company of slaves who had been forbidden to sing, is also interesting because it records the 'moan', which paradoxically isn't a moan at all but a joyful vocal expression of deep spiritual satisfaction: 'In the big meetings there was a certain set of church members set aside to lead in the moaning, a low plaintive fragment of melody, sometimes a hum and sometimes accompanied by words of striking character. This is done to help the preacher as he pours out his sermon, which is generally a vivid description of hell and destruction awaiting the sinner.'

Gradually, a recognisable body of songs emerged as the first folk music of black America – religious in character and pre-dating blues, jazz and gospel itself. The spiritual songs of the slave nation now acquired a momentum of their own, and new spirituals began to be added that owed less to England and Africa and more to the realities of life and death in the New World. Now that the 'negro spiritual' had established its own identity as a true folk music, entirely original songs started to appear that can't be traced to any particular hymn or shout. These expressed the faith of the slaves themselves. They mourned the tragedies of a slave existence, they celebrated hope in hopeless circumstances and they raised the prospect of eventual deliverance. The new spirituals were born out of the slave's own perception of divinity within bondage. Often they were tales of particular incidents, events and experiences – unique to one person but common to many.

Sarah Hannah Shepherd's story (see page 13) of prophetic deliverance on the banks of the Cumberland River, saving her and her daughter from suicide, is the reputed source of not one, but two of the most famous spirituals of all – *Before I'd Be A Slave, I'd Be Buried In My Grave* and the quintessential *Swing Low, Sweet Chariot*. The two songs burst 'from the same soul of anguish, from the same heart at the same time and under the same condition.' The story runs that, after her reunion with daughter Ella following the Fisk Singers tour, Mother Shepherd lived in love and comfort until the 'sweet chariot swung low' in 1912. On her deathbed 'she had been unconscious for some hours, but when she heard the strains of this, her heart born song which was being sung at her bedside, she awoke and made a supreme effort to join in the melody.'

Other 'spontaneous' spirituals were born 'out of hearts in a state of almost religious frenzy.' That is, they were composed on the spot in church services: 'Go out among the rural churches today and attend the Big Meetings, and there will spring up before your very eyes the first fresh shouts of songs which are soon to flourish and fructify. During slavery in some localities it was a custom to require each new convert, before allowing him to 'join the church' to sing a new song. . .'

Some spirituals like *Steal Away To Jesus* and *Go Down Moses, Let My People Go* were of both sacred and subversive intent, similes for either temporary or permanent escape:

'On a plantation down on the Red River, in the early part of the nineteenth century, a master of a large number of slaves was accustomed to allow them to go across the river, at stated times, that they might worship with the Indians, who had a mission there.

They always enjoyed themselves, and talked much of the good times on the other side. But one day the master learned that the missionary to the Indians was a northern man; and, believing that he might put ideas of freedom in the heads of his slaves prohibited his slaves from worshipping any more across the river. Doubtless the master thought the matter was settled then and there, but not so; the slaves could not forget the good times across the river: and what they could not do in the open they determined to do in secret. They decided to "steal away to Jesus", as one slave expressed it. "Steal away to Jesus" whispered at first, later chanted softly, was notice that that night there were to be services across the river. The first-born thought, "Steal away to Jesus", was expressed all day, in the fields of cotton and of corn, and in fragments of tuneful melody the slaves were all informed of what would occur that night. At night when the master, overseer, and hounds had retired to sweet sleep, the slaves would steal away from their cabins and quietly creep through the cotton, corn and tall grasses, softly humming their greetings to one another. On toward the river they crept, and the night breezes wafted their melody to the ears of the missionary, who thereby knew that his black congregation was coming.'

By the end of the 'Second Awakening' in 1830, the shout of freedom was following inevitably on from the cry for spiritual deliverance. Denmark Vesey had already led a massive revolt in South

Carolina involving as many as nine thousand slaves. The first black newspaper *Freedom's Journal* was published in New York, followed in 1831 by William Lloyd Garrison's journal of militant anti-slavery *The Liberator*. The same year Nat Turner led his famous slave revolt in Virginia, prompting the organisation of the American Anti-Slavery Society.

Two decades of intense unrest over slavery consumed the entire country, bitterly dividing it between the abolitionist Northern States and the intransigent plantation barons of the South. Increasingly, the enslaved black nation was breaking its own chains in order to stand and fight or to escape northwards along the 'Underground Railroad' established and run by ex-slaves like Harriet Tubman and Frederick Douglass.

Religious imagery in song now took on a covertly political significance, serving to communicate co-

*Frederick Douglass* (above left) *and Harriet Tubman, both used spirituals to carry coded messages during escapes*

*William Lloyd Garrison's journal of emancipation published in 1831*

ded messages within slave conspiracies. The infinitely courageous Harriet Tubman, who made innumerable trips into the South to 'conduct' other escapes to freedom, was known affectionately as 'Black Moses' and used the following spiritual to alert slaves to her arrival:

> Dark and thorny is de pathway
> Where de pilgrim makes his ways
> But beyond dis vale of sorrow
> Lie de fields of endless days.

Frederick Douglass too, used spirituals to sustain the hope of escape from slavery and later wrote: 'We were, at times, remarkably buoyant, singing hymns and making joyous exclamations, almost as triumphant in their tone as if we had reached a land of freedom and safety. A keen observer might have detected in our repeated singing of 'O Canaan, sweet Canaan, I am bound for the land of Canaan' something more than a hope of reaching heaven. We meant to reach the *north* – and the north was our Canaan.'

The census of 1860 shows that at this time there were 4,880,009 black people in the United States, of whom exactly ten per cent were free. A year later, Abraham Lincoln was inaugurated as the sixteenth President, and the remaining ninety per cent looked to him for their long-awaited liberation. On the day of his election, slaves in Georgetown, South Carolina were whipped for singing this spiritual:

> We'll fight for liberty
> We'll fight for liberty
> We'll fight for liberty
> Till the Lord shall call us home;
> We'll soon be free,
> Till the Lord shall call us home.

The Southern States were outraged at Lincoln's election, refused to accept his Presidency and promptly seceded to form the Confederate States of America under Jefferson Davis. Within months, the country was plunged into the horrendous Civil War that split the nation wide apart from East to West, taking the lives of 430 soldiers for every single day during the whole of the four year holocaust. For forty years, Northern whites had argued with Southern Whites over many conflicting ambitions and no issue had been so fiercely argued as that of slavery. Now the talking had stopped and everyone, black and white, was locked in a horrific fight to the finish. By the time it was over, more Americans had perished than in World Wars One and Two combined, $15 billion worth of property had been destroyed and vast tracts of land had been utterly devastated. Black Americans though were finally and irreversibly set free from the slavery they had suffered for almost two hundred and fifty years.

The formal Proclamation had been made by Lincoln midway through the war, declaring that from January 1st 1863 'all persons held as slaves within any State, or designated part of the State, the people whereof shall be in rebellion against the United States, shall be then, thenceforward and forever free.' Vast gatherings of slaves assembled all over America on the eve of emancipation, waiting as one group waited in a rough wooden cabin in South Carolina where an old slave said solemnly, 'By the time I counts ten, it will be midnight and the land will be free...'

In Washington, they stood on the last night of December and sang *Go Down Moses* with this verse added at the stroke of midnight:

> Go down, Abraham,
> Away down in Dixie's land;
> Tell Jeff Davis
> To let my people go.

*"We'll fight for liberty, till the Lord shall call us home..."*

# 2

# THE LORD WILL MAKE A WAY

## Baptists, Blues and Singing Saints

'I always had rhythm in my bones. I like the solid beat. I like the long, moaning, groaning tone. I like the rock. You know how they rock and shout in the church? It's a thing people look for now.'

Thomas A. Dorsey is the grand old man of gospel music. No-one has had a greater influence on gospel singing; no-one has been quite as prophetic; no-one spans the entire history of gospel music quite like Dorsey. More than any other individual, Thomas A. Dorsey *is* gospel and his story is the story of gospel.

In the years of reconstruction that followed the appalling carnage of the Civil War, a new generation of black Americans was being born who would have no first-hand knowledge of slavery. Dorsey was one such, delivered into a world that bitterly begrudged his parents their newly freed status and sought by all available means to reverse the events of history. The State of Georgia, like the rest of the South, was virtually running wild ... racism and bigotry of the ugliest kind ensuring that ex-slaves were confined to the 'rough side of the mountain', as church people put it. Depending on your convictions, the survival of the babe-in-arms to become the 'father of gospel' was either by very great luck or divine intervention.

Who can properly comprehend the chaos and upheaval of those terrible years in the South? Slaves had been turned loose in their hundreds of thousands – jubilation rapidly turned to terror as the first tastes of freedom soured into a frantic scramble for a subsistence income. Neither sympathy nor charity was forthcoming from white Southerners still licking the wounds of defeat – the unwilling price they paid for black emancipation.

As the army of the Union poured through the Southern States, imposing a new order and authority, agencies of the Northern churches followed quickly behind to cope in whatever ways they could with the flood of refugees. The American Missionary Society was the first in the field, having already established teaching programmes even before the Civil War. The AMS, formed in 1846, had consis-

*The distinctly unsaved Georgia Tom (Thomas A. Dorsey)*

tently clashed with other Missionary Societies who had been more or less acquiescent towards slavery, and the progressive record of the AMS marked them out as trustworthy by ex-slaves. Ex-slave-owners on the other hand, marked them out for special attention as dangerous agitators and a number of their (mostly women) teachers were murdered or just disappeared. By 1868, the AMS had more than five hundred teachers and ministers in the South, establishing the first black teaching and training institutions . . . Berea College in Kentucky, Hampton Institute in Virginia, Atlanta University in Georgia, Talladega College in Alabama, Tougaloo University in Mississippi, Straight University at New Orleans and, of course, Fisk University in Tennessee.

The extraordinary fund-raising tour of the Fisk Jubilee Singers inspired many imitators, all more or less unrepresentative of the common spirituals. The Tuskagee Institute Singers were perhaps the most interesting, employing harmonic patterns which were less closely related to European conventions and which more directly preceded the styles of gospel quartets in the thirties and forties. The Pace Jubilee Singers on the other hand, were one of the first to feature a solo voice – Hattie Parker, who removed herself even further from white traditions, anticipating the vocal phrasing and surging delivery of women like Bessie Griffin and Mahalia Jackson. In the main though, all the formalised attempts to present spirituals in a concert setting were solecistic, an offence to the real thing.

The AMS colleges and other similar institutions were isolated experiments in black education and advancement. As such they not only pioneered, they also divided – drawing off a tiny elite from the mass of black people, to rapidly absorb all the prevailing notions of civilised white behaviour. As in all else, black church music as it survived through the patronage of the AMS, is the laundered version of a cultural expression. Its significance is to the outsider's perception of slave songs rather than to the music of black churches generally. In short, it is the sound of a myth – a myth that endures even today.

In the churches, the division was acute and principally along racial lines. Before emancipation, black and white had often worshipped together, albeit within segregated confines. The camp meetings especially offered a forum where black people shared in worship with whites, free of any discernible animosity. After the Civil War, however, black Christians were forced into a separatism that was almost total, reflecting the growing racial antipathies in Southern society as a whole. Apart from the fortunate few who were upwardly mobilised into white sponsored institutions, there was now minimal contact between black and white Christians and this was to have a profound effect on black religious music.

In the ten years from 1860–70, the African Methodist Episcopal Zion Church grew from 20,746 members to 200,000; by 1880, the African Methodist Episcopal Church (led by Richard Allen) was claiming 400,000 members – mostly ex-slaves. Amongst the Baptists too there was a wholesale shift to separatism. The two largest black Baptist churches: the National Baptist Convention of America and the National Baptist Convention USA, were both formed in 1880. By 1894 there were no less than 13,138 black Baptist churches and 10,119 ordained black preachers.

It is sadly ironic but undeniably a fact, that the ending of slavery also marked the beginning of black exclusion. As the writer Leroi Jones pointed out, black people in the South 'became actually isolated from the mainstream of American society . . . The social repressions served to separate the Negro more effectively from his master than ever before.' One effect of isolation being to complete the synthesis of English hymn and African shout, to shed the constraints of the borrowed white Christian culture just as purely tribal traditions of Africa had already been shed, thereby creating a truly Afro-American form of worship.

Behind the political scenes, shady deals were being struck which would further deepen the racial divisions and conspire to re-impose servitude on black people. In order to negotiate a measure of civil order into the frightening social chaos, the Northern army of occupation conceded the 'right' of Southerners to inflict a vast range of punitive restrictions on the already impoverished and beleaguered 'freedmen'. In 1876, the last of the Federal troops were withdrawn, having received specious assurances that the civil rights of black people would be respected. It was like leaving a fox in charge of a hen-house; within a matter of months, Southerners had secured an authority over black

workers distinguishable from the Slave Power Conspiracies of two decades earlier only by technicalities of ownership. To be black was still to be 'beneath the underdog' as Charles Mingus put it later. Men and women weren't sold on the auction block any more – just their homes, their crops, their tools, their food, their clothes, their every means to life. Just as before, they bent their backs twelve or fourteen hours a day in the burning sun for a master, only now they had a choice: this or starvation. In many ways it was much worse than slavery – at least then there was the paternalistic provision of the basic elements of survival: food and shelter. Now it was clear that four million slaves had made the journey out of Egypt only for deliverance into serfdom. The people freed were entrapped as sharecroppers as surely as they had been by slavery.

Many fled the farms and rural areas, preferring to find a new way of life in New Orleans, Memphis, Mobile and Savannah – big bustling ports and expanding industrial centres. They loaded ships and sweated in cotton and steel mills, living packed into slum ghettoes and company shacks. Surprisingly, few fled North – the great migrations didn't come until much later – and in 1880, three-quarters of all black people were still living in the South.

The introduction of the infamous Segregation Statutes (the so-called Jim Crow laws) in the later part of the 1880s, set the seal on the fate of black people, consigning them to legally enforceable positions of inferiority. The Statutes successfully achieved their intention to maintain and, where possible, extend white supremacy.

Black music and black religion had been virtually inseparable till now, with spirituals dominating almost completely the song forms of the black people. Even the work songs were often spirituals reworked for the purpose. The first ever collection of black folk music, *Slave Songs of the United States* published soon after the Civil War, was made up almost entirely of spirituals and these songs continued to pre-occupy black folk culture for the rest of the century.

However, by the time Thomas Dorsey was born (on July 1st 1899), the first notes of a new kind of

*Ma Rainey and her Wildcat Band, with Dorsey on piano*

music were coming to be heard – the blues. Nobody quite knows how they began or where, but they coincided with an increasing social mobility and the rise of secular individualism – an ethic of lone survival in desperate circumstances. Whereas the music of the black church was almost entirely choral and communal, the blues were the voices of solo singers. One man or one woman telling a story and scraping a living – occasionally even a spectacular living. Blues singer Bill Broonzy who was born in Mississippi in 1893 recalls that the first popular bluesmen were known as 'sweet black papas' and tasted the forbidden fruits of wealth and women:

'Them men didn't know how cotton and corn and rice and sugar-cane grows and they didn't care. They went out, dressed up every night and some of them had three or four women. One fed him and the other bought his clothes and shoes. These is the men that wear ten-dollar Stetson hats and twenty-dollar gold pieces at their watch and diamonds in their teeth and on their fingers.'

The ostentatious exception was rarely the rule but, in that they articulated physical sufferings and material desires common to many, blues singers were in this and other ways setting themselves apart and coming to assume the role of secular spokesmen and women. As such they implicitly challenged the position of the church minister, and the blues implicitly challenged the consolatory function of the spiritual. The one quickly became anathema to the other, but in musical form at least the two musics weren't dissimilar: 'When you hear people singing hymns in church – these long, drawn out songs – that's the blues. Church music and the blues is all one and the same. They come out of the same soul, same heart, same body,' declared bluesman Johnny Shines. Or as singer T. Bone Walker puts it, 'Of course, the blues come a lot from the church, too. The first time I ever heard a boogie-woogie piano was the first time I went to church. That was the Holy Ghost Church in Dallas, Texas. That boogie-woogie was a kind of blues, I guess. The preacher used to preach in a bluesy tone sometimes. You even got the congregation yelling "Amen" all the time when his preaching would stir them up – his preaching and the bluesy tone.' And again: 'The blues? Why the blues are part of me,' said Alberta Hunter. 'To me, the blues are – well,

almost religious. They're like a chant. The blues are like spirituals, almost sacred. When we sing blues, we're singin' out our hearts, we're singin' out our feelings. Maybe we're hurt and just can't answer back, then we sing or maybe even hum the blues. Yes, to us, the blues are sacred.' In fact so many singers of the period testify to the correlation between sacred and profane songs that it seems that one must have been little more than a parody of the other. Some blues singers seem happy to own up to it . . . 'The blues ain't nothing but a steal from the spirituals', was the cheerful admission of one.

The use of the world 'blues' to describe a mood of sadness goes back to Elizabethan times and it was known as a slang expression in America from as early as the nineteenth century. But New Orleans piano player Harrison Barnes remembers that the music came first, the name-tag later: 'They was slow tunes, unhappy. They was what they call blues now, only they called them ditties in them days.' Rev Ledell Johnson, who was born in Mississippi in 1892, remembers that his uncle George had 'an old hobby-horse outfit' of a band and that he 'didn't know nothing about these blues. He played these little old love songs . . . see they had these little jump up songs . . . the little old blues they had to my idea wasn't worth fifteen cents.'

Whatever their value, the blues caught on, and so did another new sound born about the same time. Down in New Orleans, Buddy Bolden was putting together the first jazz band in a dance pavilion in 1895. Needless to say, neither form of music celebrated clean living, sobriety or sexual restraint and they were very soon a heresy to upright black church folk who saw in them an increasingly popular inducement to despair. Lil Son Jackson quit blues for the church and told it this way:

'You see it's two different things – the blues and church songs is two different things. If a man feel hurt within side and he sing a church song then he's askin' God for help . . . but I think if a man sings the blues it's more or less out of himself, if you know what I mean, see. He's not askin' no one for help. And he's not really clinging to no one. But he's expressin' how he feel. He's expressin' it to someone and that fact makes it a sin you know, because it make another man sin. Make another woman sin.'

The blues took its quota of sinners and the black church defiantly held to its saints. They were the two most powerful spheres of cultural influence and Thomas A. Dorsey grew up feeling the urgent pull of them both. The Baptist church was the denomination that commanded greatest support amongst ex-slaves, its various liturgical traditions of water immersion and spirit possession allowing 'Africans and their descendants to behave in what to them were the proper ways of expressing worship.' As W. C. Handy remembered from his childhood:

'The Baptists had no organ in their church and no choir. They didn't need any. The lusty singers sat in the amen corner and raised the songs, raised them as they were intended to be raised, if I'm any judge. None of the dressed-up arrangements one sometimes hears on the concert stage for them. They knew a better way. Theirs was pure rhythm. While critics like to describe their numbers as shouting songs, rhythm was their basic element. And rhythm was the thing that drew me and other members of our home town quartet to attend the Baptist services.'

Rev T. M. Dorsey was a country Baptist preacher of the old school, raising his son on Dr Watts' hymns, personal salvation and that pure rhythm. As a boy in rural Georgia, Thomas had an irrepressible urge to be a musician and he determined to learn the piano, walking more than thirty miles a week to and from Mrs Graves' music lessons. 'She was the only music teacher who taught the Black folk at that time.' Father approved the diligence but not the performing ambitions, sensing the lure of the stage in the boy. Old man Dorsey was right. Thomas was a child prodigy and wormed his way into show-business by any back door open to him. As a boy he worked for a local circus, fetching and carrying water and doing little errands. He remembers a big evangelical revival held in the circus tent, squeezing his way in on 'coloured night' to hear Calvin P. Dixon (nicknamed Black Billy Sunday). 'When he got hot, he'd take off his coat and loosen his collar and everyone would hol-ler Amen and Hallelujah. It must have just been a gesture but the people went wild.'

Even before he was a teenager, Thomas was gaining something of a reputation locally as a fair blues pianist and, within a few years, was playing for Saturday night dances and sometimes getting paid for it. How his father viewed his dalliance with the 'devil's music' isn't on record, but there were rather more pressing concerns to worry about. Dorsey Senior had been working on a farm at Villa Rica 'for forty or fifty cents a day', struggling to support his family as well as discharge his duties as a minister. Like thousands of others he found the struggle too much and eventually quit, moving the family to Atlanta where there were infinitely better work prospects. With the work came the money and the nightlife. Decatur Street was full of it all and the 81 Theater was the showplace, sandwiched between the pool-hall and the barber shop. Soon after arriving in Atlanta, Tom found work and an education of sorts there.

'As a boy I sold pop, ginger ale, red rock at the 81 Theater. And I got a chance to meet all the stars, all of the performers that came to the theatre to play. And there they'd want a pop or something, a cold drink on credit until payday, and I got a chance to know them all! I stayed round that theatre, I'd hang around the theatre and I learned a lot. And I learned blues, I could play piano, and I think it paid off very well to me.' The theatre and the street were run by black gangsters, Handsome Harry, Lucky Sambo and Joe Slocum.

'They controlled all the wild bar rooms which started rolling at 5 a.m. and closed at midnight. Any one who knew their way around could always get a belly-full of corn whiskey at Walter Harrison's, Henry Thomas' and Lonnie Reid's joint until daybreak. It was a tame Saturday night in the notorious Decatur Street section if there were only six razor operations performed or if only four persons were found in the morgue on Sunday morning.'

The city stood on a commercial crossroads, linking the Deep South with the big northern and eastern cities. White workers in Atlanta were fiercely hostile to the influx of black migrants from rural areas and the town erupted in serious race riots in 1906. Uneasy truces prevailed, but by 1915 the Ku Klux Klan was once again in business, holding mass 'Klonventions' on Stone Mountain overlooking the town. Thomas can recall the tension but prefers not to: 'I try to forget it. It was nasty as far as I'm concerned. There was a feeling someone was pressing, eventually to make the financial gain, that the black man wouldn't get a chance to do so well financially. Down there, in small towns there, if a white man came walking down the street and it was a narrow path, I'd have to get out and let him pass.' At the same time he'll also talk with obvious pleasure of childhood friendships with white boys living across the road: 'Nobody bothered us, they came to my house and played with me. I ain't never had trouble with black and white, I can get these special vibrations just coming into a room and they keep me from troubles.'

Whether directly as a consequence of the Klan revival or not, Dorsey left Atlanta the following year and joined the great migrations northwards. He was just seventeen and his head was overflowing with the conflicting sounds of church and barrelhouse. His years in Atlanta had been spent immersed in both blues and spirituals and he had moved shamelessly between one world and the other, reluctant to fully accept either's claim on his talents.

He'd rubbed shoulders with some of the classic blues names like Bessie Smith, who he heard as early as 1912, and the legendary Ma Rainey. Rainey was some thirteen years older than Thomas and distinctly outrageous, both in public and in private. She came from nearby Columbus, but was known throughout the southern entertainment circuit as the most formidable blues shouter, performing for a time with the Rabbit Foot Minstrels and then with her husband as 'Rainey and Rainey, the Assassinators of the Blues'. Thomas was spellbound. This was heady stuff for a young Baptist boy, but it wasn't until the late 1920s that he finally got to work with Ma Rainey. Ethel Waters too was around the Atlanta circuit, performing *St Louis Blues* to Bessie Smith audiences, so the secular attractions in Dorsey's home town were really something quite special.

On the other side of the fence though, he had also associated with the new breed of black church

*Clara Hudmon – the Georgia Peach* (top right)
*The first black music on record* (top left)
*A Holiness Church in full swing* (below)

QUARTETS—MEN'S VC

Negro Shouts by DINWIDDIE COLORED

These are genuine Jubilee and Camp Meetin
only negroes can sing them.

1714 Down on the Old Camp Gro
1715 Poor Mourner
1716 Steal Away
1724 My Way is Cloudy
1725 Gabriel's Trumpet
1726 We'll Anchor Bye and By

singers and preachers like the 'Famous Georgia Peach' otherwise known as Clara Hudmon and someone whom Thomas always maintains was the even match of a Bessie Smith; and the amazing Rev J. M. Gates, who went on to become the first really big selling black recording artist, with his hair-raising sermonettes.

Records, incidentally, were a whole new medium that had just begun to open up. In 1903, the very first recordings of any kind of black music anywhere in the world were issued by Victor Talking Machine Records. They featured the 'genuine Jubilee and Camp Meeting Shouts' of the Dinwiddie Colored Quartet. Surprisingly perhaps, those first six recordings lived up to their claims, displaying none of the cloying sentimentality and concert hall pretensions of other early groups like the Pace and Fisk Jubilee Singers. However, interminable patent disputes put a freeze on the new industry and no other black music appeared on record for at least eighteen years.

Elsewhere in the state of Georgia, another of the great gospel pioneers was growing up under the same sweltering oppressions. A young Sallie Martin had moved into Atlanta from the little black hamlet of Pittfield around the same time as the Dorsey family, but, though she and Dorsey were later to team up in Chicago and revolutionise church music, they never met on home territory. Like Dorsey, Sallie was brought up as a Baptist but switched to the Fire Baptised Holiness sect in 1916. The Holiness Churches (the so-called Holy Rollers) were springing up all over the South, some calling on pentecostal fire, others – the Latter Rain churches – on a spiritual down-pour.

Sallie's commitment to the Holiness church was absolute. She heard the blues but she didn't care to listen. Her music was all Holiness music, ecstatic and extempore: 'We didn't have no soloists. We would all sing together or if you felt like you were going to testify, you might start out with a song yourself.' To shout when the spirit hits you is an impulse intrinsic to real gospel, a continuous thread running through the full span of the music from camp meeting spirituals right up to the modern soul-stirrings of the Clark Sisters and the Mighty

Clouds of Joy. Musicologists and historians argue over whether the shout is rooted in African spirit possession or is borrowed from the charismatic outpourings of 19th century Christianity. The truth is surely that it is simply further evidence of the synthesis of the two.

An academic issue of course for Sallie Martin, taking such Holiness fervour and spontaneity with her as she travelled from Atlanta, first to Cleveland and then up to Chicago. Thomas Dorsey made the same journey to the same city – only *he* went via Indiana and arrived with the blues and spirituals of Georgia. They weren't to meet up until sixteen years later.

*       *       *

With the First World War in full swing, heavy industry in the North boomed and European immigration slumped. The subsequent labour famine enticed hundreds of thousands of southern blacks from share-cropping poverty to a relative prosperity in the new ghettoes. The black population of Chicago between 1910 and 1920 increased by one and a half times; in Detroit it was even more dramatic – up six-fold. In all the big northern industrial centres, vast numbers of new black city folk were picking up regular wages in the steel mills, the stockyards, the foundries and the packing houses. 'We went looking for money, man, good money,' says Dorsey, just one of the more than 50,000 black migrants who arrived in Chicago between 1915 and 1919.

They mostly travelled with more than just the hope of good money though. The North had always beckoned as a refuge from the rigours of slavery and now it also held out an imagined hope for complete racial justice. One Mississippi preacher told the US Department for Labor enquiry into the migration:

'My father was born and brought up as a slave. He never knew anything else until after I was born. He was taught his place and was content to keep it. But when he brought me up he let some of the old customs slip by. But I know there are certain things that I must do and I do them, and it doesn't worry me; yet in bringing up my own son, I let some more of the old customs slip by . . . He says, "When a young white talks rough to me, I can't talk rough to him. You can stand that – I can't. I have some education and inside I has the feelings of a white man. I'm going."'

If the preacher's son was going North in search of justice, then the reality must have been a terrible shock. Savage race riots consumed the major cities; during the seven months in 1919 there were twenty-five serious race riots led by white vigilante gangs. The worst was in Chicago itself where twenty-three black people were killed, 600 wounded and a thousand families burned out. During the next four years, more than fifty black homes were dynamited. 'I came here looking for deliverance,' says Dorsey without irony or bitterness, 'and to get deliverance you just have to wait on the movements of providence.'

Twenty-two years old now and still a barrelhouse piano player, Dorsey wasn't slow either in relocating his spiritual roots. He joined the Pilgrim Baptist Church of Chicago and began writing a few church songs, though more out of curiosity than from any burning conviction. He didn't really get himself properly converted until the summer of that year, when the (all black) National Baptist Convention met at Pilgrim. One of the great extrovert singer/preachers of the time was Rev A. W. Nix, who set the convention alight with his performance of *I Do, Don't You?*. 'He was great! He was powerful! He rocked that convention: shouts, moans, hollers, screaming. I said to myself, "That's what I want to do. That's good gospel, and I want to be a gospel singer!" That's where I first got the gospel word, and I was converted at that meeting. I wrote a song then and there, that week, for the Gospel Pearl, a song book which may still be distributed by the National Baptist Convention. It's on page 119. I never got any royalties for it, I just let them have it.'

The singer (and the song) that saved Thomas Dorsey, is of more than casual interest. Rev Nix was a shouting preacher in the mould of Rev J. M. Gates back in Atlanta. His big number, famed throughout black America, was the *Black Diamond Express To Hell* – a typically bombastic sermonette that left little to the imagination. Vocalion Records issued it a few years later, with an advert full of glee and relish: 'Here she comes! The Black Diamond Express To Hell, with Sin the Engineer, holding the throttle wide open; Pleasure is the Headlight, and the Devil is the Conductor. You can feel the

*From a Vocalion record sleeve in 1927*

roaring of the Express and the moanin' of the Drunkards, Liars, Gamblers and other folks who have got aboard. They are hell-bound and they don't want to go. The train makes eleven stops but nobody can get off . . .' Gates himself had a similar sermon – *Death's Black Train Is Coming* – and both were massive sellers in the so-called 'race market', far out-stripping sales by big secular names like Bessie Smith. It provides us with a taste of the prevailing atmosphere that encompassed all the extremes of showbusiness melodrama and religious ecstasy.

Nix's style that night at the Convention however was slightly more sombre. The song he sang that so galvanised Dorsey is often wrongly credited to another hugely influential figure of the period – Dr Charles Albert Tindley. More than anyone else though, Tindley is the man who inspired Dorsey to become a gospel songwriter, and the best of the Tindley songs have endured right through to contemporary gospel, just like the Watts' hymns. The Staple Singers in the 1960s turned in a definitively passionate version of one of his greatest compositions, *Stand By Me*, Mavis Staples paring the beautiful economy of the song even further by using only the first verse:

> When the storms of life are raging,
> Stand by me.
> When the world is tossing me
> Like a ship upon the sea,
> Thou who rulest wind and water,
> Stand by me.

Charles Albert Tindley was born of slave parents in Maryland on 7th July 1856. From as early as he could remember he was obsessed with the idea of education, collecting scraps of newspaper found on the roadside and painstakingly deciphering the words late at night by the light of the fire. In this way he gradually taught himself to read and he became known locally as the 'boy with the bare feet who could read the Bible'.

By the time he was seventeen, his self-education had been so successful that he could read and write fluently. He met and fell in love with Daisy Henry and the young couple moved north to Philadelphia,

*A rare photograph of Rev Charles Albert Tindley, standing on the right at the unveiling of a bust by sculptor M. Normil Charles.* below: *An early collection of gospel songs*

where he picked up work first as a hod carrier, then as sexton at the Bainbridge Street Methodist Episcopal Church – continuing his studies at evening classes. In 1885, Tindley became a church minister and spent the next seventeen years as an itinerant pastor, returning finally to take charge of the same Bainbridge Street church he'd originally joined as a menial. Here he remained until his death in 1933, loved and respected by the community to the extent that they later renamed the church Tindley Temple.

Renowned during his lifetime as an eloquent preacher, Tindley is best remembered now as a pre-gospel hymn writer. In his church at Bainbridge Street he combined both talents to great effect by interspersing vivid sermons with choruses and songs he'd written himself. With the congregation joining in under his direction, a form of worship developed which became known during the 1950s as a 'gospel songfest'.

Tindley was writing from 1901 onwards and must be credited with being the earliest to combine blues formats and moods with great hymn themes and spirituals. His was an entirely new genre in black religious song – directly in the tradition of Dr Watts but employing black folk imagery, distinctly innovative and afro-american but not yet gospel music as it would soon become. 'There were no gospel songs then, we called them evangelistic songs,' Dorsey points out, but the distinctions are often just semantics to the outsider. Who can really say for instance that Tindley's *Storm Is Passing Over* isn't gospel in the hands of Marie Knight or *We'll Understand It Better By And By* as performed by Roberta Martin. Still less, who could categorise the Tindley song that was adapted first as a civil rights theme song and then elevated to the status of a trans-national protest anthem:

> I'll overcome, I'll overcome, I'll overcome some day,
> If in my life I do not yield, I'll overcome some day.

Tindley's greatest strength lay in knowing his people – for them he created a form of strong, emotive worship, skilfully supported by simple yet tuneful melodies and harmonies. His songs fall into

*Arizona Dranes formulated the gospel piano styles used by later groups like the Ward Singers and Roberta Martin.*

two main groups. One of his favourite methods of composing was to take a passage from the Bible and re-word it in unembellished, everyday language. The other method which he used a lot was to tell a story or describe a situation in the form of a song – the story-line is established in the first verse and the theme is continued throughout, frequently upheld by a strong moral element. He also differed in many respects from his songwriting predecessors in that he concentrated on the plight and troubles of black Christians in the 20th century, as well as the joys of the after-life. Previously emphasis had been placed on salvation, conversion etc with very little recognition of the hardships undergone by black people in everyday life. Musically, Tindley was a great advocate of cheerful tunes, easily learnt and which enabled the congregation to join in with great abandon. Most of his melodies are based on the popular pentatonic scale and allow a great deal of room to manoeuvre in terms of improvisation and interpretation, knowing as he did that gospel music is essentially a creation of the singer, rather than the composer.

Dr C. A. Tindley published a collection of his hymns and songs in Philadelphia in 1916 under the singularly appropriate title *New Songs of Paradise*. Five years later came the publication of a hymn-book called *Gospel Pearls* aimed specifically at black churchgoers. It paid tribute to Tindley's skill as a composer by including six of his songs. One of the people involved in the selection of titles for the hymnal was Lucie Eddie Campbell Williams (1885–1963), a noted song-writer herself and greatly influenced by Tindley's works. Lucie takes pride of place as the first black female composer of gospel songs, and along with Tindley and Dorsey can be considered as one of the early pioneers in the field. Lucie wrote over eighty songs, several of which have become classics in the world of gospel. Numbered among them are *Jesus Gave Me Water* beautifully rendered by the Soul Stirrers and the Davis Sisters and *In The Upper Room With Jesus* made famous by Mahalia Jackson.

The story of Dorsey and the story of the birth of gospel music should really proceed logically from here; but it doesn't. In fact, Thomas Dorsey returned to the secular blues world to carve out a highly successful career under the name of Georgia Tom. An opportunity had come for him to join his old heroine Ma Rainey, up from Atlanta and riding exceptionally high as Paramount's biggest selling star. It's tempting but facile to cast Dorsey at this point as an opportunist and a back-slider. He was a musician by trade and blues offered a good living, just as a brick-layer might be building houses while nursing a greater ambition to build churches. The Baptists didn't quite see it that way, but Dorsey is thoroughly unrepentant of his early secular career and of course there's no reason why he shouldn't be. After all, it was this experience as a bluesman that gave gospel its distinctive qualities in the first place.

At the age of eighty-five, old Thomas looks back with evident fondness to his days with Ma Rainey and her Wildcat Band. 'She was one of the loveliest people I ever worked for or worked with. She called everybody "honey" and "darling", "baby" and so on. If you got in trouble and wanted to borrow some money or something from her, and you go to her for it, she wouldn't call you "darling", "babe" or "baby"! She said, "Why, what did you do with your money? All right, here it is . . ." She was just that kind of person.'

As Georgia Tom, he composed many of Ma Rainey's hits, giving them a kind of sleazy magic that is difficult to equate with Dorsey's later career as a gospel writer. He chuckles over the contradictions and, with only the merest hint of embarrass-

**Rev. Gates**

ment, describes the songs as "... deep moanin', low-down blues, that's all I could say!" The low-life Rainey certainly had her influence on Dorsey but there's a good chance that it wasn't all one-way and in fact, towards the end of her life she returned to Georgia and became deeply committed to the Congregation of Friendship Baptist Church, where her brother was a deacon. On her death certificate in 1939, Ma Rainey's occupation was entered as 'housekeeping'.

His marriage to Nettie brought Thomas back into the church but it was another brief sojourn. He teamed up with guitarist Hudson Whittaker (known as Tampa Red, for his Florida origins) and the new duo proceeded to scandalise the churches with their 1928 recording of the highly erotic *It's Tight Like That*, released by Vocalion. In the burgeoning race market it was an instant smash hit, spawning dozens of imitators and earning Dorsey an astounding first royalty cheque of $2,400. It also earned for him the opprobrium of the churches and, even now, as Dorsey comes to be revered in black church history almost as a saint, this episode in his life is rarely mentioned. It's not difficult to see why he was cold-shouldered a couple of years later when he tried to sell his new kind of gospel music to the churches.

Despite his great commercial success however, Dorsey was experiencing an undercurrent of dissatisfaction with his life as Georgia Tom. His partner Tampa Red noticed a sudden coolness in him as they travelled to New York to record a follow-up for Vocalion. He recalls that Tom was '... very smart', wearing his best suit and carrying a brief-case that he kept on the floor beside him as he played. Tampa guessed something was up when Dorsey skipped the usual post-recording drinks party. He was to learn later that Tom's brief-case was stuffed full of promotional material for some new religious songs he'd been writing, and that the afternoon had been spent visiting churches and choir directors in New York. Tampa Red rarely saw him after that final recording and Dorsey committed himself exclusively to a gospel music ministry from 1929 onwards.

Throughout the 1920s, black church music in America was characterised by three main forms of song and performance. Firstly by the jubilee singing groups who held to the traditional styles of spirituals and jubilee songs; secondly by the many singing preachers who built large followings with their sermons and hymns; and thirdly by the itinerant street evangelists, often self-accompanied on guitar in rural blues fashion. While it was undoubtedly a period of conservatism in terms of musical evolution, the whole of the decade is important because of the advent of recording on a commercial scale. The long years of patent disputes that followed the Dinwiddie Colored Quartet records in 1903 were over and the new record companies were eager to exploit the untapped 'race' market.

Set against a background of intense racist activity (the Ku Klux Klan were once again running riot,

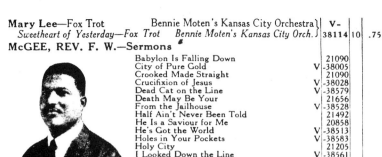

| Mary Lee—Fox Trot | Bennie Moten's Kansas City Orchestra | V- | | |
|---|---|---|---|---|
| *Sweetheart of Yesterday*—Fox Trot | Bennie Moten's Kansas City Orch. | 38114 | 10 | .75 |

**McGEE, REV. F. W.—Sermons**

| | | |
|---|---|---|
| Babylon Is Falling Down | | 21090 |
| City of Pure Gold | V | -38005 |
| Crooked Made Straight | | 21090 |
| Crucifixion of Jesus | V | -38028 |
| Dead Cat on the Line | V | -38579 |
| Death May Be Your | | 21656 |
| From the Jailhouse | V | -38528 |
| Half Ain't Never Been Told | | 21492 |
| He Is a Saviour for Me | | 20858 |
| He's Got the World | V | -38513 |
| Holes in Your Pockets | V | -38583 |
| Holy City | | 21205 |
| I Looked Down the Line | V | -38561 |
| I've Seen the Devil | V | -38583 |
| Jesus Cried | V | -38536 |
| Jesus in the Fire | V | -38574 |
| Jesus, the Light | V | -38513 |
| Jesus the Lord | V | -38561 |
| Jonah in the Whale | | 20773 |
| Love of God | V | -38005 |

**Rev. F. W. McGee**

*Blind Willie Johnson* (left). *Revs Gates and McGee were Victors's most successful preachers*

with an estimated *four million* members) black religious music was being sold into homes as a commercial product for the first time. The Paramount Records catalogue in 1924 was offering heavy shellac recordings (at 78 rpm) of their most popular male group, the Norfolk Jubilee Quartet, led by Norman 'Crip' Harris. (In 1969, long after the Quartet stopped recording, the totally blind Harris was murdered by thugs in Harlem.) Paramount were one of the earliest companies in the field and even sponsored their own Paramount Jubilee Singers, but the most interesting item offered for sale in that catalogue is the first recording of that great Tindley song *Stand By Me*.

There were some early attempts to set up black owned record companies but they didn't last long. One such was Meritt Records owned by Winston Holmes, who recorded sermons by Rev H. C. Gatewood and Rev J. C. Burnett, who had great success with his *Downfall Of Nebuchadnezzar* and *I've Even Heard Of Thee*. Shortly after, Columbia Records moved in, snapped up Burnett and put Holmes out of business. It was no consolation to Holmes that he was merely the victim of a historical precedent.

Columbia were the second major company into the market place. In 1926 they sent a field unit down to Atlanta where they recorded the Birmingham Jubilee Singers and also discovered the famous Rev J. M. Gates. The Birmingham Jubilee Singers' first record was *He Took My Sins Away* and *Crying To The Lord* and it sold almost 5,000 copies. Their second did even better, selling 13,000 copies

and establishing them as the first big recording name in the quartet style of singing.

The most significant find for Columbia however was the magniloquent Rev Gates, and on that first Atlanta session they recorded four of his 'sermons with singing'. On *Death's Black Train Is Coming*, Gates is joined by two female members of his congregation and declares: 'I want to sing a song tonight, and while I sing I want every sinner in the house to come to the angel's feet and bow and accept prayer – you need prayer. Subject of this song, *Death's Black Train Is Coming* – it's coming too.' Somehow the engineers had managed to get a train whistle to blow in the background and the band of singers launch into dire warnings of the railroad to hell. As the first sermons on record to feature singing, the Atlanta recordings were a sensational success, and when the remaining two sides were issued in October 1926, the advance order alone was a massive 34,025 copies.

Rev J. M. Gates was quite a star but somehow he escaped contractual ties to Columbia and worked for as many as six different labels, recording an astonishing forty-two sides within the space of three weeks. He loved to put dramatic and topical titles to his records and would preach sermons like *Tiger Flower's Last Fight, God's Wrath In The St Louis Cyclone, Hitler And Hell*, or *Will Hell Be Your Santa Claus*. He influenced just about every other singer preacher and many of them, like Rev H. R. Tomlin, Rev W. M. Mosley and Rev Moses Doolittle were signed up by record companies. During a single nine month period (from September 1926 to

June 1927) sixty records of sermons were put out by the various companies and no less than forty of them were by Rev J. M. Gates.

More companies moved into the market. The Victor catalogue of 1929 has some old recordings of the Taskiana Four and the Pace Jubilee Singers as well as sermons by Rev F. W. McGee, Rev E. D. Campbell and Rev Gates himself. McGee is interesting as an example of the new instrumental groups that appeared in Holiness churches in the late twenties. This was a controversial move and condemned by many black churches as irreligious but the music is joyous in the extreme. Rev McGee's *Fifty Miles Of Elbow Room* features a jazz band with the congregation and his recording in Detroit in 1929 of *Jesus The Lord Is A Saviour* sounds like an enthusiastic amateur jazz orchestra doing a Sunday School chorus.

Of all the great preachers in the 'sermon boom' though, Gates remains the most important and most influential representative of the music that was typical in churches at the time. In southern junk shops even today, heavily played copies of Rev Gates' records are as eagerly sought after as old Bessie Smith records.

The itinerant guitar-playing evangelists were meanwhile also getting their chance to record; the first being Blind Joe Taggart in 1926 singing *Take Your Burden To The Lord* and *Just Beyond Jordan* followed later that year by Rev E. W. Clayborn. Clayborn was a strident country blues singer who also played 'a singing bottle-neck guitar' and his first record for Vocalion was *The Gospel Train is Coming* backed by *Your Enemy Cannot Harm You (But Watch Your Close Friend)*. When first issued, the record was listed only as being by 'The Guitar Evangelist' but they were highly popular and later pressings gave Clayborn proper credit.

A year later, Columbia took a field unit to Dallas and Memphis and recorded two of the great religious singers of the South: Washington Phillips, who was noted for playing a curious instrument called the dulceola, and a singer much revered by blues collectors, Blind Willie Johnson. Willie was a Texas farm boy, blinded at seven by his stepmother during a fight with his father. With few options

other than to beg for a living, he became a kind of religious busker, standing in the streets of Marlin, Hearn and Dallas with a tin cup tied to the neck of a battered guitar. In 1927 the tall, gangling twenty-five year old with a thin moustache married Angeline, who taught him many of the songs he became famous for. Most of them came from old songbooks she kept in a trunk in the back of their house, like the *Redeemer's Praise, For Sunday School, Church And Family* by T. C. Okane, published in 1881.

Blind Willie Johnson's records – thirty in all – are intense and moving testimonies sung mostly in a tortured, rasping voice over his astonishing guitar style, often swapping their functions at the end of a line for dramatic effect. The first record, issued in the last week of January 1928, was *I Know His Blood Can Make Me Whole* and *Jesus Make Up My Dying Bed*, advertised by Columbia as 'The new sensation in the singing of sacred songs – and what guitar accompaniment!'

The success of the records made little difference to Willie's life-style. He never got more than a few dollars from the company and he remained a street beggar all his life. Even in the late 1940s, when his name had become a legend among sophisticated jazz collectors, he was still living in obscurity down in rural Texas. After putting out a fire in his house one night in 1949, Angeline lay newspapers over the wet bedding and they were both soaked and cold by morning. Standing out in the winter winds the next day, singing to earn a little money, Willie got sick and within a few days was dying of pneumonia. When Angeline took him to hospital he wasn't admitted. 'They wouldn't accept him. He'd be living today if they'd accepted him. They wouldn't accept him because he was blind. Blind folks has a hard time. . . .'

During the late 1920s, itinerant evangelists were doing so well on record that even secular bluesmen like Blind Lemon Jefferson were putting out religious items . . . in his case under the pseudonym 'Deacon L. J. Bates'.

But the great recording successes of the period were the preachers, and in the peak year of 1926 Rev J. C. Burnett's re-recording of *Downfall of Nebuchadnezzar* sold a staggering 80,000 copies soon after its release. A measure of its popularity is that the best-selling blues artist of the time, Bessie Smith, could only manage a quarter of that figure. But perhaps the best known popular sermon of the whole decade was the *Black Diamond Express To Hell* by the Rev A. W. Nix, the man who can take the credit for singing so powerfully at the National Baptist Convention that he turned the heart of a certain Thomas Dorsey to gospel singing:

'This rhythm I had, I brought with me to gospel songs. I was a blues singer, and I carried that with me into the gospel songs. These songs were not just written. Something had to happen, something had to be done, there had to be a feeling. They weren't just printed and distributed. Somebody had to feel something, someone had to hand down light for mankind's pathway, smooth the road and the rugged way, give him courage, bring the Black man peace, joy and happiness. Gospel songs come from prayer, meditation, hard times and pain. But they are written out of divine memories, out of the feelings in your soul.'

# 3

# WORKING ON THE BUILDING

## Professor Dorsey and the Gospel Mothers

Thomas Dorsey's gospel music started a revolution. It upset the spirituals and it upset the people who sang them. Black styles of worship in America may have been from the beginning infinitely more exuberant than white, but it doesn't follow that the black churches are any the more receptive to radical changes in direction. At best it's an instinct for survival, a defensive closing of ranks against an external threat. Black churches in white societies don't tend to have either the wealth or the power of their established counterparts. They tend to be communities of the common people with a superhuman ability to carve out places of worship in the hostile city rocks, against all the odds. They know about the hard sweat that goes into real miracles. Every brick, every song book, every choir robe has been bought and is maintained year by year from tithes and donations that come gladly out of wage packets that contained precious little in the first place. The elders and the mothers didn't just build churches, they built homes where they and their God could dwell together. A sacred household living in constant danger of bankruptcy, eviction and exploitation. In many cases the household faced actual physical attack and desecration.

Not surprisingly, black church leaders were (and still are) tenacious defenders of the faithful as well as of the faith. By the same token though, they're often extremely conservative, regarding internal pressures for change with a similar defensiveness and suspicion. It's one reason for the astonishing proliferation of different doctrines and churches – it being easier for rebels to launch new denominations than to effect reform from within. Even today, in black churches on both sides of the Atlantic, one pastor's righteousness is another's schism.

Nowhere is this intransigence more apparent than in styles of worship, where the faith is poured out in tangible form in a manner that is familiar and comforting to the elders of the church. Even in the Pentecostal churches, where the worship is subordinate to the movement of the holy spirit, there is nevertheless a hierarchy and a culture that will dictate the form of a service as much as any Liturgical Commission would for Roman Catholics. Perhaps it's only human nature that an omnipotent and unchanging God should inspire a hundred different, and equally immutable, forms of worship.

Small wonder then that the churches most definitely did not take kindly to the attentions of a

*Mother Willie Mae Ford Smith (foreground).*

famous barrelhouse bluesman and his new line in 'gospel' songs. However much Dorsey tried to smarten himself up and exploit his old Baptist connections, he was still the ignominious 'Georgia Tom' who'd made his name with Ma Rainey and Tampa Red, the man who'd co-written the erotic smash hit of the decade. Not only that, he was trying to bring all that blues stuff and mix it with the spirituals, with the Tindley and the Watts hymns. He had hawked his songs round to ministers and he had mailed out hundreds of copies to churches all round the country but the response was predictable. 'I'll tell you how it happened. I had about $13 in the bank, and I had to spend that. I got addresses of missions from a magazine of the National Baptist Convention. I borrowed $5 and got 250 two-cent stamps (you could mail a letter for that much then). I put the songs in the mail and sent them off to the churches. What do you think happened? Nothing! Do you know it was a year and nine months before I got a reply?' When he looks back to that time now, there's a rare trace of bitterness in his voice: 'I got thrown out of some of the best churches in them days. If they'd been good ministerial men they would have helped me . . . I felt like going back to the jazz field of music!'

The year it all began to happen for Dorsey and for gospel music was 1932. In a matter of a few months, a confluence of events turned the whole of black church music upside down.

The supplanting of spirituals by gospel songs was a major controversy within the black churches and, though we can now take for granted that the two musics are naturally compatible, the introduction of gospel incited great antagonism. From the earliest moan to the latest digitally recorded shout, spiritual and gospel music together can be considered to have a history spanning about two-and-a-half centuries, but only the last fifty years really belongs to gospel. Gospel you see, was the great usurper, the new wave of youthful black worship, the defiler of sacred hymnody with downhome blues, the sweet sounds of heaven thrown together with the noise of hell. Preachers and pastors throughout black America would try to force it back but the weight of two hundred years of Afro-American church music tip-ped over into gospel music in the space of this one year.

Thomas A. Dorsey wasn't so much the founder of gospel music – that's a convenient piece of mythologising – but he was certainly its major catalyst. He tipped the balance in 1932 but only because the extraordinary pattern of events allowed him to. He was an ordinary person with a particular talent and a vision of how best to use it, but he also had the advantage of being in exactly the right place at the right time. The place being Chicago and the time . . . the Great Depression.

'I don't know what brought on the Depression,' he says with a quick shake of his head, 'I don't know. I didn't feel so depressed for I didn't have a thing to start with.' When it began with the Wall Street Crash in 1929, Dorsey was still outside the church and, as earnings tumbled and rents trebled, he was kept busy but not rich, playing piano at 'rent parties'. 'I had a circuit, I had a place to play every night. If you got 50 cents, or 35 cents a night for playing piano for three or four hours you had good money. They'd have to raise this rent money and they would have these house-rent parties to raise their money. I got in with a bunch there, so I walked round dressed up in the day and played at night. It wasn't much, they give you a little something. Best you got was all that you could drink, all you could eat and a good-looking woman to fan you, that's about the best you'd get.'

The statistics of the Depression are almost beyond belief. Unemployment rose from 3 million in 1930 to 11 million in 1932, then to as many as 15 million the following year. More than 5,500 banks and over 100,000 businesses had collapsed by 1932. A quarter of all the railroads were bankrupted. 'The gulf between rich and poor was so great that the 36,000 wealthiest families had incomes that equalled the total combined income of the 12 million poorest families. The living conditions of these 12 million families, or 42% of the population, barely reached the level of subsistence,' was the estimate of one writer.

No prizes of course for guessing which group the black population was consigned to. Whether in the devastated cities of the North and East or the rural wastelands of the South, black families endured privation on an unprecedented scale. The government of Herbert Hoover was not only unable to cope with the disaster, it was also unwilling, believing as he did in the all-American notion that recourse to public relief would undermine the individual's will for self-help!

The hundreds of store-front churches that had sprung up in city ghettoes in the 1920s were swamped by the needs of the community they served. Many set up 'thrift shops' selling clothes and shoes for a few cents. Some black churches were already highly organised, like the Olivet Baptist Church in Chicago which had a social welfare programme involving 42 departments with over 500 officers – 24 of them paid full-time, but even they were overwhelmed. Other religious figures, like the messianic Father Divine, traded public assistance for personal deification, establishing 'a massive co-operative, based on the biblical Last Supper' which provided meals free or very cheap and organised supplies of coal at cost. (Father Divine went on to become an influential figure in black politics, calling for 'a plan for a righteous government in which there will be equality for all mankind, with the abolition of such evils as lynching and Jim Crow practices.')

It would be difficult, if not impossible, to fully comprehend the initial significance of gospel music without appreciating the context of the Depression within which it took shape. Those first gospel songs were all set against this great tragedy. The antagonism with which they were received wasn't just because they had the profane taint of the blues about them; it was also because they communicated an exceptional joy during a time of exceptional sorrow. Churches that were overcome with the poverty of a desperate flock were just not in the mood

*"I got thrown out of some of the best churches in them days..." Professor Dorsey remembers*

for songs that they regarded not simply as secular but as frivolous.

In this sense, Thomas Dorsey was a prophetic figure in the church, affirming the central Christian theme of good news in a bad time. When he fixes you with a long bony finger and demands to know, 'Down through the ages, gospel's what? What'd they say it was? You mean you don't know that . . . good news?', you can be sure that he's not just talking about a bunch of songs, however good they may be.

The Baptists succumbed first. The Jubilee Session of the National Baptist Convention was meeting in Chicago and Dorsey was there to drum up business. At least one of his songs had got there before him however and he was stunned to hear his own composition *If You See My Saviour* ringing round the huge Coliseum and 'laying them in the aisles'. He promptly struck a bargain with the Convention's musical directors and began selling his music right there and then. Not all the Baptists were so easily persuaded but down at 4501 South Vincennes Ave, in the Ebenezer Baptist Church, Thomas Dorsey organised his first choir and established a base for the exhilarating new sounds of gospel.

People came to Ebenezer from all over Chicago, and many more were getting to hear about this dynamic 33 year-old who was revolutionising black church music. Sallie Martin was one who got to hear and she was down there like a shot, making her debut with Dorsey's little choir in February 1932. Dorsey ignored her completely at first, but Sallie isn't the kind of person who'll take a back seat graciously and besides, she knew just how to handle the bull-headedness of men from Georgia. She had been raised in Atlanta just like Dorsey, she'd made the same pilgrimage to Chicago for work and she'd not long since walked out on a boorish, drunken husband. Thomas A. was small fry for the combative Sallie and they quickly teamed up for what was to be an eight-year mission to spread the gospel of gospel.

If Dorsey was the creative inspiration, Sallie Martin was the promotional genius. She was no great shakes as a singer's singer, she never could hit

*Sallie Martin in the early 1930's*

the sweet high notes nor could she seduce with the low, resonating moans of a gospel blues, but she knew that rare art of charging up an audience out of her own strength of conviction and very little else. She performed as a great preacher performs, going out a little way in front of the audience then pausing, then articulating exactly what everyone else is on the point of articulating. Her way wasn't to impress by vocal skills but to catch hold of the spirit in a room and allow it to flood through her in a torrent of home truths and eternal wisdoms. It was something she'd brought with her from the Holiness churches and when it was harnessed to the vehicle of a Dorsey gospel song, there were very few listeners who weren't touched by the intensity of the moment.

That same year they set about organising the very first National Convention of Gospel Choirs and Choruses (or the Gospel Singers Convention, to give its original name). The two of them were ambitious enough, shifting over to Dorsey's home church, the three-thousand-seater Pilgrim Baptist Church. Come the day of the Convention though and South Indiana Avenue was solid with people trying to get in. The place was so packed that there was barely enough room for the choir. 'We had to put the director's stand halfway up the aisles, back of the church,' Dorsey remembers with pleasure.

That first time, the young people just couldn't get enough gospel singing. The elders and the pastors weren't quite so sure about the merits or de-merits of this rocking, bluesy gospel but Thomas was quick to point out to them that putting a beat into a spiritual was only a way of bringing out what was there already anyway. 'There's always been a beat as you call it in the church. If they didn't have a piano organ, they did it with their feet, pat their feet, pat their hands. There are moaning blues that are used in spirituals and there are moaning spirituals that are used in blues.' Privately he'd also continued to scorn the false divisions between sacred and secular. 'You know, the blues ain't nothing but a good woman feeling bad, while a good spiritual is something that lifts the heavy heart. Now tell me what's wrong about that?'

The man who wrote the new gospel songs and the woman who first sang them, were beginning to sense that something momentous was taking shape. The Dorsey/Martin combination was starting to pack them in at Pilgrim and at Ebenezer Baptist Churches and people were eager to catch the new songs almost before the ink dried. With the city still in the depths of the Depression, the black church movement was growing daily as a focus and a refuge for the dispossessed. People were hungry enough for food and clothing, but they were even hungrier for reasons to be hopeful. Governmental relief was one thing but no public body was supplying relief from spiritual poverty. Community programmes were saving people's lives but they weren't saving their souls. The churches weren't bulging at the seams because they were giving away soup and bread; they were filled with people starved of hope, strength, courage, dignity and happiness. The gospel music of Thomas Dorsey spoke directly to these needs in these circumstances, af-fording real comfort and affirming real joy. His revolution didn't lie in any kind of trivial musical rebellion but in creating a means whereby the poor could discover unfathomable riches. 'I wrote to give them something to lift them out of that Depression. They could sing at church but the singing had no life, no spirit.'

Hide me in thy bosom till the storm of life is over,
Rock me in the cradle of thy love.
Feed me until I want no more,
Then take me to my blessed home above.

The classic Dorsey tunes were selling for 10 or 15 cents, but the recording industry had all but collapsed in the climate of austerity, with every big company taking its share of the common tragedy. The gospel movement, born as it was out of this tragedy, was running against the tide. Insofar as material suffering increased, so did the need and the demand for spiritual release – gospel boomed as society collapsed. The Dorsey songs directly reflected the experiences of the human condition in all its sufferings and its triumphs, because they reflected his own sufferings and triumphs. His most perfect song is the best example. . .

By the middle of the year, Thomas Dorsey could walk past any of the thousands of store front churches and not be too surprised to hear one of his tunes filtering through the door. But this was just Chicago and both he and Sallie set out on the road to 'liven up' the churches in the other big cities, conducting revivals and setting up gospel choruses – the first in Cleveland, where Sallie was already known. Tragedy caught up with Thomas on the road though: 'I was in a revival and my wife was to become a mother and I was feeling that she'd make a lovely, lovely mother when I got back. They said for me to come to the door of the hall where I received a telegram. I read it – I almost fell out. "Hurry home. Your wife just died." I don't know how you would accept that. I couldn't accept it at all. A friend of mine put me in the car and dropped me right home. When I got home I just ran in to see if it was true and someone goes "Nettie just died, Nettie just died, Nettie just died." The baby was still alive but within the next two days the baby just died.'

For a full week Dorsey was utterly stricken and inconsolable but he roused his spirits sufficiently to visit close friend Theodore Fry and pour out his anguish with some singing. 'Right there and then I began to sing, "Precious Lord . . . take my hand . . . lead me on . . . let me stand! . . ." and I cast my burden on the Lord.'

Precious Lord is the most majestic of all the gospel anthems. There can be very few gospel singers who haven't at some point wrapped their vocal chords round the consummate beauty of its simple tune, who haven't revived a somnolent congregation with its lyrical supplication, who haven't been irresistably *compelled* by the sheer economy of its themes, to take this song and make it their own. It's a masterpiece of gospel hymnody – part spiritual uplift, part blues melancholy – and it cries out to be sung with all the dramatic phrasing and curlicues that characterise the emotive gospel performance. It almost never fails to draw a response, even when sung by the most mediocre singer. In the hands of a front-rank gospel singer it assumes an awesome spiritual power. 'I don't know anyone that has written songs as heart-searching as *Precious Lord*. They come out of the experience in him, that's what he says. There's no sound that could equal *Precious Lord*; he wrote it when he was discouraged and his spirit was broken,' said another great pioneer, Willie Mae Ford Smith.

Amongst those pioneers, Sallie Martin was the first of a stream of young singers who took up with Dorsey in 1932. His disciples were many and, curiously, all of them were women – or at least all of those who came to any prominence. None of them have hinted that there might have been romantic attachments to Dorsey, though photographs taken at the time reveal him as a sharp dresser with a knowing smile and his past reputation as an erotic songwriter wouldn't have gone unnoticed. Perhaps though it's simply a quirk of history that invites retrospective speculation and certainly at the time Dorsey was in no fit emotional state, after the deaths of his wife and daughter, to mix the Lord's business with his own pleasure. There's no doubt however that the women singers were the first into the field with Thomas Dorsey's songs and that they

Tony Heilbut

*Willie Mae Ford Smith and the Ford Sisters, Detroit 1940*

all came to idolise him as a father figure.

By the autumn of 1932, Dorsey and Sallie Martin were back on the road, taking the new songs to black churches throughout the country. It was while they were down in St Louis, Missouri that they first met up with Willie Mae Ford Smith who became Dorsey disciple number two. Thomas summed her up in the typical manner of a bluesman. 'He said I had the vocal power to surpass Bessie Smith', remembers Willie Mae with some pride – like so many other young singers out of strict Baptist homes, she was a closet fan of the blues. Like Dorsey, she was surrounded by all the delights of the Devil's music while rooted solidly in spirituals and church songs. 'My maternal grandmother, who had been a slave, used to baby-sit us while my mother worked. She used to amuse us by singing, clapping and doing the 'Rock Daniel', her name for the holy dance. She'd be in the spirit and we'd just copy her, playing like. I didn't shout till I was grown, when I had something to shout about.'

Willie Mae came up the hard way. Originally from Rolling Fork, Mississippi, she was raised in Memphis along with her thirteen brothers and sisters. Father was a railway brakeman and a devout local deacon to whom singing came as natural as breathing. The kids slept four to a bed with their own coats as blankets but she's long forgotten the hardships. The memories that endure are of family love and homespun music. 'In 1922, I joined the family quartet, called the Ford Sisters, who were entertainers as well as evangelists. We were more like the spiritual version of the Mills Brothers!' Two years later the Ford Sisters caused a minor sensation at the National Baptist Convention and a singing career became inevitable – though at that stage it might as easily have been in secular as sacred music. Even after meeting up with the Dorsey/Martin team and committing herself to organising St Louis for them, she still didn't consider herself saved, and there was always as much chance of her singing Cab Calloway as Thomas Dorsey. The Church of God Apostolic finally took her in the late 1930s, but pentecostal fervour had always delineated her singing style and many a Baptist convention was thrown into serious commotion by Willie Mae's scorching solos. She worked in front of a congregation with the same emotional pitch of Sallie Martin, but unlike Sallie she was also a formidable voice in her own right. Even at the age of eighty and, like Dorsey and Martin, fêted by an adoring new generation of gospel lovers, she still retains a vocal control and intensity of feeling that most singers half her age could never achieve. It's almost inconceivable that in all those years she was never recorded but, once committed to gospel she sang only to evangelise and there were few personal considerations of career or recognition. Willie Mae was (and at the last count, still is) one of those few who never sold out, never gave up and never made a thing out of gospel other than the satisfaction of working for her Saviour. 'My voice may crack as deep as the Mississippi River, but you know like the river, I just keep on rolling.' If anyone qualifies as a gospel saint it's Willie Mae Ford Smith.

Back in 1932 though she was just another child of the Depression, a church kid with a big voice and big ideas, shaking up the Baptists as a Dorsey

Disciple. She had that same blend of blues and sanctified and she got herself into the same kind of trouble for it. 'They said I was bringing the blues into the church' she says in tones of real outrage, '"You might as well be Mamie Smith, Bessie Smith, one of those Smith sisters, you make me sick with that stuff". Well, I said, that's all the stuff I know. When I first started out singing gospel they said "We don't want that coonshine stuff in here, we don't want that ragtime singing in here", but that didn't stop me. I kept going because that's what the Lord wanted.'

Willie Mae took on the job of organising the Soloists Bureau for Dorsey's National Convention of Gospel Choirs and Choruses and in so doing she inspired a whole string of young singers who all went on to become gospel legends – most of them gaining the kind of kudos that should have been hers. Up in Washington she fired up a young Edna Gallmon Cooke who later had successful albums with Nashboro Records; in Chicago it was Myrtle Scott, a reclusive figure who makes legendary once-a-year appearances when she'll sing just one song and completely wreck a church; in her home town of St Louis it was Martha Bass, who became a mainstay of the Ward Singers and a successful solo artist; Brother Joe May was her pupil too and gained considerable fame as 'The Thunderbolt of the Mid-West' with a straight copy of her style. Mother Smith, as they now all know her affectionately, trained them all and inspired them all.

Someone else though was in the wings and getting inspiration from Willie Mae and Thomas Dorsey. Someone who would become the greatest Dorsey protegé and take gospel music to unimaginable heights. Someone who in that same year of 1932 was not far away, singing leads with Chicago's Greater Salem Baptist Church Choir and with its offshoot, the Johnson Gospel Singers.

Mahalia Jackson was twenty one and already a singer of extraordinary power. She'd come up to Chicago at sixteen, having absorbed all the music that her home town of New Orleans could offer. Hers was the most heavily blues-drenched background of any of the major gospel singers of the time and everyone who heard her said she could be

*Mahalia Jackson cuts her 41st birthday cake in Paris, 1952*

Bessie Smith number two. She got offers of course – from big name jazzmen like Earl Hines, but she showed them all the door. Others would have been tempted, some would have wavered, still more would have capitulated, but there's not the slightest hint that Mahalia Jackson ever considered singing blues for a living. Not that she disapproved in any way – in fact she secretly played all the records just like Willie Mae. 'When did I first begin to sing?' Mahalia Jackson had been asked the question by Studs Terkel, the Chicago journalist and critic. 'You might as well ask me when did I first begin to walk and talk. In New Orleans where I lived as a child, I remember singing as I scrubbed the floors. It would make the work go easier. When the old people weren't home, I'd turn on a Bessie Smith record. And play it over and over . . . Bessie was my favourite, but I never let people know I listened to her. Mamie Smith has a prettier voice, but Bessie's had more soul in it. She dug right down and kept it

in you. Her music haunted you even when she stopped singing.' She spurned the blues for herself not because it was incompatible with her voice, but because it didn't suit her attitude to life. 'Blues are the songs of despair,' she once said. 'Gospel songs are the songs of hope. When you sing gospel you have a feeling there's a cure for what's wrong. When you're through with the blues you've got nothing to rest on.'

The real musical inspirations of her girlhood in New Orleans probably lay outside of both the blues and her own Mount Moriah Baptist Church. In the latter case, literally outside it – the Holiness Church right next door, in that part of the city sandwiched between the river and the railway. Mahalia was endlessly fascinated with the Holiness manner of worship, with its echoes going all the way back to West Africa. 'These people had no choir or no organ. They used the drum, the cymbal, the tambourine and the steel triangle. Everybody in there sang, and they clapped and stomped their feet, and sang with their whole bodies. They had a beat, a rhythm we held on to from slavery days, and their music was so strong and expressive. It used to bring tears to my eyes.' Whether through family ties or theological choice, Mahalia never converted to Holiness but she always favoured their style, even within the more decorous Baptist services. 'I loved best to sing in the congregation. All around me I could hear the foot-tapping and hand-clapping. That gave me the bounce. I liked it better than being up in the choir singing anthems. I liked to sing songs which testify to the glory of the Lord. Those anthems are too dead and cold for me. As David said in the Bible: "Make a joyful noise unto the Lord." That's me ... We Baptists sang sweet ... Where these Holiness people tore into *I'm So Glad Jesus Lifted Me Up!* they came out with real jubilation. I say: Don't let the Devil steal the beat from the Lord! The Lord don't like us to act dead. If you feel it, tap your feet a little – dance to the glory of the Lord!'

Mahalia Jackson took the Holiness fervour and she matched it with these hymns of old Dr Watts that were still so popular with black Baptists. 'Dr Watts?', she exclaims with delight, 'Now you're talking about the *power*. Those songs, *hmmmm*, they come out of conviction and suffering.' And though it's clear she's talking about the adoptive article rather than a London hymnwriter of comfortable means, she's nevertheless touching on the kind of universality that is in the work of any great spiritual songwriter – whether it be Isaac Watts in Stoke Newington or Thomas Dorsey in Chicago; 'The worst voices can get through singing them, cause they're telling their experiences.'

Chicago was alive with the new black church music of Dorsey, of Sallie Martin and of Willie Mae Ford Smith. Willie Mae was an especial influence on the young Mahalia and encouraged her out of her little cosmetics business. 'She often told me, "Willie Mae, I'm gonna leave this beauty shop, I wanna be like you" ... I liked her right off, she was more like me, a mover and a go-getter.' The raw southern sounds of Willie Mae's gospel singing so inspired Mahalia Jackson that she took all the various elements of the older woman's style and stirred it with her own into a potent brew of down-home shouting. She wasn't above playing a little on the element of nostalgia either. 'Gospel music in those days of the early 1930s was really taking wing,' she recalls in her book *Movin' On Up*. 'It was the kind of music colored people had left behind down South, and they liked it because it was just like a letter from home.'

The more sophisticated and middle class black people in the northern cities weren't quite so taken with the idea of shouts and moans and Holiness excesses. It was all so retrogressive to them, a harking back to old indignities and to old African roots they would quite happily prefer to leave behind. She tells the story of her 'one and only singing lesson' when professor Dubois, a refined black tenor, tried to get her to adapt. 'You've got to learn to stop hollerin'. The way you sing is not a credit to the Negro race. You've got to learn to sing songs so that white people can understand them.' Even Thomas Dorsey, when later she partnered him as Sallie Martin's successor, tried in vain to polish her up a bit. 'I tried', he recalls, 'to show Mahalia how to breathe and phrase, but she wouldn't listen. She said I was trying to make a stereotyped singer out of her. She may have been right.'

By the middle of the 1930s, Mahalia was an established and popular solo singer, and on May 21st 1937 she did her first recordings for the Decca-Coral label, with Estelle Allen accompanying her on piano and organ. She'd been married a year then, to a graduate of Fisk University, and the world must have seemed a very rosy place indeed for her; but neither the marriage nor the recording career lasted long. Her first record – *God's Gonna Separate The Wheat From The Tares* backed up with the old Baptist hymn *Keep Me Every Day* – is something of a gospel masterpiece and was a fair hit in the still depressed race market; but she didn't record again until more than ten years later. The intervening period was spent with Thomas Dorsey, who had parted company with Sallie Martin, and needed a replacement who could do his songs equal justice. Mahalia became his perfect musical foil and they travelled continuously together, raising the temperature at every church and programme they attended. One young singer remembers them at a convention in Birmingham, Alabama: 'It was amazing. Mr Dorsey would just keep handing Mahalia these ballads, and she'd stand there reading the words while she sang. She'd do fifteen, twenty songs a night like that.' For many churches they raised the temperature higher than was proper and decent, for not only was Mahalia an excessive shouter, she was also a flirtatious entertainer known for her 'snake-hips' and for lifting her robe an inch or two when she got happy. It's difficult to believe that the matronly figure who later came to personify gospel music at its most imperious, was once so outrageously sanctified in her performances that she'd get barred from respectable Baptist churches.

It didn't worry her, all this criticism from the 'high-up society Negroes'. She was happiest anyway amongst those who had nothing to lose – the poor in everything but spirit who thronged the storefront churches to hear her magnificent contralto voice. She rocked them like a New Orleans ragtimer with Dorsey's *What Could I Do?* and she made them faint dead away with his *Precious Lord*. She roared and shouted like a pentecostal preacher, she moaned and growled like the old southern mothers, she hollered the gospel blues like a sanctified Bessie Smith and she cried into the Watts' hymns like she was back in a slave cabin. They say that, in her time, Mahalia Jackson could wreck a church in minutes flat and keep it that way for hours on end.

In 1946, Mahalia Jackson re-launched her recording career with four songs cut for Apollo in New York City on October 3rd. It was a first appearance for the young pianist Mildred Falls who became Mahalia's permanent accompanist for more than two decades. Mildred was there again the following year, together with organist Herbert Frances, for the second recording with Apollo. On September 12th, back in her Chicago stamping ground, Mahalia recorded a further four songs, one of which – *Move On Up A Little Higher* (parts 1 & 2) – provided her with her first (and gospel's first) million selling record. Three months later she was back in the Chicago studios to make the sequel –

*Dig A Little Deeper* – which sold over half-a-million copies.

Mahalia Jackson was the first super-star of black gospel, though at this stage she was still virtually unheard of outside the black churches and the 'race records' market. The transition from store-front Queen of Gospel to national matriarch, came in the early 1950s. A triumphant appearance at Carnegie Hall as soloist with the National Baptist Convention in 1950 was about as far as she could go within the confines of the black church, and a wider audience beckoned when her Apollo recording of *I Can Put My Trust In Jesus* won a prestigious French award and led to a first European tour. She sang in London in 1952 – the first gospel artist to do so since the Fisk Jubilee Singers eighty years earlier – and Max Jones of the *Melody Maker* reviewed the Royal Albert Hall concert in glowing terms, adding: 'And she has charm, so that when she dances those little church steps at the end of a rocking number, you need a heart of stone to remain unsmiling.'

Back in America she began to be courted by the big white-owned media companies, who saw in her an opportunity for high earnings with little risks. By 1954 she had her own TV program on Chicago's WBBM, which was part of the CBS network, and the same year she dropped Apollo after royalty disputes and signed to Columbia Records. It was a calculated business decision on Mahalia's part, that reflected a growing pre-occupation with things material – firstly as just recompense, later as a crude commercialism. John Hammond, the legendary A&R man for CBS (who later discovered and signed Aretha Franklin and Bob Dylan) told this story after her death, 'Mahalia was recording for Apollo Records and getting gypped, like all the artists. She called me in the early fifties to tell me that she had got an offer from Columbia. This was before I was working for Columbia. I told her: "Mahalia, if you want ads in *Life*, and to be known by the white audience, do it. But if you want to keep on singing for the black audience, forget signing with Columbia, because they don't know the black market at all." She took up the offer from Columbia then . . . and she lost the black market to a horrifying degree. I'd say that by her death she was

*Mahalia Jackson – the stately Queen of Gospel*

playing to a 75 percent white audience, maybe as high as 90 percent. Columbia gave her the fancy accompaniments and the choirs, but the wonderful drive and looseness from the Apollo recordings was missing. Did Mahalia miss the black audience? Mahalia was only interested in money, to be specific with you.'

This is a pretty gross assessment. Mahalia Jackson was weaned on poverty and raised on exploitation and she was one of the first gospel singers to apply business acumen as a line of first defence against the parasites who attached themselves to black religious music. Many are the gospel singers today who'll pay tribute to the shrewd good business sense they learnt from Mahalia Jackson. It's a romantic, and ultimately demeaning, notion to hold that a gospel artist should simply stand and sing the Lord's praises while leaving to others the distasteful business of calculating the profits. Mahalia Jackson did become a successful entrepreneur and it's true that it did curtail her artistry and her appeal to black audiences. It's also true that her concern for financial enterprise led her into all kinds of bizarre ventures; she converted her reputation for southern cooking into a chain of Mahalia Jackson Chicken Dinners that, at one stage, rivalled Colonel Saunders! She used to say, 'He calls his finger-licking good . . . I call mine tongue-licking good.' But Mahalia had always been enterprising in that way – early on she'd had the beauty parlour and later a florist's shop. By the time she was earning huge sums on the international concert circuit, she'd set up a string of property deals which generated an estate worth more than a million dollars at her death.

But she wasn't one for extravagance or personal luxuries and she never wavered once from her gospel mission. When she returned to Britain in 1969 for a concert at the Royal Albert Hall, she told Max Jones, 'I don't work for money. I sing because I love to sing. I don't care for luxuries like jewelry. This is the only diamond I ever kept . . .' And she proffered him the same ring that had been on her finger when she first visited seventeen years earlier.

Rather, her acquired wealth enabled her to establish the Mahalia Jackson Scholarship Foundation and to become a loyal and active supporter of fellow Baptist Dr Martin Luther King. King adored Ma-

*Facsimile of a page from 'Our World' magazine, June 1949*

halia, who in turn pulled political strings for him in Mayor Daly's Chicago. She stood with him at the historic climax of the March on Washington in 1963 and sang *I Been 'Buked and I Been Scorned* to the quarter-million strong demonstration assembled below the Lincoln Memorial. On the day of his assassination, King had been planning the evening church service, specifically requesting his favourite hymn – Thomas Dorsey's *Precious Lord*. Fittingly, Mahalia travelled down to Atlanta for Martin Luther King's funeral on April 9th 1968 and, at the open air service in the grounds of Morehouse College, she distilled all the triumphs and tragedies of black America into an unbearably moving performance of *Precious Lord, Take My Hand*. It was the ultimate that gospel music could ever, and can ever, become – a work of the most profound hymnody conjoined to an awe-inspiring public witness during a single moment at the greatest depth of human experience. It was then impossible not to be touched by it.

One man who was with Martin Luther King planning that service on the day of the shooting was Rev W. Herbert Brewster – a sixty-seven year old civil rights radical and a gospel hymnwriter who has been described as 'at the very least, a Milton to Thomas A. Dorsey's Shakespeare'. Brewster is indeed an enormously significant figure in the early development of gospel who was, in the early 1930s, doing much the same thing in Memphis as Dorsey was doing up in Chicago. He it was who wrote that first million-selling song for Mahalia Jackson – *Move On Up A Little Higher* (though for many years she claimed to have written it herself with Dorsey's old colleague Theodore Frye), and Mahalia recorded at least as many Brewster songs as Dorsey songs, including the classic *How I Got Over*.

W. H. Brewster, with Arts and Divinity degrees, arrived in Memphis as a teenager from the rural Tennessee town of Somerville. Like Dorsey and Mahalia and Willie Mae Ford, he absorbed all the secular sounds of blues from Bessie Smith and Ma Rainey to W. C. Handy and, like those other pioneers of gospel he effected a kind of marriage between blues and hymns. East Trigg Baptist Church in Memphis became famous for the new music of its minister. Lyrically daring, as well as musically, Rev Brewster was known for his use of Christian metaphors to intimate the political advancement of black people. His 'movement on up a little higher' wasn't simply a pietistic gesture heavenwards, but a conscious statement about black progress here on earth. In the heart of Tennessee in the wake of the Depression, *that* required real courage. His great singing disciple was named after Queen Candice of Ethiopia, and joined East Trigg Choir in the late thirties. Within a few years, Queen C. Anderson was the greatest gospel name throughout the South and, though her voice never really transferred to record, she drew huge crowds to her enthralling performances of Brewster's songs. In many ways, Brewster rivals Dorsey as a gospel songwriter, blending a rich and hopeful biblical imagery with a succession of timeless melodies. Above all, his songs combine literary insight with folk wisdom. 'A gospel song,' he says, 'Is a sermon set to music. It must have sentiment and doctrine, rhetorical beauty and splendour.' It's evident even in the titles of his classic songs, still in common currency today: *Treading The Wine Press Alone, How Far Am I From Canaan, Weeping May Endure For A Night, These Are They, My Soul Looks Back And Wonders How I Got Over* and *Surely God Is Able.*

Brewster's genius has largely gone unrecognised while others have made their names and their fortunes with his songs. He remained at East Trigg throughout his life, becoming as much a political figure as a religious one in Memphis. During the 1950s his reputation, and that of Queen C. Anderson, was such that the young Elvis Presley is said to have turned up many times to services at East Trigg, absorbing the gospel music he later combined with blues and country music to launch white rock 'n roll. There were no Brewster songs amongst the Presley big sellers and royalties aren't payable on inspiration, but Elvis did sell a million copies of another classic black gospel song – Thomas Dorsey's *Peace In The Valley.*

Gospel publishing, as distinct from recording, was in its infancy when Dorsey began to issue his songs in 1932. Sallie Martin spotted the opportunity first on her initial trip to Cleveland in 1933, when she sold some of Dorsey's sheet music for ten dollars. 'People would come into Mr Dorsey's home to buy music, and so one day after they had finished, you see, he was living with his uncle you see, he had a sack on his drawer in which he'd keep his money, and if his niece wanted to go to the store, she'd just go and get the money out, and never say how much out and how much in and I noticed that. "Really you have something here but you don't know what to do with it."' Dorsey didn't always take to Sallie's abrasive and inquisitive ways but he recognised her organisational skills 'You think you could do better?' he asked, drawing an emphatic response from Sallie. They struck a deal and he paid her the grand sum of four dollars a week.

By the time Sallie split up with Dorsey in 1940, through petty misunderstandings and personality clashes, gospel music sales were once again in full flood. The collapse of the race records market during the depression had been all but complete.

During the years of 1932 and 1933, the number of spiritual records was cut back even more drastically than blues. Bluebird Records did an isolated recording of the eternally popular Rev Gates in 1934 but not again for the next five years. Rev J. C. Burnett cut six titles near the end of the 1930s but the boom in sermon records (over 300 were issued in five years up until 1931, most of them by Rev Gates) had come to an end. Insofar as there was any great recording activity in the 1930s, it fell mainly to the jubilee quartets, and even then much of it was re-issues of earlier sessions. Discographers Dixon and Godrich have found that, 'In 1934 there had been only eight quartet records, but the number gradually built up until in 1938 there were over fifty, the level of the peak years. Every label had its regular quartet – Mitchell's Christian Singers on Vocalion, the Heavenly Gospel Singers on Bluebird, and Paramount's Norfolk Jubilee Quartet on Decca.' The guitar evangelists fared little better. Joshua White did some sacred recordings in 1934 and Decca brought back Blind Joe Taggart the

same year. The following year they added a few spiritual songs from Blind Willie McTell but interest was fading fast. In 1938, not one single new recording was issued, but a year later the market had recovered to the extent that gospel records formed a quarter of all race releases. Once again it was Rev Gates, with increasingly outrageous sermons like *Will Hell Be Your Santa Claus?* and *Smoking Woman On The Street* recorded for Victor in 1939. The Golden Gate Jubilee Quartet were also very popular – with their acapella close harmony entertainment based on the old spirituals. Between 1920 and 1942, about 1,250 spiritual and gospel records were issued.

Almost none of this mass of recording activity reflected the activities of the Dorsey pioneers. Gospel music proper was a radical departure in the middle of a depression. It would have represented a commercial risk to the companies at the best of times. In the 1930s it was even beyond elementary consideration as a selling prospect. Whatever small budget there was for recording got spent on the

*The Original Roberta Martin Singers in 1945 (Roberta at top left)*

Tony Heilbut

safe bets – the big name preachers and the jubilee quartets – and the rest of the catalogues were padded out with old recordings, sometimes put out under different artists' names and often issued many times on different labels. The business therefore for the new breed of gospel artist lay, not so much in recording, but in publishing.

Having left Dorsey, Sallie Martin gravitated to the First Church of Deliverance on Chicago's South Wabash Avenue, where the extrovert Rev Clarence Cobb presided over a Spiritualist congregation. Cobb wasted little time in setting her up with one of his pianists cum songwriters called Kenneth Morris, and together they founded the Martin and Morris Publishing Company. Their first hit was with an arrangement of *Just A Closer Walk With Thee* and it was Kenneth Morris who later wrote *Dig A Little Deeper*, which sold half-a-million copies for Mahalia Jackson in 1947. Until 1945, however, there was still no recording of the new gospel music and sheet-music was the only outlet, garnering sales in the hundreds of thousands. At ten or fifteen cents a time, that added up in a big way.

Roberta Martin wasn't any kind of relation of Sallie's, but she was yet another ardent Dorsey disciple of the early 1930s, emerging from his first choir at Ebenezer Baptist Church. Her career isn't so well documented as Mahalia's, but she grew in stature and reputation until she rivalled Queen Mahalia in the people's affections. Roberta and Sallie teamed up briefly, using some of the best young male singers – Robert Anderson, Eugene Smith, Norsalus McKissick and Willie Webb – to form the Martin and Martin Gospel Singers. The liaison of namesakes was short-lived, neither woman ready to risk being in the shadow of the other, and Roberta took the group on to international fame. The Roberta Martin Singers presaged all the other thousands upon thousands of gospel groups that followed. Roberta became, like Sallie, a powerful publisher of gospel through her own Martin Studio of Gospel Music and the name of Roberta Martin came to personify black gospel every bit as much as Mahalia. The people of Chicago especially idolised her – when she died in 1969, more than

50,000 passed through Mount Pisgah Baptist Church to view her body and pay their last respects to a gospel madonna.

Sallie Martin, meanwhile, had formed her own group of singers – the first ever all-female group in gospel. The Original Sallie Martin Singers' line-up, in a 1940 photograph taken at a Virginia revival, shows Sallie with a very young Ruth Jones (who later changed her name to Dinah Washington and became the mother of rhythm and blues), Necie Morris (Kenneth's wife) and Sarah Daniels. The personnel changed frequently and early on, Sallie brought in her adopted daughter Cora as soloist.

Through the Singers and through the publishing company, Sallie Martin extended the orbit of gospel music over the next few years, travelling to programmes thousands of miles apart even as far as Los Angeles, which had yet to encounter the new music. At home in Chicago, Rev Clarence Cobb had broken into radio and was spreading the word through his Sunday night broadcasts, all full-throated gospel choir and roaring exhortation. More than fifty years later, his weekly broadcasts still go out today, a measure of the sheer endurance of the music, if nothing else.

The Chicago pioneers were building the gospel highway. Thomas Dorsey, Sallie Martin, Mahalia Jackson, Roberta Martin, Willie Mae Ford Smith all set out on that journey in 1932, travelling in different directions with evangelistic zeal. These weren't just singers and songwriters concerned with simply making a way for themselves; they were quite literally, ministers of the Christian gospel, communicators of good news through a brand new medium of song. In some ways, the excellence of their art makes it easy to forget that we're talking about a liturgical phenomenon as much as (if not more than) a musical one. The tradition of Afro-American worship as it evolved from slave songs and spirituals, was making a quantum leap here which would set it once again centre-stage in an increasingly secular drama. The Chicago pioneers set out to save souls but ultimately their achievement was to rescue black culture from despair. Nothing that followed in black music and very little that happened in popular music generally, would remain untouched in some way by the new sound of gospel.

# 4

# NONE BUT THE RIGHTEOUS

## The Golden Ages of Gospel

The Second World War marked the watershed of gospel music and ushered in its golden age. Between 1945 and 1965, countless thousands of gospel groups formed, toured, recorded and disbanded. Every town, every city, every county with an identifiable black community could boast a few quartets or gospel singers who mostly sang for free-will offerings at local church programmes and snatched the odd chance to make a few records. Immediately following the War, dozens of independent record companies were set up to serve the renewed demand for gospel, offering the artists a chance of wider exposure but very little else. The standard agreement being around $50 per selection and the slimmest possibility of royalties. With so many superb groups emerging and keen to record, few escaped the double-dealing and exploitation unless, like the legendary Kings of Harmony who originated from Alabama to become one of the finest of gospel quartets, they avoided record companies altogether. Fortunately for us, even groups such as the Kings of Harmony were occasionally enticed into a studio for perhaps only two or three songs, leaving us with just a taste of their music. The Kings' one session in 1946 included Dorsey's *Precious Lord* and *God Shall Wipe All Tears Away*, hinting at a vocal imperative which was said to induce religious convulsions in their audiences; house-wrecking they called it.

The hard men of gospel quartet, the house-wreckers who took the older style of jubilee quartet and set its meticulous harmonies against a roaring lead voice, had been gathering their forces throughout the pre-war years. Independently of Dorsey and the Chicago pioneers, quartets – almost exclusively male – had been developing out of two main regional sources. The fount of quartet in the South was the area of Jefferson County in Alabama (the towns of Birmingham, Bessemer and Fairfield) and traceable in fact to the work of one man – R. C. Foster. Foster had arrived in Jefferson County in 1915, schooled in the art of university quartet singing by a Tuskagee Institute graduate, Professor Vernon Barnett. This of course was the measured, even way of spiritual singing we know from the Fisk Jubilee Singers – '. . . when it come down, it come down just like one solid voice and it sound just like a brass band! And that's what the

*e Jackson Harmoneers (later to be known as the Five Blind Boys of Mississippi)*

During the program last Sunday night at Radio church, Mr. Carey Bradley, tenor-baritone of the famous Kings of Harmony, became over-heated while singing with his group, "God Will Wipe Away Your Tears," and was carried off the floor by spectators.

After several hectic moments he revived, but was too weak from his experience to continue. The scheduled ap-

*The legendary Kings of Harmony and a newspaper report from 1943*

white folks said, "I can't understand how you manage to do that?" Well me either! I can't explain it.' The original Foster Singers never recorded but they primed the whole area for magnificent quartets like the Birmingham Jubilee Singers formed by the ubiquitous Charles Bridges in 1925 and Silas Steele's Famous Blue Jay Singers, formed a year later. The Blue Jays, along with the Kings of Harmony, are often cited as progenitors of the hard gospel quartet style and by 1930, the entire county was fired up with groups of extraordinary power and quality – The Heavenly Gospel Singers, The Four Great Wonders, the Dunham Jubilee Singers, the Sterling Jubilees of Bessemer and the Ravizee Singers.

Out of Jefferson County, the groups began touring on a hand-to-mouth basis, spreading the word. Rev Isaac Ravizee recalled for Doug Seroff his first out-of-town trip: 'One of our first trips was in Mississippi. Laurel, Hattiesburg, Picayune, Amory, Jackson, Mississippi. We went from there to Vicksburg and we left Vicksburg going to Monroe, Louisiana. Where we really got stranded was in a little old place called Bass Trap, Louisiana. There was a Baptist State Convention going on there and it was largely attended. There were some people from Mobile there, one of the ladies was Daisy Fisher.

When she saw us on the yard she said "Oh, here are the Ravizee Singers!" She went in and contacted the president of the State Convention and made a request to allow the Ravizees to sing. When we sung, we were stranded. We really didn't have any money and the car was broken down. When we got through singing they took up a collection of about $170. After we sang, the people were shouting and they heard it across the street at the church where the Women's Auxiliary of the Convention was meeting and they wanted to hear the Ravizee Singers too. So we went over there and it was almost pandemonium over there. They wanted to know how much the men raised and someone told them and they said "We're going to beat them." And they gave us $200.'

Thus the groups, and the Alabama innovations in quartet singing, travelled the country.

While the Jefferson County singers fanned out across the South and Mid-West, the other great source of gospel quartet was serving the East Coast. For some curious reason, the Tidewater region of Virginia was the birthplace of numerous fine male quartets which by 1923 included the innovative Norfolk Jubilee Quartet (who also recorded as the Norfolk Jazz Quartet) as well as the Silver Leaf Quartette, the Excelsior Quartet, the Pearly Gates of Suffolk and many others. Like the Jefferson County groups, a direct descendency can be traced from the Tidewater groups to the university quartet tradition – in this case the local Hampton Institute Quartet – and indeed, the traditions were largely maintained. Tidewater's churches were known to be stiff and conservative, vigorously opposed to syncopation and any form of exhibitionism. Since they provided the venues, they also called the tune but one group at least managed to bust out and became the most widely copied and successful of all the gospel quartets – the Golden Gate Quartet.

The Golden Gates are generally credited as being the first to introduce the rhythmic spiritual and there are certainly no recordings in this style before 1936, when they cut their first sides for Bluebird Records. Again it's a Dorsey song that features, with Henry Owens, William Langford, Willie Johnson and Orlandus Wilson contributing perhaps the earliest known version of *Standing By The Bedside of A Neighbour*. In later years they clowned their way to show business prominence, moving to Paris where they still sing today, but in their time they were both entertaining and revolutionary. Interviewed by Doug Seroff just before his death from cancer in 1980, founder member Willie Johnson recalled the formation of the Golden Gates: 'We used to get together in Eddie Griffin's barbershop. At that time we weren't singing the type of stuff that we sang later. We were singing the run-of-the-mill things, like the old Fisk songs. The slow beat songs . . . we were singing in every church that let a quartet sing in it. And particularly, the main churches that got to me were the Holiness Churches, because they sang with a beat. And whenever I got around to training the group, I'd give our things a beat, upbeat it you know. That, in some churches the preachers wouldn't allow you to do! That was sinful stuff! You was singing the Lord's song with a beat and that was like dancing! So we overcame that . . . I think with this quartet what we tried to create was what I used to call "vocal percussion". It was just like a drum but it had notes to it, it had lyrics to it you see. And you had different beats, you had different accents. Like

*The Golden Gate Quartet*

a bunch of guys beating a tom-tom somewhere, and that's what it had to sound like. It all had to be done sharply and together, along with the harmony, and we sang simple chords. We were trying to sing chords that sounded good to the ear.'

The Golden Gates were Tidewater's ambassador group, pioneering the new forms of male gospel quartet at the same time as the Chicago team around Thomas Dorsey was starting out. Chicago too had direct links with the quartet tradition from the Southern regional source of Jefferson County. Norman McQueen, who had sung lead in the original Foster Singers of Bessemer, had moved up to Chicago and formed the Chicago Progressive Quartet Association in March 1931 with the motto 'Do all the good we can in all the places we can find'. The Association of more than twenty-five local quartets was very active during the 1930s, opening up the airwaves for the first live broadcasting of gospel quartet and organising benefit programmes during the Depression years.

By the 1940s, many hundreds of black gospel quartets were on the road as full-time professionals and many thousands more worked as weekenders. Singing nearly always *a capella* (without instruments) it was the era of greatest artistic importance for black male vocalists, producing such works of the human voice as were never heard before and have rarely been heard since. A great deal of the music was captured on record but much of the history of the groups themselves is tragically missing. Ironically, the period of gospel's most fertile activity is also the most hidden and it's only in recent years that a picture has begun to emerge through the dedication of a handful of researchers, collectors and historians who are painstakingly tracking down surviving group members and interviewing them in depth. It warrants – and one day will hopefully get – a three-volume history all to itself.

Notwithstanding that event, we're able to find out, for instance, that very few gospel groups who recorded before the Second World War also continued to record after it. It was a whole new ballgame for the great quartets who dominated gospel music over the next decade or so; the only real exception being the magnificent Dixie Hummingbirds, organised by James B. Davis in the mid-1930s, who managed to cut sixteen sides for Decca just as the war broke out. Even though they scored a regional hit with *Joshua Journeyed To Jericho*, it was five years before they recorded again – this time for Regis-Manor – by which point they'd picked up long-termers Willie Bobo from out of the Heavenly Gospel Singers and the legendary hard lead voice of Ira Tucker. Both Apollo and Gotham recorded them (twice in collaboration with the all-female Angelic Gospel Singers) until they finally settled with Don Robey's Peacock label in 1952, where they consolidated their formidable reputation.

The Hummingbirds – and Ira Tucker especially – remained at the head of gospel quartet for almost thirty years, becoming the grand masters of the style. Always versatile and progressive in their har-

monies, they could also pile on the emotional pressure and slay an audience in the Spirit . . . once literally; at a Sunday concert in Ohio a woman collapsed and died from the intensity generated by Tucker as he sang *I'm Still Living On Mother's Prayer*. They toned it down a little after that but retained a distinctive urgency which they combined with more than a dash of showmanship. It was they who introduced the hip-slapping that male quartets became famous for and they took audience involvement to new extremes way back in 1944 when Tucker first broke out from the stationary posture of male leads and leapt off the stage. 'I was singing *I Don't Know Why* by Thomas A. Dorsey and the folks had fits!'

*The Dixie Hummingbirds* (opposite, top); *Rev Claude Jeter* (below) *reflects on life with the Swan Silvertones*

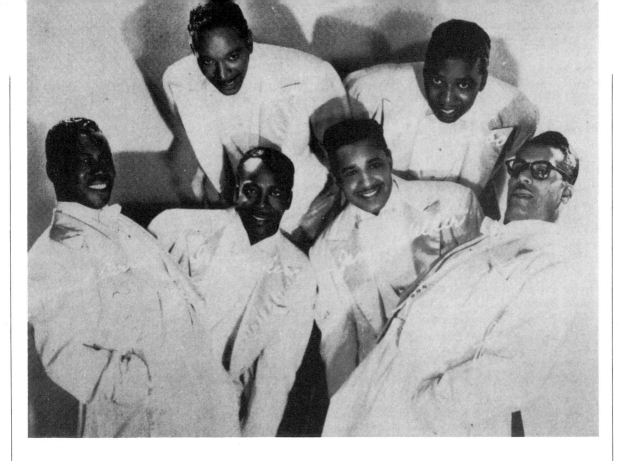

Sue Cassidy Clark

Later years saw them in the role of elder statesmen – still employing lush, progressive harmonies and shouting leads but also indulging the huge crowds with wicked impersonations of younger rivals – a feature they called 'Let's Go Out To The Programs'. In 1966 the Dixie Hummingbirds took the Newport Jazz Festival by storm and they seemed set for widespread popular acclaim but, despite occasional guest spots with Paul Simon, their harmonic innovations became the stuff of legend and reference only.

It would appear to be the cross that all of the great quartets must bear. The Swan Silvertones and the Spirit of Memphis go back almost as far as the Hummingbirds and both created a vocal music which holds up even today for both its spiritual depth and awe-inspiring technique. The former quartet were organised by the Alabama born master of falsetto singing, Claude Jeter, out of the Four Harmony Kings. Jeter and his brother had relocated to West Virginia and formed the group in 1938. Fearing confusion with the original Kings of Harmony, they changed names and became the Silvertone Singers. A weekly broadcast over WBIR in Knoxville, Tennessee captivated the local Swan Brothers Bakery, who became the group's sponsor over the next five years and bestowed on them the Swan prefix. 'There were only a few stations across the country playing gospel on the air so it was rough,' Jeter remembers. 'It was just like nothin'. People had to put out handbills, posters, go through the city with a sound truck. That's how we had to make it. We were cutting down hedges and pavin' the way for singers today. Once in Pulaski, Virginia, we got ready to leave and we had 20 cents between all four of us! A ticket to a church program was 15 cents for children, 20 cents for adults. The sponsoring church or auxiliary in the church would take 50 percent of the house money, say $40, which left the four of us with $20. By the time we'd fill up the car, pay expenses (we'd pay $1 each to stay overnight someplace) we weren't making anything. It's something I wouldn't want to go through anymore, but we survived. We were born into singing gospel – if it hadn't been a part of us, we wouldn't have stayed out there and done it. We would have quit

SPIRIT OF MEMPHIS GOSPEL SINGERS
MEMPHIS, TENNESSEE

Standing left to Right:
Freddie Johnson, Leader.    Ramond Sanders, Bass    Hermon Paul
Baritone   Lewis White, Tenor                        Robert Reed, Tenor Sec'';
Earl Malone, Bass Asst. Mgr    End Jethro Bledsoe Leader and Mgr
To Communicate this Quartette Call 5 6937
or write to 462 Concord St.        Memphis, 7, Tenn.

Jethroe Bledsoe/Kip Lornell/Memphis State University

Lawrence Jasud/High Water Records

and got a job.' Hundreds of radio hours spent around a single microphone honed the group to unusual smoothness, which they later contrasted (not altogether willingly) with a succession of hard, shouting leads – first Soloman Womack who recorded with them for King Records in the late 1940s and early 1950s, joined by the amazing Robert Crenshaw who screamed ecstatically all over their early Speciality recordings. Most of their unencumbered vocal music remains unmatched for subtlety, tension and dramatic counterpoint. That it also imposes its intentions on the human soul with such deft artistry, is nothing less than miraculous. Claude Jeter and the Swan Silvertones created a religious music equal to the finest in any other field and their best songs – *Saviour Pass Me Not, Jesus Remembers, My Rock* – may be counted as spiritual masterpieces.

In the mid-1960s, Claude Jeter quit the Swan Silvertones and became an ordained minister of the Church of Holiness Science in Detroit. The tall, skinny genius of falsetto gospel reflected later that '. . . this is a thing where you can only survive by

*The Spirit of Memphis Quartet c.1939* (left) *and still going strong today.*

being real. Out of all the people we can fool, we can't fool God. He knows our intentions. So I'd rather fool nobody in the gospel field. If I don't feel the spirit, I won't move. I believe in the soft approach. The Bible tells us, "If you pray in secret, I'll reward you openly." I tried to practice that during my career.'

The Spirit of Memphis go back even further than the Silvertones – some reports suggest as early as 1928 with original members Arthur Wright, Luther McGill, James Peoples and James Darling. They were re-organised a few years later, taking their name from Lindberg's plane, Spirit of St Louis. One of their longest serving members is Earl Malone, who joined the group out of their junior section when he was 18 and still sings with them today – almost fifty years later! Yet even he can remember a time when he was looking up to them from the sidelines. 'I was a small lad at that time when it got started,' he says. 'And they used to walk everywhere they'd go. They used to walk up and down the street singing, and I used to sit in my porch and see them going by. And that's all that was

in my mind, to one day be a member of the Spirit of Memphis.'

Through the 1930s the group stuck mostly to the Memphis area, keeping up their day jobs – Malone worked at the National Biscuit Company – and singing on weekends. Not until they were well into their second decade did the group begin travelling outside of Tennessee. 'It was just before we made our first recording,' Malone recalls. 'Silas Steele had joined us. He was a member of the Blue Jays – they were already famous – and they were in town and heard us. He was impressed. He said "Y'all are good enough to go on the road." So he joined us, and we started riding trains.' Leaving their jobs, they took on another phenomenal lead voice in the form of Jethroe Bledsoe and set off on their professional career in the autumn of 1949. 'We went to Birmingham, and there was a fellow down there, and he made a cut on us. The record didn't really go anywhere, but he made some money on it. But then Deluxe Records came in and bought the rights to the master from him, and then King took over, King bought De Luxe out.' The much dealt-over first recordings were in fact issued under the name Memphis Gospel Singers and comprised just two tracks – *Happy In The Service of The Lord* and *My Life In His Hands*.

It was the beginning of an illustrious recording career for the Spirit of Memphis – their work for King and later Peacock Records having a peerless quality, especially with Wilbur 'Little Axe' Broadnax joining Steele and Bledsoe in a triumvirate of leads. Their trademark was their subdued emotional intensity. 'Our first trip to Chicago, the Soul Stirrers brought us up there as a favour because we'd brought them to Memphis. The people up there, they couldn't believe it. They thought we were the greatest thing that'd ever been up there. Because we didn't sing real loud at all, we just sung a bit above a whisper. We were all harmony – we didn't go for all the hollering.'

The Spirit of Memphis, like the Swan Silvertones, were on the road for a good twenty five years and they're still active even now, though only Earl Malone and Robert Reed survive from the early line-up. Over the years they included O. V. Wright and Joe Hinton who both got taken into R&B by the boss of Peacock Records and Brother Theo

Wade who moved into radio with WDIA until his death in 1980. The great Silas Steele had a stroke on stage and died in California. 'Now he was the sort of guy, you just didn't know what he'd do next. When he sang at our concerts and you might say the house had been *demolished*, with all the people going out the door at the end of the night, he'd just stop them right in their tracks. And he could re-open the house again . . . never did give up. If he felt there was something left to do he'd do it!'

A year or two back they celebrated their fiftieth anniversary at Mason's Temple in Memphis, with Earl Malone reflecting on a lifetime in spiritual music, 'The people who've come to Christ after hearing us sing, I think that's the best part of what we've done.'

At the other end of the post-war quartet spectrum stand the Sensational Nightingales and another legend – Rev Julius Cheeks. Where the Silvertones and the Spirit of Memphis captivated audiences with exquisite understatements, the Sensational Nightingales devastated them with diamond hard harmony and the primeval roaring lead of Julius Cheeks. Jo Jo Wallace, who sang tenor with the Nightingales for thirty years, was brought up on the softer jubilee stylings of the Golden Gates and the Jubalaires and remembers the shock of joining the Nightingales. 'It was almost like pulling my insides out, trying to sing behind Cheeks. I'd be hoarse every night. I nearly killed myself trying to make it with the Nightingales! I wasn't used to that style.'

Julius Cheeks was born into grinding poverty in the same South Carolina town Ira Tucker comes from. 'It were bad, man. We didn't have a clock, we told time by the sun. We didn't eat right, we lived off fat-back and molasses. All us kids worked in the cotton fields, and Mama would whip me every day . . . but she kept us straight.' No proper schooling meant that he couldn't read or write, but he got himself a recorded Bible when he was twenty-four and played it to death. His first singing group was the Baronets, who managed to impress the Nightingales when they passed through for a pro-gramme. The next day they came and collected him from the filling station where he worked and began

training him. 'Our manager made us get up at eight or nine and we'd rehearse till lunchtime. Man, it was like gettin' out there plowin'. We'd hang a broom from the ceiling like a mike, and we sang all around it. After lunch, we'd get right back into rehearsal.'

The Nightingales made their first recordings in the same year as the Spirit of Memphis – 1949. They went on to record for both King and Decca but their best material is preserved on the Peacock recordings of the mid-1950s with songs like *Standing In The Judgement*, *The Blood of Jesus*, *It Is No Secret* and *Burying Ground*. They're classic hard quartet tracks and essential in any gospel collection – stirring songs performed at the outer limits of vocal harmony.

Julius Cheeks died in 1980, having left instructions that his body not be taken further South than the Fourteenth Street Bridge in Baltimore, signifying his fierce hatred of southern racism. His voice was lacerated from his twelve years on the road with the Nightingales and some say he just about sang himself to death, impervious to the warnings of doctors, until his voice – never a refined instrument at the best of times – began to sound like gravel in a tin bucket. His was the rawest of gospel's baritones – moving and painful in its evocation of the roughest side of the mountain. Listening to the Nightingales, it's possible to understand that Cheeks wasn't simply indulging in nostalgia when he said towards the end of his life, 'I sit home sometimes and play my old records. I just cry. It'll make you cry, you know.'

Archie Brownlee died early too. At 2 o'clock on February 8th 1960, the hardest quartet singer of all time gave way to pneumonia in the New Orleans Charity Hospital. He was Cheeks' big rival on the circuit, the inheritor of Silas Steele's title as the star voice of quartet. One old time singer recalled, 'My style wasn't broken until Archie Brownlee, he come in . . . I mean, I seen him at Booker T. Auditorium jump *all the way* off that balcony, down on the floor – *blind*! I don't see how in the world he could do that. People would just fall out all over the house!'

Brownlee was the high-pitched screaming lead

Ray Funk

Savoy Sound

*The Sensational Nightingales with the late Julius Cheeks*
(inset)

PEACOCK RECORDS

OUR FATHER

FIVE BLIND BOYS
"JACKSON HARMONEERS"
Lead: ARCHIE BROWNLEE

1550

*Clinkscale*

Rev Percell Perkins

70

The original Five Blind Boys of Alabama.

*The Blind Boys of Mississippi* (left) *and Alabama (top) with
Peacock Records boss Don Robey* (above)

*Clockwise from right: Christland Singers, Harmonizing Four, Salem Travelers, Swanee Quintet*

Ray Funk

Ray Funk

singer of the Five Blind Boys of Mississippi and they had a *formidable* reputation as a live gospel act. So much so that for a while in New Orleans they were required by the mayor to put up a Peace Bond because they were sending so many members of the congregation to hospital. The spirit ran so high when the Blind Boys hit a church that people went into comas – those who didn't come out of it were ferried off in ambulances.

The Five Blind Boys came out of the Piney Woods School for the blind, near Jackson, Mississippi, where they had learned to sing spirituals while still young boys. The Principal of the school, Lawrence Jones, had been organising fund-raising quartets as early as 1922 which all went under the name Cotton Blossom Singers. Archie Brownlee, Lloyd Woodard, Isaiah Patterson, Joseph Ford and Lawrence Abrams were just kids when they set out in the early forties to do their bit for the School's funds, touring as the Cotton Blossom Singers for several months at a time and singing to audiences of wealthy white benefactors. Leaving the school in 1944, they began a professional career as the Jackson Harmoneers, travelling first up to Chicago and to programmes all over the South. By the time they cut their first records for Excelsior in 1946, they'd been joined by Rev Percell Perkins, an experienced lead singer who'd worked with groups like the Fairfield Four and the Soprocco Singers.

Perkins took them over as manager and is fond of telling how he shaped their style from steady spirituals to the hard driving quartet they were later famous as. Now with their nickname formalised, the Five Blind Boys recorded ten songs for Coleman in New Jersey before signing a five year contract with the crafty boss of Peacock Records, Don Robey. They were Robey's very first gospel group in 1950 and he was so impressed with their record sales that he moved on to sign up the biggest roster of gospel groups in the golden era.

Archie Brownlee and the Five Blind Boys began to hit big, moving out of the church programmes and packing auditoriums with anything up to 40,000 people – the Cow Palace in Dallas, the Keil Auditorium in St Louis, Convention Hall in Los Angeles and the Golden Gate Auditorium. One time in Dallas, Rev Perkins recalls that the Blind Boys got paid as much as $5,000 for one night's

appearance, but that was exceptional and mostly their tale is a familiar one of big crowds, small fees and regular short-changing by tricky promoters. The music took them through it all, some of the most electrifying in all gospel and a great deal of it was captured on record. Even after Brownlee's incredible falsetto screams had been finally silenced and the personnel had altered dramatically, the Five Blind Boys continued to make intense, committed records. When they made their only visit to Britain in the mid-1960s, they displayed a rare Christian fervour and proved that in Rev Willie Mincy and Henry Johnson they still had lead singers who could rattle the windows of Hell. There's a verse in Isaiah 42 that seems to have been written just for them:

> And I will bring the blind by a way they knew not; I will lead them in paths that they have not known: I will make darkness light before them, and crooked things straight. These things will I do unto them, and not forsake them. . . .

By a complete coincidence, a second gospel quartet emerged around the same time from the Talladega Institute for the Deaf and Blind over in Alabama. The Original Five Blind Boys of Alabama were formed by the late Velma Traylor, who was killed in a road accident in Blowing Springs, Georgia in 1947. A year later, the original line-up of lead singer Clarence Fountain, Olice Thomas, Johnny Fields and George Scott had been joined by Rev Paul Exkano, minister of the King Soloman Baptist Church in New Orleans and a member of that city's Chosen Five quartet. Paul Exkano shared the group's management duties with bassman Johnny Fields – an outstanding student at the Blind School who had majored in business administration – and guided them to their first recording session for Coleman. Like the Mississippi Blind Boys they often went under a different name – in their case they were also known as the Happyland Singers.

After Paul Exkano left in 1952 to return to the ministry, the Alabama Blind Boys reached their performing peak with a series of classic recordings for Speciality, joined for a while by Rev Percell Perkins from the Mississippi Blind Boys. While they never quite matched their Mississippi counterparts, neither artistically nor in terms of popular acclaim, they were nevertheless a major force among the hard gospel quartets largely due to the savagely commanding voice of Clarence Fountain . . . a screamer of epic proportions. After a spell with Savoy Records in the sixties, the Original Blind Boys of Alabama gradually lost their hard edge, finally being reduced to singing dispirited versions of songs like *Danny Boy*. Humiliation and indignity were regular burdens heaped on the back of gospel groups, never sadder than when self-inflicted.

During the 1940s and 1950s there were far more exceptional quartets than a book like this can possibly do justice to. Rev Sam McCrary led the great Fairfield Four out of Birmingham during those two decades, but he was also their front man (boy) in their original 1921 line-up at the age of seven *and* occupies the same position in the re-activated group today, when his duties as pastor of St Mark's Baptist Church in Nashville allow. The Jubalaires took gospel quartet into the rock 'n' roll era, appearing in several Elvis Presley films and with people like Ry Cooder. The Chosen Gospel Singers were a fine, emotional quartet with Lou Rawls and Joe Hinton in their early line-up, eventually changing their name to the Gospel Keynotes in the mid-1960s when they began featuring the stratospheric voice of the young Paul Beasley. The Pilgrim Travelers were possibly the first gospel quartet to be heavily promoted and they earned huge sums for Specialty Records from 1948 onwards. Like the famous Soul Stirrers (see Chapter 5) they hailed from Texas and copied many of their stylings, but they had the powerful voices of Kylo Turner and Jess Whitaker to carry them through. From Richmond in Virginia came the Harmonizing Four with their polar opposite to the star falsettos of other groups – the incredible bass voice of Jimmy Jones. And so many others – the Paramount Singers, the Selah Singers, the Flying Clouds of Detroit, the Swanee Quintet, the Highway QC's, the Bells of Joy. . . .

T he era of male group dominance of gospel began to be overthrown towards the end of the 1940s with the emergence of their female counter-parts, singing three-part harmony arrangements. By the middle of the 1950s, the male quartets were in rapid decline and only a tiny handful survived on into the 1960s with anything like the success of their hey-day.

From out of the heart of the deep South came the Angelic Gospel Singers – Margaret Allison, Lucille Shird, Josephine McDowell and Ella Mae Norris. Their downhome versions of the old hymns and gospel tunes, loosely sung to piano and some-times organ accompaniment, turned them into one of Gotham Records' hottest properties in the early 1950s. Some of the earliest records were as joint ventures with the Dixie Hummingbirds and they formed a popular double bill for many years with songs like *Standing Out On The Highway* and *Jesus Will Answer Prayer*.

In the North at about the same time, the ill-fated Davis Sisters were beginning to rise to prominence. An initial line-up had Ruth Davis, her sisters Audrey, Thelma and Alfreda, Imogene Greene and Curtis Dublin on piano. Imogene Greene, a child-hood friend of James Cleveland's stayed for only a few years, later replaced by Jackie Verdell, a contemporary of Aretha Franklin. At the height of their fame the Davis Sisters rivalled the Ward Singers and were one of the young Jessy Dixon's great idols, 'I remember when the Davis Sisters sang – there were five ladies and one man at the piano – but they sounded like a choir. They didn't have to hover round the microphone, they stood way back and directed their voices to it. That was some of the best singing that the world has ever known.'

Their seemingly limitless vocal power might have put them at the very top but they were continuously dogged by tragedy – no less than four of the group's singers met with untimely deaths. One Davis Sister was burned to death in a horrific accident but the story of Ruth 'Baby Sis' Davis, is perhaps the saddest of all. In her prime she thundered forth with consummate ease, her lustrous contralto as hard as nails, but she was dragged down physically by diabetes and by the kidney and liver disease that finally killed her in 1970, a veritable shadow of her former self.

# NEWARK ARMORY
### SUSSEX AVE. & JAY ST. – NEWARK

## SUN. OCT. 20 3 P.M
### 1968

★ ★ ★ ★ ★

# RONNIE WILLIAMS ★ 24th. ★ ANNIVERSARY CELEBRATION!!
## WORLD CHAMPIONSHIP QUARTET BATTLE ★ ★ AUDIENCE WILL BE THE JUDGE

# DIXIE $500. CONTEST
# HUMMING BIRDS
# CLOUDS OF JOY
## REV. WILLINGHAM

# SWANEE QUINTET
## REV. CLAUDE JETER
# SWAN SILVERTONES

# PILGRIM JUBILEES
## BRO. PAUL FOSTER
# SOUL STIRRERS
# VIOLINAIRES
# GOSPELAIRES
# 5 BLIND BOYS
### · THE SONS OF THE ·
# DIXIE
## HUMMING BIRDS

5 BLIND BOYS
of ALABAMA

### EATS · Drinks · Bar - B - Q ·

Tickets on sale    BROOKLYN, N. Y.    Newark, N. J.    Pee Wee's, 260 Belmont Ave.
at: Gottesman's, 1560 Fulton St.;    J. & Z. Record Shop, 441 Springfield Ave.;
Birdell's, 540 Nostrand Ave.;    N. Y.    Rainbow Records, 125th St. & Lenox Ave.

TICKETS  $2.50
$3.00  $4.00  $5.00
CHILDREN $2.00 ·

NEWARK, N. J.
PHONE 242-2910
2 43-9419 — 248-3287

# WASHINGTON TEMPLE 1372 BEDFORD AVE. BROOKLYN, N. Y. SAT. OCT. 19

At the National Baptist Convention in 1943, Mother Gertrude Ward of Philadelphia introduced her 14-year old daughter Clara, and caused a sensation that carried through two decades. The fabulous Ward Singers were far and away the most successful female group of gospel's golden age, tearing up churches by the hundred with an intoxicating repertoire of old Watts' hymns matched with the pick of the new Dorsey and Brewster songs.

Clara Ward was the star of the group and star is definitely the right word. Acutely aware of her ability to shout an audience by moaning a hymn like *The Day is Past and Gone* or *Amazing Grace*, she became ever more flamboyant in both dress and manner until it all became an elaborate spectacle. People went wild for it and turned the Wards into a travelling phenomenon. 'They were like the Supremes,'

smiles Jessy Dixon. 'They wore fabulous gowns and they travelled in this long limousine with a trailer on the back that carried their costumes. They would go to different churches on Sunday mornings and sing just one song and then announce that they would be back that evening. At night you wouldn't be able to get near the place because all the people would have telephoned around to say that the Ward Singers were in town – it was like an underground movement.'

At their peak during the 1950s they were the ultimate female gospel stylists, blessed with a vocal chorus that for eleven years included the illustrious voice of Marion Williams, a Holiness singer out of Miami. The Clara Ward spectacle and charisma drew the crowds, but it was Marion who increasingly took over the job of delivering the goods. It's

*The Davis Sisters (Below). Right, the funeral of Ruth Davis in 1970 drew massive crowds. Bottom right, Gertrude and Clara Ward (wearing outlandish headgear) view the body of Ruth Davis*

Ray Funk

her voice on the Ward Singers' million-selling hits – Brewster's *Surely God Is Able* and *Packin' Up* – soaring up from growling blues to a staggeringly high soprano. Clara could still slay them with the odd hymn or two and her fame was so great that she was still able to beat Mahalia Jackson into second place in the polls, but Marion's was the voice that really mattered.

Towards the end of the 1950s, when the Ward Singers were the undisputed queens of gospel, Clara pushed the group to undignified extremes, decking them out in bizarre wigs and showy outfits, milking her massive reputation for all it was worth. 'There were occasions,' remembers Madeleine Bell, 'when people turned up to see the Clara Ward Singers and Clara wouldn't even be there. It got so that she had three or four different groups and they

were all called the Clara Ward Singers. If you were an agent you had to specify you wanted Clara *and* the Ward Singers or you didn't get her. I remember she was a very small woman, Clara Ward. She was thin but she was *not* thick!'

In 1958, the main group including Marion Williams, decided to go it alone and split off as the Stars of Faith, soon to become the featured group in Langston Hughes' smash hit play *Black Nativity*. Clara, scarcely daunted, quickly regrouped and went all the way into show business. In 1961 she scandalised the churches by signing a 40-week contract with a Las Vegas nightclub to do mock gospel routines for a fee of $200,000. They re-signed her for another 40 weeks and then another until she was finally as tragic as Las Vegas itself. She died on January 16th 1973, when she was still only 48 – a bizarre self-parody at the end, but a great gospel adventuress in her time. 'I watched her carry gospel into many, many places where it hadn't been before and where it hasn't been since . . .,' said her old friend James Cleveland, adding 'Giants fall and little chips grow. Many young persons who were inspired by her as I was, will pick up and carry on like Clara would have wanted them to.'

If the Wards' mantle of female supergroup was passed to any of the little chips in gospel it must be considered to have passed to the legendary Caravans. Though other fine groups followed more directly in Clara's footsteps – the Imperial Gospel Singers from Philadelphia's Christian Hope Baptist Church for instance – few female gospel acts had that same stardom written all over them in the way the Caravans had.

Organised originally in 1952 as the backing chorus for Robert Anderson (striking out on his own after leaving the Roberta Martin Singers), their early recordings for States focussed on the powerful lead voice of Albertina Walker on traditional songs like *What A Friend We Have In Jesus* and *Blessed Assurance*. When the famed contralto Bessie Griffin moved up from her native New Orleans to join the Caravans in Chicago, Albertina stepped aside to let Bessie lead on most songs, including *Since I Met Jesus* and *Ain't That Good News*. Putting Bessie out front was Albertina's tactical ploy to gain

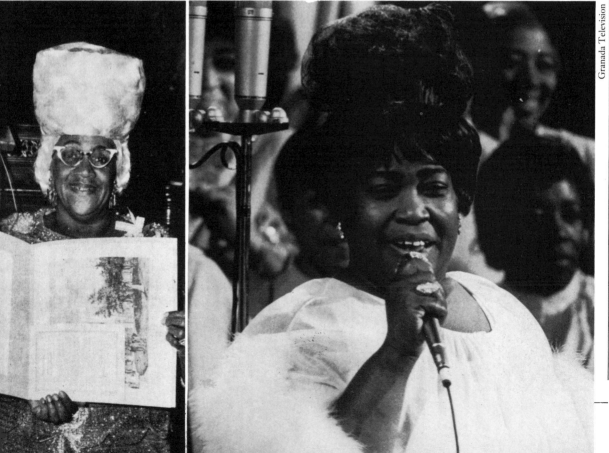

Clara Ward (opposite page, above and centre top). Gertrude Ward receives her citation from the City of Philadelphia (centre below). Marion Williams (below right)

national attention but it didn't work out and Bessie moved on to continue seeking a recognition she deserved but never did receive.

As Bessie Griffin moved out, the young James Cleveland, rising composer and arranger for Roberta Martin's Studio of Music, moved in. The new Cleveland arrangements were distinctly hot and classy, propelling the Caravans into the avant garde of female gospel and attracting a rush of phenomenal young singers – Cassietta George joined in 1955 followed by Dorothy Norwood, Inez Andrews and Imogene Greene from the Davis Sisters. The excess of vocal talent made for a highly volatile group existence and the Caravans were always an explosive unit. When properly motivated, they sparked one another into compelling antiphony but petty rivalries and money problems forever intruded and the great voices came and went.

Albertina was always there and the hugely popular Inez Andrews – a statuesque Alabaman with the most uniquely melodic shriek in the whole of gospel – stayed for about five years. Madeleine Bell was with the Alex Bradford Singers at that time and has vivid memories of Inez, 'We did a couple of programmes with the Caravans and I remember her singing lead – she had an amazing voice. She was about six feet tall, very thin and I remember her standing on stage at the Apollo Theater leaning on the Hammond organ – she was eight and a half months pregnant – singing *Oh Mary Don't You Weep*, and I *cried*. I could not believe this woman.'

Lippman + Rau

*Inez Andrews – the High Priestress, with the Andrewettes* (above)
*Bessie Griffin* (below) *and the famous Caravans with Shirley Caesar*

With evangelical dynamite added to the Caravans in the shape of the diminutive Shirley Caesar, the group was unbeatable on the road. Shirley had the task of opening the show and rousing the audience to fever pitch, hurling graphic sermonettes at them like an old time preacher. By the time Inez and Albertina came to the front of the stage, the place was already in uproar. Not surprisingly, Shirley wasn't content to be the little warm-up girl for long

and when Inez left in 1961 she seized her promotion and effectively led the Caravans through their peak years with her big crowd pleasers – *Comfort Me, Hallelujah, It's Done, Running For Jesus*, and *Sweeping Through The City.*

Not even the Caravans could hold Shirley for long though and after she left in 1967 to concentrate on evangelism, Albertina found herself deserted by all the rest a few months later. She pulled in new members but the magic was gone and she eventually resigned herself to the solo role that her protegés had all chosen. As a skilful organiser she threw herself into Chicago politics, working with Rev Jesse Jackson and organising the Operation PUSH People's Choir. For a time she restricted her appearances to special occasions, like the Caravans' Twentieth Anniversary Celebrations, when she was honoured by no less than eighteen singers who had all at some time been privileged to serve in the group she'd struggled so long to hold together. For once it seems there's a happier ending and Albertina Walker, the woman who launched more gospel careers out of one group than anyone else, is now at last finding her own mass audience and ironically rivalling Shirley Caesar for the title 'Queen of Gospel'.

Numerically, the quartets always dominated the golden age but there were many female groups travelling the same hard road. All through the years when Albertina Walker's flock ruled the roost and back further through the heyday of the Ward Singers, Dorothy Love Coates and the Gospel Harmonettes were perhaps the main female challenge to their double supremacy.

Dorothy is fiercely uncompromising and has good reason to be. She was a lone voice in the Alabama heartland of male quartet and married twice directly into it – first, briefly, to Willie Love of the Fairfield Four, then much later to Carl Coates of the Sensational Nightingales. The Original Gospel Harmonettes were Birmingham's great female counterpart to the stentorian excellence of its finest sons, but Dorothy was always way ahead of them. While they harmonised with precision and restraint she declaimed with extreme urgency, pushing herself physically to the limit.

She spent two long periods as leader of the Gospel Harmonettes, taking a three-year break in 1959. The rigours of the gospel life, the punishment she imposed on herself through performance and the miseries inflicted by southern racism were constantly undermining her spirit. She never let any of it beat her. When the Civil Rights movement swept the South, she threw herself into the local campaigns of Martin Luther King, marched the streets of Birmingham and accepted jail as an honour. When she returned to gospel with a reorganised Harmonettes, her abrasive spirit was more than re-charged and she captured a mass audience with defiant lyrics of faith and struggle:

'Old Satan is busy stirring up wrath,
Gathering stones to block my path.
Enemies inflicting all the hurt they can,
Throwing their rocks and hiding their hands.
If you dig one ditch you better dig two,
The trap you set just might be for you.
He put it in my heart, you can't change me,
My soul's on fire, and the world can't harm me.'

She was never the greatest voice in gospel but she spoke a greater truth than most. Where others were as docile off stage as they were frenetic on, Dorothy Love Coates lived out her righteousness to the full, commanding a special sort of respect from black audiences. Without any of the Wards' clowning or costumes or hairdos, she rivalled their popularity by becoming a trusted spokeswoman and a heartfelt performer. There is a specific injustice in the comparative obscurity of the Gospel Harmonettes.

With any number of small aggregations blanketing the country throughout the 1940s and 1950s, it might seem that there was little room for solo gospel singers but they had their niches too. Mahalia Jackson of course ploughed her own furrow with spectacular success, but singers like Madame Edna Gallman Cooke found a big southern audience with her country sermonettes on Nashboro Records, Bessie Griffin might have been the greatest of all but she was cheated every step of the way, Brother Joe May had a huge following for his

*The Original Gospel Harmonettes with Dorothy Love*
(inset)

Specialty

Pub: Hill & Range
BMI
Time: 2:15

YOU BETTER RUN
(T. Dorsey)

THE ORIGINAL
GOSPEL HARMONETTES
SP-887

*Sister Rosetta Tharpe, minus guitar for once, with Marie Knight* (standing)

rocking gospel blues, the Reverend Cleophus Robinson packed them into his Greater Bethlehem Baptist Church in St Louis through the 1950s and sold prodigiously for Peacock, Mother Mattie Moss Clark's albums for Savoy achieved gold status but she's been wilfully ignored by historians, Professor Charles Taylor, Reverend Robert Ballinger, James Cleveland – all built their own followings.

Inevitably, they tended to be slightly eccentric, even by gospel's broad standards – iron willed characters who were too brash, too stubborn or too unique for subordination into someone else's group. Sister Rosetta Tharpe, preceding even Mahalia Jackson, was forever her own woman and her music defies all of gospel's categorisation. Essentially a Holiness singer, she nevertheless exuded

jollity rather than passion and her rollicking guitar-based gospel is quite unmistakable 'Rosetta was a great inspiration to me,' Inez Andrews recalled. 'She used to tease me all the time and say, "Come on Inez, you can do it!" I couldn't see no woman picking no guitar like she did, but she did it, and with a lot of grace and dignity.'

She was born Rosetta Nubin in Cotton Plant, Arkansas and debuted as 'Little Sister' with her mother Katie Bell up in Chicago at the age of six, singing *I Looked Down The Line And I Wondered* to an audience of a thousand. The song turned up on her first Decca recordings in 1938 and she was instantly the brightest star in gospel. Moving to New York, her jazz affinities and stylings attracted sinners as much as saints and she took a plum job with the Cab Calloway Orchestra where her rousing, foot-stomping spirituals found an unlikely home. *Didn't It Rain*, *Up Above My Head I Hear Music In The Air* and *Strange Things Are Happening Every Day* have become jazz classics every bit as much as gospel gems and she somehow managed to keep a foot firmly in each door for much of her long career. Listening to her now, it's easy enough to see why the jazz fraternity were happy to take a little religion with her music but quite how she got away with recording *I Want A Tall Skinny Papa* and still face a gospel crowd is a mystery. Even *Life* magazine was surprised to find her still welcome as a church singer on Sundays, having ripped up the clubs all week.

By the time gospel's golden age was beginning to roll, Rosetta had given up the double life and was back with the church exclusively. Teaming up with Marie Knight, a young singer from Oakwood Avenue Baptist Church in Newark, Sister Rosetta Tharpe became one of the great attractions on the gospel circuit, drawing huge crowds – 17,000 to a song-fest in Ponce de Leon Park in Atlanta, 27,000 to Griffith Stadium, Washington DC in 1950 and capacity audiences elsewhere in every State. When she married in 1951, the open-air gospel wedding was reported to have attracted a phenomenal 25,000 paying guests!

She could do no wrong, or so she thought, but uproar followed a blues recording she did with Marie and the two split up – Marie for a chance at pop success which failed badly and consigned her finally to a job as a Brooklyn telephone operator; Rosetta to face the wrath of churches who had forgiven past indiscretions but were more resolute now. She suffered badly this time, the more so because in her heart she was still solidly with gospel. It got so she had no option but to move into Mahalia's orbit – playing concerts on the national and international circuit to largely white audiences who were there for the music but not the message.

Up until her death in 1973, Sister Rosetta Tharpe came to personify gospel to the rest of the world almost as much as Mahalia Jackson did but she was never typical of the gospel mainstream. Like another guitar playing evangelist, Rev Utah Smith (famous for his incredible version of *I Got Two Wings*) Rosetta created a hybrid music, a fusion of swing jazz and jumping spirituals. There had certainly never been anyone quite like her.

Gospel's always been full of people who didn't quite fit the mould. Bessemer in Alabama for instance was renowned for its sensational quartets and any local guy with half a voice would fight tooth and nail for a place in the Kings of Harmony or the Blue Jays or the Swan Silvertones or any of a score of others. Yet in that town there was still Prophet Jones, bedecked in gorgeous robes, playing piano with his feet, who in turn inspired the young Alex Bradford to become everyone's favourite gospel showman through the 1950s and 1960s.

Immediately post-war, Bradford (as he became known to all and sundry) shipped himself out of Alabama and into Chicago where Mahalia and Roberta Martin reigned supreme. Roberta would introduce him at a programme as part of her regal patronage. 'So I got up, and they'd never heard a man make all those high soprano notes before. Baby, they were carrying folks out *bodily*.'

In the mid-1950s he formed the very first all-male gospel group – the Bradford Specials – stunning the gospel circuit with falsetto approximations of the Wards' material and an unprecedented line in choreography. Signed up by Speciality in a rash moment, they suddenly hit with Bradford's own song and subsequent gospel standard *Too Close To Heaven*. It sold well over a million copies and Bradford camped it up all over as the 'singing rage of the gospel age'.

By the end of the 1950s he was using the occasional female voice in his group and Madeleine Bell joined him out of the Glovertones in 1960, and toured Europe with him in *Black Nativity*. 'He taught me just about everything I know as far as singing goes. One time we travelled 2,000 miles by bus from New York to New Orleans for a programme and when I got there I lost my voice – couldn't speak a word, but he taught me how you can sing right over that even though you still can't speak. And the volume I got from him. I'd sing as loud as I could but he'd come up behind me at rehearsals and punch me hard in the back – I trebled my volume and he said, "sing like that all the time – just think I'm going to come up behind you and punch you in the back if you don't". And I still think of that now.' His oblique training techniques earned him the title of Professor Bradford.

On the road, the hardest thing was getting money out of promoters – no less for gospel singers than any other. Bradford's temper was legendary and he had his own way of dealing with those who crossed him. 'One time we were on stage and Bradford suddenly couldn't see the promoter. He was off after him in a flash, leaving us still singing. Caught the man red-handed, climbing out the window with the money-bag in his hand.'

'When he died about eight years ago, my mother tried to go to the funeral in New York but she couldn't even get into the block. So many people turned out, the whole block round the church was roped off.'

There's precious little room now in gospel for eccentric genius in the Bradford mould. As the electric age came down over the music like an avenging angel, singers and choirs, songwriters and publishers, quartets and gospel groups all adapted to its conforming influence or died resisting it. Mostly they died. A religious folk-art founded entirely on the human voice and acoustic music, doesn't sit gracefully alongside an amplified backbeat and a show-time band. Rhythm and blues may have been great dance music but it proved a lousy bedfellow of gospel, inflicting most of its lesser talents on the hapless groups under record company pressure to modernise. Don Robey at Peacock, with a heavy R&B rosta as well as the pick of southern quartets, began to insist that *all* gospel recordings included at least a drummer and preferably a full band. Other companies – Vee Jay for instance – even over-dubbed drums and bass onto gospel tracks after they had been recorded.

Under the onslaught of cheap, badly recorded rhythm sections it seems that solo voices survived easier than groups and women fared better than men – perhaps because the female voice was more naturally able to ring out clearly over the noise. Thus the Caravans (and their graduates like Inez Andrews) and the Patterson Singers who toured Europe in 1968, were able to incorporate an R&B backing into gospel successfully while the Blind Boys of Alabama were not.

The male groups who did survive were the young bloods coming in at the end of the long quartet tradition. Sharp dressers and hard shouters, they met R&B head on and matched it for tearing excitement – exceeded it even. Sometimes they also produced music as compelling as any in gospel's golden age. The Gospelaires of Dayton, Ohio were one of the most expressive of the young male groups with a harmonic range and vocal intensity that is almost inconceivable today. Founded by Melvyn Pullen, Clarence Kendricks and the ecstatic Paul Arnold in 1954, they were virtually unbeatable in the late 1950s and early 1960s with a front rank that included Arnold, ultrahigh tenor Charles McLean and the almost gutteral ragings of Robert Washington. Recording exclusively for Peacock Records with brilliant guitarist Robert Lattimore, they contributed a series of definitive hard gospel performances, including the magnum opus – *Remember Me Jesus*. If I were forced to pick just two records out of the whole of gospel music this would be one of them, for it captures the religious passion and vocal perfections of gospel most completely. Only once did I see them in person and then without Robert Washington, but they damn near laid me out for a week.

\*     \*     \*

'The Mighty Clouds of Joy have been together for about twenty-five years and we're totally dedicated to it. We've had so many offers to go commercial you know . . . if we'd have gone into singing rock and roll, we'd be millionaires several times over, but gospel's in my blood and we'll keep on until they listen.' Willie Joe Ligon sat in a pokey West London hotel room and reflected on a quarter century at the helm of the only hard gospel quartet to survive successfully into the 1980s. 'I started this group when I was fourteen years old and my big inspiration was Rev Julius Cheeks of the Sensational Nightingales. I went to a concert they did in Los Angeles and he became a kind of father figure.'

Young Joe Ligon had moved to LA from Troy in Alabama where he was born, bringing with him the urgency of southern church singing and matching it

*The Mighty Clouds of Joy c.1965;*
*Rev Cleophus Robinson* (top right)
*Professor Alex Bradford*

against the more sophisticated city voice of California born Johnny Martin. The two lead voices then added bassman Richard Wallace from rural Georgia and baritone Elmo Franklin from Florida, and began to sing at small church events around the poorer parts of booming Los Angeles. Soon after, Elmo's brother Ermant joined them and also became their first manager, together with two new members – Leon Polk and David Walker.

A single radio programme broadcast over a local Watts radio station in 1959 was their debut proper, recorded but not issued until nine years later when Hob records in their wisdom chose to dub in organ, piano and drums to songs like *Amazing Grace* and *Take Me To The Water*.

Within a few months, they got their own recording break and the original seven members of the Mighty Clouds travelled down to the Goldstar Studios in Houston, Texas. Word of their great vocal prowess had reached the ears of Don Robey, who was looking to beef up his ailing catalogue of older quartets. He'd already made a small fortune out of the Five Blind Boys, the Nightingales and the Dixie Hummingbirds, but those days were nearly over and only the Gospelaires showed any chance of repeating that kind of success and as he once joked, the Clouds were going to be his 'silver lining'. The day was September 28th 1960 and the two songs they recorded that day for their very first single were *Jesus Lead Us Safely* and *Ain't Got Long Here*. Both songs appeared subsequently on the debut album Family Circle a couple of years later.

For ten years they painstakingly built their reputation as the hardest male gospel group on the road, employing all the vocal weapons in the quartet armoury and dressing them up in a devastating show of youthful charisma. Sporting exaggerated pompadour hairstyles and slick mohair suits they descended on one town after another and left audiences reeling from their wildly emotional performances of songs and sermonettes. The latter was their trademark – spirit-filled tales and exhortations that exploded into screaming climaxes.

*A Bright Side* is their archetypal sermonette – a hair-raising tale of mother/son tragedy in the classic shouting preacher style, that has all the Clouds stretched to their limit, over hovering organ and guitar chords. With Joe Ligon roaring and screaming, forcing the group up higher and higher, it scales a peak of intensity that is almost frightening. 'When we recorded that in 1964,' Joe remembered, 'we put out a call over the radio station and got people to come on down to the studio so we could do it live and get some church going. Just one take we did it in.'

The Clouds have always been full-time on the road since then, rarely doing less than 200 concerts a year and eventually sharing stages with everyone from Andrae Crouch to the Rolling Stones and Earth, Wind and Fire.

In the mid-1970s, the Clouds were on the verge of following the Staple Singers into the gentler pastures of 'inspirational music' – soul with a minimum of stirring. Johnny Martin was pumping it up in the wake of a bitter split with Don Robey's Peacock Records and a prestigious new deal with the ABC conglomerate: 'We intend to go right to the top as an R&B group,' he told one writer. 'See, we've all been around a long time, and we've done our fair share of dues paying on the gospel circuit. It wasn't until 1963 that we could even afford to stay in hotels. When we were on the road, we just had to sleep in our van. You know, the situation with gospel is really weird, nearly all black people are behind the music and its message, but few actively support it, buy the records, go to concerts, etc., and the situation's getting worse. People just seem to play gospel music cheap. The thing we recently found ourselves in with Peacock was a living example of the Lord moving in mysterious ways. Ever since we signed with that company, we had been doing most of our own writing, producing and arranging, but it wasn't until about three years ago we discovered how much they'd been ripping us off for. You see, although we've all been around for a long time, we were pretty naive when it came to being hip to publishing rights and that type of stuff, but what we did realise was that we weren't getting as much money as we were entitled to. So we took our contracts to a lawyer for his advice, and he nearly flipped. He described the terms as "slavery". He was right too, because all that time we had been getting just one-eighth of a penny on what we had written, and we'd been steady selling albums for fifteen years! So we took out a lawsuit against the company, and it was around that time that ABC

Clockwise from top left: *the Mighty Clouds of Joy; Joe Ligon; The Gospelaires of Dayton, Ohio; The Violinaires*

took over. We figured we were finished then because we had gotten pretty cold, no new releases for three years. But the vice-president, Otis Smith, was hip enough to realise that even without new stuff on the market, we were still selling more than some of their established artists. He introduced us to Dave Crawford, who just gathered together a pile of our old albums and disappeared. When we next saw him, he'd written a whole set of new material for us. They didn't need to talk us into recording more commercial sounding stuff, we were all for the idea, because we saw it as a way of getting our message which was, is, and always will be, the word of God, to a far wider audience. The younger generation for example, a lot of the kids in our black ghettos are in pretty bad shape with the drugs thing and crime on the increase. Those are the people who need some kind of spiritual guidance and we weren't really reaching them before. To get to them you have to wrap your message in an R&B sound.'

But Alex Bradford for one, was distinctly less enthusiastic for the new ways of selling the music: 'You know those little men that sit up in their ivory towers and decide what is going to be a hit next month. They have raped the gospel for 25 years trying to kill it. Now ABC is going for it, but they want to prostitute it still. They don't want you to say anything about Jesus or God. They want you to be negative, but if you take the feeling away from it, you got nothing but a plastic kind of thing.'

For a while there in the mid-1970s it looked like Bradford's prediction was going to be the Clouds' reality. They hovered right on the brink of commercial success in the big league and appeared to capitulate to the claims it made on them. The now-familiar ambiguity over lyrics crept in, so that any one track could be taken either as a romantic love song or as a song of divine adoration. Now, someone like Al Green can get away with this because he is clearly perceived as travelling from pop deeper into religion, but if the movement appears to be in the opposite direction – away from gospel and closer to pop – then the motives of the artist are liable to be called into question. The Mighty Clouds began to look as if they were care-fully hedging their bets, preparing to drop gospel altogether and go for gold.

No doubt they could have done it too, but something drew them back into gospel proper. Despite big R&B chart hits like *Time* and *Ride The Mighty High* and the prospect of a phenomenal secular career ahead of them, they chose to get back off the fence on the less profitable side. Even so they were doing pretty well. Their recording of *Live And Direct* earned them a gold album and they won Grammy Awards in 1978 and 1980, with plaudits coming thick and fast – 'no singing group on the face of the earth produces a more joyful sound . . .'

These days, Joe Ligon doesn't strain his vocal chords in quite the way he used to, preferring to share the lead duties with new member Paul Beasley, the amazingly high-voiced singer from the Gospel Keynotes. Nevertheless, he's still regarded as one of the greatest male gospel singers to have survived from the hard quartets. His three original co-founders – Johnny, Richard and Elmo – are still with him and the current group are without doubt the finest male vocal chorus in existence. It was fascinating to watch the effect they had on European audiences in 1983 during a seventeen-day tour that included an audience of 7,000 in Holland and a capacity crowd of 30,000 in England at the Greenbelt Festival who were left reeling after a fantastic late-night performance in the open air. It was quite something to stand among the vast throng of youthful Christians and feel them respond, first in awe and disbelief, then in roaring, shouting support as Beasley's heart-breaking voice took hold of them bodily until, by the end of the night, the whole place was literally jumping several feet into the air.

I realised then, looking out over the thousands of bobbing heads in the cold night air, that there were probably no more than a handful of people out of that entire audience with the merest inkling of gospel's long hard journey. Even among the new generation of young black churchgoers there is little recognition that the Mighty Clouds of Joy – and other current stars like Shirley Caesar – are the last surviving links in a chain that stretches right back through gospel's golden ages.

It's a whole new programme now.

# 5

# WILL THE CIRCLE BE UNBROKEN?

## From Gospel to Soul

'We have a lot of rock-and-roll singers out in the audience,' the gospel singer Inez Andrews said over the telephone from New Orleans last Sunday. 'They come purposely to see what they can learn – or what they can steal. They'll come backstage and say, "Hey, girl, I've got to know what you did on those last eight bars." Rock-and-Roll singers steal even worse than the gospel singers. Because we had something to steal from the very beginning, while they had nothing.'

*New York Times* – Friday, March 9th, 1979

One Sunday in Gary, Indiana a few years later, Stevie Wonder turned up unannounced with Deniece Williams at her local church. Sitting down at the piano he began to sing *Have a Talk With God* to the congregation but, finding the piano badly out of tune, switched over to the church organ. 'He was jamming on that organ too, man. He made it sound like a synthesizer and stuff. He can't even see and he made it sound like a synthesizer. And he swayed back and forth like this here. Then the choir – there were three choirs and they turne it into a mass choir – sang *Oh Happy Day* and he was leading the solo. And my cousin was playing organ and another dude was playing drums, and after church they were trying to get that contract!' Stevie later gave them a new piano.

The route from gospel obscurity to secular acclaim is not quite as well-worn as legend would like to have it. Even at the peak of the soul music boom in the 1960s, when record company men looked on the black church the way oil men suddenly looked on the North Sea, there were always twenty exquisite voices who stayed behind for every one that left. This book is mostly by way of tribute to those who stayed, but it would be a perverse history that ignored the impact of gospel music on popular culture. Besides, the biblical injunction about the minority who stray is appropriate here. Faith is sustained by the many who keep it, but it's also given urgency by those who don't.

*retha Franklin at eighteen, ponders her next step*

Most people approach the gospel/soul nexus as complete outsiders – familiar with the resolutely public face of soul music, curious perhaps about the church confines from whence it came. Nearly twenty-five years ago, when Sam Cooke was enjoying the first flush of commercial success, I chanced on the first recordings in church of the fourteen-year-old and, at that stage, completely unknown Aretha Franklin. The fervent outpourings of such a young girl as she extemporised on the old Watts and Dorsey hymns, was a stunning revelation and sparked a journey of exploration into the roots of soul. It didn't take long to discover that the view is very different for those on the inside looking out.

This is a church that defends its children like a lioness. The fellowships of young people are clutched tight to the bosom of Abraham, schooled in Baptist or Pentecostal mystique, subject to strict disciplines over dress and behaviour. It's rarely brutal or unlovely though and most who grew up under its brooding tutelage turn wistful at old memories of getting dressed up in 'Sunday going-to-meeting clothes' for church outings and family occasions. 'I can remember those church picnics like it was yesterday,' says one ex-gospel singer, 'They were such real happy times for us kids and though we used to kick against the rules, I can see now that it was the church that kept us out of trouble. If we hadn't been in the church we'd have been just hanging around the streets, getting picked up by the police. The church had us so busy with the Lord's work, there wasn't no time left to get into trouble.'

Music holds a peculiar fascination for young people in the church, not least because it flirts with secular temptation. Ever since Thomas Dorsey married off blues and spirituals to create gospel, the sights and sounds of black church music have influenced those of the devil and vice versa. The sense of danger generated thereby, is one of the great attractions for teenagers of gospel music. Despite the familiar claim that 'when you join the black Pentecostal Church, you don't stop dancing,

*Ruth Jones left the Sallie Martin Singers to become Dinah Washington – the 'Queen of Rhythm & Blues'*

you just change partners', it remains an area of considerable tension. Just where devotive worship leaves off and sensual pleasure begins is anyone's guess, but the elders and the pastors will draw arbitrary lines and stick to them. Music that entices pubescent youth is subject to the same kind of church law enforcement as the other pleasures of the flesh – only if divinely inspired and in their rightful Christian context. Musical virtue is as fiercely protected as any other virtue in the black churches.

For many though, it is this very inclusion of temporal pleasures into the religious sphere that makes the black church so down to earth and full of humanity. There's no false asceticism and worship is a thing of riotous exuberance that extends over long periods. It's a form of therapy for the soul, healing the wounds inflicted on it by the heartlessness of the world. James Baldwin's oft quoted description of a store front service, captures it: '. . . we all became equal, wringing wet, singing and dancing, in anguish and rejoicing, at the foot of the altar.' Strength regained didn't always become power realised, but the resurgent qualities of black church worship sustained the saints through two centuries of bondage and oppression.

From this perspective it may now seem that out of such strength cometh forth . . . well, weakness would perhaps be too extreme, but a diminuation certainly. The forms of gospel – the chord changes, the call-and-response, the melismatic styles – are evident in soul music, but the incredible passion and power is watered down to facilitate the crossover.

Sam Cooke is the classic case. Along with Dinah Washington (who began her singing career as Ruth Jones in the 1940s with Sallie Martin) Sam Cooke was one of the most important figures in the transition from gospel to soul. He was born in Clarksdale, Mississippi but the family of eight joined the great migration up to Chicago in the early 1930s just like Dorsey and Sallie Martin and Mahalia Jackson and all the other gospel pioneers. Father Charles became a Baptist minister and by 1940, Sam had his first taste of gospel with the Singing Children – a family group that appropriately enough included his two sisters and a brother. When Rev C.S. Cook (Sam added the 'e' to his last name later) moved to the pastorate of Chicago's Highway Baptist Church, the teenagers organised themselves as the Highway QCs under the guidance of R.B. Robinson, who was at that stage baritone singer with one of the most famous gospel quartets of all time – the Soul Stirrers.

The history of the Soul Stirrers is a book in itself. They were formed in Texas in 1934 and were already breaking out of the mould of traditional jubilee quartet. Even back in 1936 when they were still working as farm hands, the veteran folklorist Alan Lomax was recording them for the Library of Congress and remembers being overwhelmed by 'the most incredible polyrhythmic stuff you've ever heard.' The only surviving member of that original group is Jesse Farley who recalls: 'Back then, we took things as they came. I can remember one time in 1936, the Soul Stirrers held a revival in this all-coloured town, Boley, Oklahoma. Do you know, the whole group made two

*R.H. Harris – the genius of quartet and the idol of Sam Cooke*

Stash Records

dollars sixty five for the entire week? But nobody was married, everybody was young, the fellows wanted to travel.'

Their first time into Chicago created a huge stir in gospel circles. Not only were they applying the Southern quartet style to the Thomas Dorsey songs (*Precious Lord* was early in their programme) but they had also introduced the most revolutionary development in harmony group history – the use of a second lead voice, allowing the first to stand prominent and be a focal point. The innovation may not seem so extraordinary now, but it opened up the way for all the great lead voices of quartet to come through – Julius Cheeks, Ira Tucker, Claude Jeter et al, each owe a debt of *space* to the Soul Stirrers. Within the Stirrers themselves, the man who made the greatest use of the space was Rebert H. Harris. His contribution to gospel quartet is quite phenomenal. Almost all the trademarks of the modern quartet style are traceable to Harris – the lyrical ad libs, the delayed time signatures, the antiphony and especially the falsetto leads. 'Even women didn't sing falsetto in church back then,' he claims and no-one's challenged him on it.

Harris epitomised the new wave of quartet lead and his work with the Soul Stirrers was widely imitated. Sam Cooke was heavily under the Harris spell himself, appearing with the Highway QCs on the same bill as the Stirrers and other quartets like the Blind Boys of Mississippi and the Pilgrim Travellers. During the late 1940s, quartet had become exceptionally popular and a moral laxity had subsequently infected the circuit – even to the extent of female groupies following the male groups around for casual affairs. R.H. Harris was raised to carry himself with integrity and this new thing wasn't his style at all. 'I believe there's this *virtue* that goes along with gospel. There's more to it than good singing. It's a beaconing thing that other folk can see without you talking it.' In 1950 Harris quit the Soul Stirrers 'because the moral aspects of the thing just fell out into the water. The singers didn't care anything about it. They felt they could do anything they wanted.'

Roy Crain was the forceful tenor voice of the Soul Stirrers and the number two man of the group, but he was no substitute for the genius of R.H. Harris. Crain had spotted the still teenage

*Sam Cooke and the Soul Stirrers (Sam far left)*

Cooke singing with the Highway QCs and judged him to be the perfect replacement. Not that he was anything truly exceptional as a singer, but his boyish good looks and lean build matched the mood of the moment. For Sam it was the main chance, fronting the premier gospel group of the time and still not yet come of age. Cooke and the Soul Stirrers were almost permanently on the road through the US, Canada and Mexico and Sam spent a glorious six year apprenticeship with them. 'I had a wonderful time, a wonderful life', he recalled later. 'I was doing the thing I liked best and getting paid for it. The fifty dollars or so a week I got at the beginning seemed like a fortune. I was just a teenager then. Later I earned more and more money until my salary more than tripled. It was one church after another on the one-nighter trail, and at that age, who cares about inconveniences?'

Sam Cooke at first settled for a poor imitation of Harris but gradually evolved his own way with a song. 'Sam was a great thinker,' says Harris. 'He was a singer who could stand and within the process of just singing, create without throwing the background off. I taught him that.' His first recor-

dings with the Soul Stirrers were for Specialty in 1951 and included Thomas Dorsey's *Peace In The Valley* and Roy Crain's song *I'm Gonna Build On That Shore*. Even at that early stage it's clear that the Cooke voice was shaping up as an exceptional asset and within a year or two the group was selling out everywhere they played. Jesse Farley remembered Sam's emergence as a youth idol: 'In the old days, young people took seats six rows from the back, the old folks stayed up front. When Sam came on the scene, it reversed itself. The young people took over... They started this pattern of standing up when the lead singers start bearing down.'

Finally, it all became too much of a commercial prospect for the gospel world to contain. During a Los Angeles appearance by the Soul Stirrers, Sam was quietly approached by the Specialty Records A&R man, Robert (Bumps) Blackwell, an old-time musician and arranger who formerly worked for Billy Eckstine, Earl Hines, Benny Carter and others. 'Bumps told me I ought to switch to the pop field,' said Sam later. 'He said I had the voice, the confidence and the equipment to work as a single, and that I ought to give it a try. Frankly, the pop field hadn't much attraction for me up until then. I was happy enough on the gospel trail and making myself a nice living. I liked the people I was working with and I was learning more and more about show-business every day. But the more I thought about the pop field the more interesting it became. Bumps, of course, had a good deal of influence. He was constantly prodding me to make the change whenever he got the chance. Then there were a lot of things I wanted to do. I wanted to do things for my family, and I wanted nice things of my own. Making a living was good enough, but what's wrong with doing better than that?'

Sam Cooke took the bait, quit the Soul Stirrers and studied the pop market. He listened to all the records, read all the trade papers and rehearsed with Blackwell. He even went to drama school for a while, but he wasn't entirely convinced that he was doing the right thing and his first secular record in 1957, *Lovable/Forever*, was issued under the pseudonym Dale Cook as if to hedge his bets. This fooled no-one and the record sold only modestly. The second was under his own name but *I'll Come Running Back To You* didn't do much better, prompting second thoughts all round.

Then Sam's brother, L.C. Cooke came up with *You Send Me* which they recorded for Specialty the same year. 'We had a lot of help on the session,' Sam remembered. 'Bumps conducted the orchestra and S.R. Crain, my old mentor with the Soul Stirrers, helped on the arrangement. It was he who taught me to use my voice the way I do; the "Oh, oh, oh" gimmick, which is now becoming so popular.'

Ironically, Specialty rejected the song which subsequently went to No.1 and sold two and a half million copies. The company who picked up the recording was Bob Keene's own West Coast Keene Records, with whom he stayed for nine chart entries including the classic *Only Sixteen*. The rest is soul history. Cooke took his place as the greatest of all black male singers in commercial music, fawned upon by the press, idolised by women for his excessive charm and looks, revered by the rising generation of young gospel singers who would soon themselves dominate the pop market. He was the very first true superstar of soul but he was forever looking over his shoulder at the church he'd left behind. 'In those days, everybody who sang gospel believed that if you switched over to popular music, something bad would happen to you,' said Sam's old guitarist Bobby Womack (himself an ex-gospel singer and now a bona-fide soul star in his own right). 'I grew up believing all that and I was afraid to make the change. See the gospel world used to be a lot more sacred than it is now.'

Even though Sam was now making the kind of money in a week that he'd have made in a year with the Soul Stirrers, he was continually drawn back to gospel, as if guilty of deserting it. When he formed his own record label SAR, he recorded the Stirrers and Harris's new group, the Paraders and he gave both Womack and the young Billy Preston their first starts. He even considered returning to gospel completely at one point in the early 1960s, but when he appeared at the Soul Stirrers anniversary in Chicago, the church put on its hardest and most unforgiving face. All the past group members were in attendance at the program and old Pop Harris himself was the master of ceremonies. 'While the Soul Stirrers were on stage, they called Sam up. I was the MC but I didn't know anything about it. Somehow when Sam hit the stage, the crowd went dead and stayed dead till Jimmy Outler and Paul Foster came back. Folks were hollering, "Get that blues singer down. Get that no good so-and-so down. This is a *Christian* programme." And it pierced me to my heart, it *shamed* me how he was rejected by the home people. He walked off stage, tearin'. He was hurt badly.'

Bobby Womack was even rejected by his own parents for leaving gospel. 'Our parents put us out of the house when we started singing pop music. My father said "you will not bring the devil in here! If you gonna aim his pistol, I want him to know who to shoot." In his last years he finally began to accept what I've done with my life. I told him, "Dad, I just want you to see I'm the same guy. I coulda sung gospel to make you happy, but when you died we wouldn't have had the money to bury you."'

Sam Cooke was gunned down in a Los Angeles motel on December 10th 1964. The woman who shot him alleged rape; Cooke's manager said he'd simply stumbled into the wrong room by mistake. Other stories claim it was a mafia killing. Whatever the truth, one of the finest soul voices – in or out of the church – had been silenced.

**'At the Mt. Sinai Baptist Church in Los Angeles, a crowd of 5,000 persons, some of whom arrived five hours before the scheduled last rites, over-ran facilities designed to accomodate 1,500. In an emotion-packed atmosphere, super-charged by the singing of Lou Rawls, Bobby Blue Bland and Arthur Lee Simpkins, women fainted, tears rolled down men's cheeks and onlookers shouted. Gospel singer Bessie Griffin, who was to appear on the funeral program, became so grief stricken she had to be carried off. Blues singer Ray Charles stepped in from the audience to sing and play** *Angels Keep Watching Over Me.*

**Outside someone started a fistfight, and people paid freelance photographers to take pictures of them on the scene of Sam Cooke's funeral posing with a celebrity. One photographer was banished from the funeral parlour after he snapped pictures of Sam Cooke's casket, then peddled them outside for 25 cents apiece. Both in Chicago and Los Angeles, crowds crushed against the doors of the churches and around the cars so much that it took a flying wedge of security guards to get the family in and out. It was 40 minutes after the West Coast services ended before the cortege to Forest Lawn Cemetery in Glendale where the singer was buried, could begin. Two hundred cars were in the funeral procession. Whatever the reasons for the crowds – genuine love or mere curiosity – they indicated thousands of persons' concern for facts about Sam Cooke's life and death.'**

*Ebony Magazine*, February 1965

By consensus, Sam Cooke's very best work was with the Soul Stirrers. While the world remembers him for songs like *Twistin' The Night Away* and *Cupid* and *Having A Party*, surely his real magic is enshrined in all the exquisite Specialty sides he cut with the Soul Stirrers. Nothing he ever did in pop can compare with the searing beauty of *Wonderful* or the urgent narrative of *Touch The Hem Of His Garment* or the falsetto masterpiece *Jesus Wash Away My Troubles*. Amid all the relative pop trivia he later came to record, perhaps only one song rises to the majesty of these gospel gems. Issued the year of his death, Sam's own song *A Change Is Gonna Come* is a modern soul classic. The tune is pure gospel hymn, the lyrics are all hope. Contributing a soaring vocal performance that goes right back to R.H. Harris, Cooke evokes the mood of pilgrimage – both political and spiritual – that is black America at its best:

'I was born by the river, in a little tent
And oh, just like the river I been running ever since.
It's been a long time coming, but I know
A change is gonna come!'

\*     \*     \*

The change, for Aretha Franklin, came when she was eighteen. Cooke was a close friend of the Franklin family and if he could make it in commercial music, why shouldn't she? After all, they all said she could sing as good as Sam – some even reckoned she was better – and as he said himself, 'I'm making good money, and the devil ain't got me. I ain't left gospel.'

Aretha Franklin epitomises church-based soul singing. Neither James Brown nor Ray Charles – who along with Sam Cooke are always cited as the progenitors of soul – carry the same degree of gospel power over into their music. Aretha is altogether more deeply embedded in the gospel mystique, more so even than some of the great gospel names themselves.

It issues from the Franklin family background rather from any particular group experience like

*Mahalia Jackson passes a few things on to a very young Billy Preston*

Cooke. Though Aretha made a handful of recordings as a gospel singer, she was never a household name in the way that Sam was. In fact, in many ways she is overshadowed as a performer by her father, Rev Charles L. Franklin, who pastored Detroit's 4,500 member New Bethel Baptist Church. He's recorded more than seventy albums of his sermons, which all sell heavily even today; for two decades he was one of the most famous of the black gospel preachers, commanding thousands of dollars per appearance. At New Bethel, Franklin Snr would preach so hard that they had two white-uniformed nurses standing permanently by to revive the overcome parishioners!

Rev C.L. Franklin may not have been a member of the Baptist Ministers Conference, but he could boast a Cadillac, diamond stick-pins and alligator skin shoes – all testifying to an eminently successful pastorate. In 1967 the Federal Government took a direct interest in the level of his success and fined him $25,000 for tax evasion. This is all a long way removed from St Francis of Assisi, but the Franklin sermons have an extraordinary power nonetheless throwing echoes back through the sermons of Rev Gates and Rev McGhee to Franklin's own roots in the country churches of Mississippi.

After short pastorates in Memphis and Buffalo, he moved into Detroit and set up home on the fringes of the city's East Side ghetto. The Franklin house was big, ramshackle and tree-shaded with a neatly kept lawn and Aretha grew up there, alongside many other kids who would eventually become huge stars – Diana Ross, Smokey Robinson and all the Four Tops to name but a few. Half a block away, all the pursuits of the ghetto were in full swing. 'The people that you saw who had any measure of success were the pimp and the hustler, the numbers man and the dope man,' recalls Aretha's older brother Cecil. It wasn't a happy childhood for Aretha, despite the fame and fortune of her father. Her mother deserted the family when she was six and died four years later, traumatic events that she never really got over. 'After her mama died,' said Mahalia Jackson, 'the whole family wanted for love.' Franklin's long-time friends were the Clara Ward Singers and two of them – Frances Steadman and Marion Williams – stepped in to comfort Aretha and 'show her how to take care of herself.'

The Wards were always in the house, so was Mahalia and Sam Cooke and James Cleveland. Any excuse for singing the good old gospel songs was taken up and Aretha would often sit in the corner and watch as the shouting, clapping and moaning went on all through the night. When one of her aunts died, she became mesmerised at the funeral as Clara Ward shouted herself into a trance on the old Dorsey song *Peace In The Valley*. In her fervour, Clara tore off her hat and hurled it to the ground. 'That,' says Aretha, 'was when I wanted to become a singer.'

She was just twelve then and her first attempts at public performance were in New Bethel, mimicking all the mannerisms of Clara Ward. The church went wild over her from the very beginning; after her first solo, Franklin Snr was mobbed by his parishioners, telling him 'Oh, that child can sure enough sing!'

Within two years, Aretha was a featured performer with the Franklin gospel caravan, an evangelistic team who toured endlessly by car – except for Rev Franklin himself, who chose to save his

*The Franklin Superstars: Aretha* (bottom) *and the Reverend C.L. who finally passed away on July 27th 1984 after five years in a coma*

strength and travel by plane. The experience of the road encouraged her performing skills, but it also aged her prematurely. Cecil Franklin remembers it: 'Driving eight or ten hours trying to make a gig, and being hungry and passing restaurants all along the road, and having to go off the highway into some little city to find a place to eat because you're black – that had its effect.' In later years, Aretha would say only half-jokingly, 'I might be just 26 but I'm an old woman in disguise – 26 going on 65.'

By the time she was eighteen, Sam Cooke was hitting with pop records and Aretha's generation of young church singers were listening intently. One close friend was the young Jackie Verdell who'd been singing leads with the famous Davis Sisters, and the two girls decided to try out the commercial field that same year. For years it was touch and go who'd make it first. In fact it looked at first as if Jackie would be the most assured probability – her voice was the equal of Aretha's and she had a confidence in front of club audiences that Aretha lacked. 'I was afraid,' said Aretha, 'I sang to the floor a lot.' Despite the commercial clout of a Columbia Records contract, nothing happened for Aretha Franklin until years later when she switched to Atlantic Records, dismissing her Columbia material by saying 'It really wasn't me.' Jerry Wexler was the producer at Atlantic and was shrewd enough to spot what was missing from the jazzy froth she'd been given to work with. 'I took her to church,' he said, 'sat her down at the piano, let her be herself.' To that he added the hardest R&B backing that Memphis could offer and the result was some of the very best music that has ever emerged from the soul factories of the 1960s. The first to take off was *I Never Loved A Man The Way I Loved You*; it sold a million copies in a matter of weeks. 'It had looked for the longest time like I would never have a gold record,' said Aretha when she got the news, 'I wanted one so bad.'

The subsequent stream of immaculate soul hits followed the same formula of church feel matched to R&B, and the Baptist preacher's daughter became the undisputed Queen of Soul. The public face of Aretha Franklin was of a woman in her element, at the very peak of her creative power, supremely successful as a commercial artist, a model for any young church singer with ambition.

They weren't to know the personal agonies and the remorse she was suffering away from the stage lights. Her marriage to a Detroit street-hustler had been a disastrous mistake, the more so since Ted White had also taken over the management of her career. In 1967 there was a much publicised incident when White's private brutality spilled over into public and he openly beat her up in the foyer of Atlanta's Regency Hyatt House Hotel. Nor was it the only such incident, prompting Mahalia Jackson to comment tersely, 'I don't think she's happy. I think somebody else is making her sing the blues.'

When she visited Britain that same year she was still intensely neurotic – 'peeping out from behind her self-imposed curtain,' wrote Leonard Feather in the *Melody Maker*. On stage at London's Hammersmith Odeon though, she opened up sufficiently to turn the audience inside out, especially when seated alone at the piano for songs like *Dr Feelgood*. Even coasting on a blues tune, Aretha is more emotion than most people can handle.

Within two years, her isolation was virtually complete. On a David Frost British TV show in November 1970, she was monosyllabic and defensive until they sat her at the piano. She chose to sing *Precious Lord*, defying show-business conventions by shouting to camera 'I'm strong in my religion. I wish other people knew Him like I do.' Valerie Wilmer, writing in *Down Beat*, found her to be 'plagued with a feeling of insecurity. She seems to come to life only on the stage.' And in the *Observer* Sunday newspaper, Tony Palmer commented that Aretha 'has become impenetrable, even to her friends.'

This wasn't the childish petulence of a prima donna. At the heart of her trouble lay the realisation that she wasn't simply a great voice who happened to learn her stuff singing for the Lord. She was a gospel singer through and through and the commercial music business was anathema to her soul. Her gospel family were the only ones who properly understood this and she confided her anguish only to them. She went eventually to Mahalia Jackson, as a daughter to her spiritual mother, and told her, 'I'm gonna make a gospel record and tell Jesus I cannot bear these burdens alone.'

For some reason, Aretha had never drawn the same sort of violent censure from the church that other deserters had. Perhaps it was C.L. Franklin's status that inhibited the critics or perhaps it was because they sensed that she had never really left them. Aretha was like an icon that had been borrowed for an exhibition and whose owners were expecting its return. The demons that she wrestled with were very private but the battle for her soul was public enough. 'I'm looking for Aretha to come back one of these days,' said a close church friend, 'She won't be happy till she does.'

Finally, she did it. In January 1972, James Cleveland assembled his Southern California Community Choir and Atlantic set up their mobile recording unit in the new Temple Missionary Baptist Church in Los Angeles. Aretha was back home in front of an ecstatic congregation and she turned the whole building out. Not since her first recordings in New Bethel had Aretha hit this level of emotional intensity and, over a two day period, she improvised on the hymns and gospel tunes closest to her heart: the Clara Ward classic *How I Got Over* (Clara was in the congregation with mother Gertrude, who moaned away in the background), Inez Andrews' song *Mary Don't You Weep* and of course Dorsey's *Precious Lord*.

It's one of the oldest of spirituals – *Amazing Grace* – that inspired her to the greatest heights however, and she took ten and a half minutes to practice her extraordinary art to the utmost limit. This was the Queen of Soul's finest moment and she drew on all her prodigious vocal powers to wring every drop of pathos and meaning out of the hymn. Even on record, it is almost unbearable in its extremity and it can still move the hardest heart to tears. If anyone should doubt Aretha's true musical calling, they should be placed alone in front of an efficient sound system and made to experience the full explosive intensity of this event. Even at second-hand, the home-coming of Aretha Franklin is the ultimate gospel encounter.

As the entranced choir and congregation attempted to recompose themselves, James Cleveland brought Rev C.L. Franklin up to address them. This, he said as they dabbed their eyes and fanned their brows, 'took me all the way back to the living room at home, when she was six or seven years of age. I saw *you* crying and I saw *you* respond, but I was ready to bust wide open. You talk about being moved – well, not only because Aretha is my daughter . . . Aretha's just a *stone* singer. If you wanna know the truth,' he declared with bursting pride, 'she has never left the church!'.

It should have been a happy ending, but nothing's quite that simple it seems. Just one month later, the great Mahalia Jackson's heart gave out and Aretha went to the funeral of one of her closest and wisest friends, singing *Precious Lord* over mother Halie's body just as the gospel matriarch had sung it over the body of Martin Luther King. If the constraints of the music industry hadn't been so overpowering, then she might have picked up Mahalia's mantle at that point and kissed the world goodbye. As it was, she returned to an increasingly lack-lustre career in pop music and the church got by without her. The last time I saw her in 1982, she was such a sad and pathetic caricature of her former glory, lumbering half-heartedly through her least demanding pop hits, grossly underselling a bitterly disappointed audience. I can't really believe that it's by free choice that she wastes herself in this way, to the extent that she even hires a third-rate session tambourine player so lacking in feel that she must provide him with sheet music. More than anything else in her performance, this was the most poignant symbol of gospel music corruption by commercial property ethics.

When C.L. Franklin sank into a coma after a shooting incident, Aretha drew back to nurse him and share in his silent isolation. After years of devoted seclusion she consented to break her vigil and take the lead in 'Sing, Mahalia, Sing'. Preparing to open in Detroit in the summer of 1984, the fates once again intervened in her life and daddy C.L. slipped from his coma into glory. Mahalia's story should perhaps have been Aretha's own but she never got to play it for real and now was unable even to play it as make-believe.

Neither Aretha nor Sam Cooke were the first to market their soul. For many people, Ray Charles is the greatest gospel singer who never was.

Arguably, he was the first major artist to take the essential black church sounds and fashion them into an attractive commodity. Maybe because he was never a gospel singer in the first place, Brother Ray has never had the same kind of traumatic relationship with the church that Sam and Aretha had. Ray had no compunction about taking the moans of the saints and the cries of Archie Brownlee, underpinning them with down-home gospel piano and calling it soul. He is the great paradox of black music – the father of the soul movement who was brought up in the Baptist faith but who has studiously avoided any *direct* gospel references, while embracing every other genre from modern jazz to country and western. 'All music is related,' he tells Gary Kramer, 'A gospel music background is important to a jazz musician for it draws out feeling. What you speak of as *soul* in jazz is *soul* in gospel music. The important thing in jazz is to feel your music, but *really* feel it and believe it – the way a gospel singer like Mahalia Jackson obviously feels and believes the music she is singing, with her whole body and soul.'

Like most bona-fide legends, his own history requires little more than a recap. Born Ray Charles Robinson in Albany, Georgia on September 23rd 1930, he was blinded totally by glaucoma at the age of six and orphaned at fifteen. Though he never sang in a church, religion was a big influence. 'Everyone in a small town went to church, and I mean you had to go too. Sunday school in the morning, then regular services, home for dinner and back for Baptist Young People's Union. Then there were the evening services, and you'd get home about ten at night.'

There are stories told that he did at one stage sing gospel, even that he was once a member of the Five Blind Boys (a story put around by a press-agent) but none of them are true. 'If you love something, it's bound to rub off on you. But I never sang in any church choir or anything. My first singing was in a rhythm and blues kind of thing. No I didn't have too much time for choirs and things; I was too busy trying to make two dollars 'round about then.'

Ray is almost on the defensive about gospel music and he'll usually try to change the subject, as if embarrassed about the use he's made of it to turn

*Ray Charles – the greatest gospel singer who never was*

those two dollars into two million. It's not generally known for instance that Ray has a huge collection of gospel records, mostly duplicated onto tape and carried round with him. Alex Bradford, the hard shouting gospel professor from Alabama, was a big influence on him; 'Ray Charles told me I was his ideal as a gospel singer, and if I ever wanted to send him a song, all I'd have to do is announce my name and he'd give it first preference.'

Charles' predilection for a good gospel song provided him with some of his biggest commercial successes. *What'd I Say, Hallelujah, I Just Love Her So* and *This Little Girl of Mine* are all fairly direct parodies (the latter being the most blatant steal from Clara Ward's *This Little Light of Mine*) but his plagiarism extends even to the more obscure material – in *Lonely Avenue* he does a note-for-note copy of *How Jesus Died* as sung by Jess Whitaker of the Pilgrim Travellers. Big Bill Broonzy was scathing of his method: 'He's got the blues, he's crying sanctified. He's mixing the blues with the spirituals. I know that's wrong . . . he should be singing in a church.'

For all this, Ray Charles must still be reckoned as a musical genius. We can only speculate what he

*Dionne Warwick graduated from the Drinkard Singers –*
*"the best singers I ever heard."*

A lot of young gospel singers went through the door that Ray Charles had opened. Apart from Sam Cooke and Aretha, Lou Rawls came out of the Pilgrim Travellers, Wilson Pickett left the Violinaires, the Fairfield Four said goodbye to Roscoe Robinson and Joe Henderson, David Ruffin moved on from the Dixie Nightingales and the Soul Stirrers produced another graduate in the person of Johnnie Taylor. Don Robey, boss of Duke-Peacock Records, took Joe Hinton from his lead position with the Spirit of Memphis with the idea of making 'another Sam Cooke' out of him. Clearly, not all who defected found their fame and fortune.

\*      \*      \*

The Drinkard Singers of New Jersey were one of the more successful 'academies' of soul, having launched the singing careers of no less than four popular artists – Judy Clay, Cissy Houston and sisters Dee Dee and Dionne Warwick. Contrary to popular myth, Dionne never actually recorded with the Drinkard Singers but, as she told me recently, 'You might say I cut my teeth on this music . . . coming from a gospel singing family, that was the music and teachings I grew up with. It was, and it still is, the happiest sounding and feeling music that I know. Church life was quite steady, because my grandfather was a minister and his family played an important role as part of the congregation and as choir members. The Drinkard Singers are all my aunts and uncles and my mum. They're still very active in our church – New Hope Baptist Church. They were the best singers I ever heard – I'm proud to be part of the family.'

During the early 1960s, Dionne Warwick began her famous association with songwriters Burt Bacharach and Hal David after doing session work for them. The team scored an immediate hit with *Don't Make Me Over* followed by the 1963 million seller *Anyone Who Had A Heart*. A second gold disc a year later with another Bacharach/David song *Walk On By*, firmly established her in the very front rank of sweet soul singers and today she enjoys phenomenal success on the international concert circuit.

I tried to draw her out on the issue of crossing

might have been capable of had he sung gospel, but his performances (particularly his live performances) of heart-tearing songs like *A Fool For You* are among some of the most moving moments in soul music. At the Newport Festival in 1973, on the same bill as Aretha Franklin and the Staple Singers, he held a vast crowd spell-bound with *Just A Man* – solo at the piano with his own song of the most profound lyrical beauty. Outside of gospel, it is one of the few recordings that can be counted as an ultimate artistic statement; and if that sounds like pretension then it's a necessary inadequacy in the face of such expressive music.

Brother Ray opened the door to commercial acceptance for ambitious young gospel singers and in so doing he fathered the soul movement. LaVern Baker and Dinah Washington married church and pop music before he did, but he was the catalyst for its final emergence as soul. As Nesuhi Ertegun says, 'Ray wasn't the first to do this, combine gospel and blues. He is the best of a long tradition – there were people singing this way twenty years ago. But Ray was able to bring so much of his own to it.'

over from gospel to secular music, but she was noticeably on the defensive. 'Taking the word secular on its face value, the answer to this question is simple – I'm making an honest living. To go into depth would take hours, so I'll simply say that as long as I'm able to look out and see smiles on people's faces, then I believe that secular music is *not* what I'm singing. I'm using a God given talent to provide those smiles on people's faces. My grandfather was probably my biggest fan – he felt as I do that the honesty I approach my singing with cannot ever be criticised by anyone.' Pressing the point further though, I put it to her that she was now reaping benefits that would have been impossible if she'd stayed in gospel and I wondered if perhaps she had *any* regrets about making the choice; whether maybe she'd be poorer but happier now. The implicit cliches drew a suitably sharp response from her. 'To set you straight, the names James Cleveland and Shirley Caesar are very well known and popular and these are just two recognised gospel singers. They also display gold and platinum albums on their wall as I do. They both live in spacious homes with pools and tennis courts as I do. None of us are poor but we're all extremely happy, so I hope this dispels your preconceived notion that one has to be in the pop field to be a recognised public figure. As far as I'm concerned, there's no conflict between church music and popular music – my church upbringing always did allow me to voice my own opinion and it still does.'

It's not generally known that Dionne Warwick still works behind the scenes to educate people about gospel music and she clearly retains a great sense of its importance. Her personal catchphrase for instance is taken from the letters GOSPEL: God's Orders Sung Portraying Everlasting Love and she's also written a foreword to Dr Joan Hillsman's textbook on *The Progress Of Gospel Music*. In it she lists some of the great pop names who've grown up with gospel and demands to know 'Why is it then if gospel played such an important part in all of these lives, it has not been recognised in our music teaching in our school systems? It has been said "no-one would be interested enough to study it". How then did we become interested in Beethoven, Bach and Brahms? Simply because these were the chosen masters of music to study . . .'

Watching her shimmy out onto the concert stage, transfixing thousands of fans who'd payed £12 a head for fifty minutes of sheer pop artistry, it's difficult to accept that it's the same gospel daughter who once sang only to God's greater glory. Unlike the phoney nostalgia of other superstars though, Dionne acknowledges a tangible debt to her roots and sees herself almost as an unofficial envoy for gospel music. As far as she's concerned, it isn't that her beliefs have changed, merely the way in which she earns her living. Her parting shot was 'I'm still a very religious person and that still plays a very important part in my daily life.'

\*     \*     \*

While it became commonplace for individual singers to leave gospel groups and take up pop music, it was much rarer to find whole groups crossing over to the secular field and even rarer for them to achieve anything at all by it. In the early 1950s the Selah Jubilee Singers, who had given twenty-five years to gospel quartet singing, were persuaded to switch to pop by Bess Berman of Apollo Records and they ended up ignominiously as The Larks. The long established New Orleans Humming Four heeded the call of the Imperial Record Company and became The Hawks. Another New Orleans quartet, the Delta Southernaires, were marginally more successful in rock 'n' roll as The Spiders; not exactly a 'Hall of Fame'.

One of the very few groups to have enjoyed real success in both gospel and pop is the Staple Singers. As a family group, the Staples can look back over a career spanning thirty-four years, dividing almost exactly into two parts. In 1950, Roebuck Staples strapped on his sixty dollar pawnshop guitar and presented three of his kids to the Mount Zion Baptist Church in Chicago where his brother Rev Chester Staples was pastor. Cleotha, Pervis and Mavis sang country spirituals over the blues chords of Pops' guitar and the congregation, in their white shirts, slicked hair and fancy clothes started crying and wouldn't stop. There's something in the way the Staple Singers harmonised back then that immediately evoked memories of the old South for the hardened city exiles and the family group were immediately in demand around the Chicago churches.

Roebuck of course, was one of the exiles himself. He was born in 1915 in Winona, Mississippi and started out learning the blues guitar styles of Big Bill Broonzy and Barbecue Bob while working in the plantations. He got converted when he was 15, started singing in the Baptist Church and joined up with local spiritual group the Golden Trumpets a year later. For a couple of years he toured with them round the Mississippi churches but the Depression was destroying the cotton industry and he and his wife Oceola and their two children added themselves to the long trek northwards in search of work. Like so many others, they settled in Chicago and Roebuck took up with another gospel group, the Trumpet Jubilees. The explosion of new gospel sounds was happening in Chicago at exactly the same time and all the excitement generated by Thomas Dorsey and Sallie Martin over at Pilgrim Baptist Church, had a profound influence on the young Roebuck. He had a family to look out for though and he served long hours in the steel-mill, the docks, the construction site and the car wash, bringing them all safely through the Depression and the war years.

While Yvonne and Mavis were still at school, the family group were called to the studios of United Records in 1953 where they cut about eight sides. United only issued two of them – *Sit Down Servant* (issued as *Won't You Sit Down*) and *It Rained Children*, selling the rest off later to the Sharp and Gospel labels. *Sit Down Servant* was just another traditional spiritual on a two-bit label and it didn't set the world on fire. 'It sold about 200, that first thing,' said Roebuck. They heard us – a lady from the record company – and liked us, so we recorded. But the man who owned the company, he wanted us to do rock 'n' roll . . . we wanted no part of rock 'n' roll. So he held us for two years on contract with that one record. When his contract was up, Vee Jay asked us to come and do a record, so we did and that record sold 1,000. The first Vee Jay record we made was *If I Could Hear My Mother Pray Again* and as it sold 1,000 I thought Vee Jay was disappointed with us, so we were ready to quit. But Vee Jay said "No, no, when will you be ready to go into the

*The Staple Singers* (left and below) *are the first family of gospel cross-over, with a continuous stream of hits from the 1950's right up to today.*

Dennis Morris

studio?" And I said, "I'm ready to go in now". So we went in and we made *Uncloudy Day* and it sold like rock 'n' roll!'

*Uncloudy Day* isn't by any stretch of the imagination the stuff of a conventional smash hit, but it is undoubtedly one of gospel's masterpieces. A ponderous blues hymn, it ushered in the two dominant features of Staples' music – the tremeloed, economic beauty of Roebuck's guitar and the awesome, sensual voice of Mavis Staples. Their years with Vee Jay produced their greatest artistic triumphs – 30–40 tracks that are quite unlike anything else in gospel music. They are instantly recognisable from the thousands of groups of the time, not simply by their sound but by the controlled intensity of their performance. Roebuck is one of the most under-rated of guitarists, possibly because he is a master of the under-statement, using the absolute minimum of notes, sometimes almost as if he can't bear to actually touch the strings. Mavis, on the other hand, is one of the most moving singers ever produced by black America. Particularly on these early recordings, her breathy exhortation and searing entreaties are the embodiment of all the traditions of gospel and she is an incredible communicator on stage. On the few occasions I've heard her in person, she seems to be able to summon up super-human qualities from the depths of her soul, leaving her audience breathless and dumbstruck. Even during the more recent programmes when much of the time they'll sound like a disco outfit, Mavis will pick out a slow spiritual and stalk up and down the stage with her arms jacking downwards, piling on the emotive fervour until those standing open-mouthed beneath her can't take it any more. Then she'll pause and savour the moment, shaking with exhaustion, until she gets her breath back. And just when they think she's coming back down, she'll start in again and force them up and over the limit.

There was always a degree of speculation about whether the Staple Singers would cross-over. One of the last recordings they did for Vee Jay was a version of the Tindley hymn *Stand By Me* which featured Mavis at her most impassioned and vibrant best. Had it been secularised and given a lush backing it would have halved the effect but doubled the sales potential. (Leiber and Stoller saw the chance and did just that for Ben E. King.) Another of the Staples' 1958 recordings *This May Be The Last Time* was stolen by the Rolling Stones and turned into big money.

When they did finally make moves in a commercial direction, it wasn't at first into soul music but into folk. Bob Dylan went around for years eulogising over the group and especially over the voice of Mavis Staples and they eventually signed to Riverside Records where they did a series of tepid 'folk-gospel' albums. The white folk music fans loved them and they enjoyed celebrity status at all the big folk festivals for a while, but Pops wasn't too happy. 'Riverside really tried to put us in a folk bag so we could be more commercial so we could sell records, but we still didn't quite make it with them. When it didn't work we tried Columbia. Our first producer there, Billy Sherill, couldn't find us either so they brought in Larry Williams.'

Their material till then had been strictly devotional – either traditional spirituals or Roebuck's own gospel tunes. In 1967 they were persuaded to secularise the message – take out any direct references to God or Jesus, and substitute vague concepts of love and understanding. That way the label got themselves a saleable commodity and the Staples were able to convince themselves that they hadn't sold out. The first of the Larry Williams productions was *Why Am I Treated So Bad* and it proved the label's point by entering the Hot 100. A year later they switched to Stax, where Al Bell began to produce the kind of soul hits that finally took them to international acclaim. *Heavy Makes You Happy* was the first to go really high in the charts and Mavis was both relieved and delighted. 'We knew Al had the sound we were looking for. We started doing much bigger shows, rock concerts. We just got bigger and bigger. *Respect Yourself* earned us a gold disc of course. It started with the kids, you know they had little slogans saying *Respect Yourself* which they'd attach on the backs of their shirts and stuff.'

Fame bought them the respect they deserved from the rest of the world but they were fast losing it from the church. In an incident remarkably similar to one experienced by Sam Cooke, Tony Heilbut describes how deeply their rejection was felt. 'On Thanksgiving Day 1969, they made a rare gospel appearance in Philadelphia, where Mavis' latest ballad was a smash hit. They went back to the same routine that had sustained them for years; the Staples are probably the only gospel group who still feature the songs they sang in 1956. Mavis shook hands on *Help Me Jesus* and groaned with suffering on *Tell Heaven I'm Coming Home One Day*. Philadelphia remained very still. The girls walked off stage shyly and obviously hurt. But Roebuck wouldn't give up. "Listen church, you have to look out for yourself," he said strumming the guitar. "Don't nobody want to go to heaven more than I do, children, but we got to live down here too." The message was clear, but no "Amens" resounded. Finally Roebuck brought Mavis back to sing *Precious Lord*. I've seldom seen her work harder. She was all over the audience, crying, roaring, running. Four ladies screamed, the least such effort deserved, but the rest of the church remained very still. The applause was barely polite as Cleotha led the entranced Mavis out.'

*Sam Cooke*

Motel manageress says
SHOTS

Mavis always defends the move into commercialism, but she doesn't come across with any great conviction. 'You know since we become "stars", whatever that is, it's been pretty hectic and everything moves kinda fast. *Be What You are, I'll Take You There, If You're Ready, Come Go With Me* – our records are kinda funky but we still do message songs. But we had to move with the times. Now we try to get our message across to a bigger audience, that's all. I don't think the message in our lyrics has changed since those times. Sure, the beat's got harder, but the message is the same.'

These days it's almost obligatory for famous soul stars to allude to a gospel background – mostly real but occasionally imagined. It does a grave disservice though to gospel music, to conclude that it functions merely as a training ground for promising singers. There are dozens of singers who *choose* to remain exclusively in gospel who stand head and shoulders in every way over the big names of soul – Vanessa Bell Armstrong and Twinkie Clark are just two from the current spiritual crop. And for every one who crossed over and made it big, there are hundreds who crossed over and didn't. Whereas Aretha Franklin lives in fabulous, if troubled, luxury – Jackie Verdell, who made the same move at the same time made nothing at all and is now back singing gospel to a faintly suspicious audience.

It's difficult to escape the conclusion that the music industry has attempted to colonise the black church for its own financial gain. That some have been tempted by its offers of glittering reward is hardly surprising. What is more surprising is that so many of the best gospel singers remained and resisted the decimation of black church music. Maybe with good justification they can say, 'What shall it profit a man if he gain the whole world and lose his own soul.'

*The original Soul Stirrers re-union in Spring 1984. L-R: Rev Paul Foster, Lawrence Stickman, S.R. Crain, Ernest Smith, Leroy Crume, R.H. Harris*

Opall Nations

# 6

# THE STORM IS PASSING OVER

OH HAPPY DAY / JOY, JOY / TO MY FATHER'S HOUSE
PAVILION
THE EDWIN HAWKINS SINGERS*
LET US GO INTO THE HOUSE OF THE LORD
*Formerly The Northern California State Youth Choir

## Contemporary Gospel Music

'For months now (and in the record business, months are decades), desperate music hustlers have been searching for the new groove . . . Last week, with appropriate fanfare, they proclaimed they had found the sound: pop gospel. Waving contracts and recording tape, Columbia Records moved into a new Manhatten night club called the Sweet Chariot and began packaging such devotional songs as *He's All Right* for the popular market. "It's the greatest new groove since rock 'n' roll", said Columbia pop A&R Director David Kapralik. "In a month or two, it'll be all over the charts.'

While such fatuous predictions had uncanny parallels in Britain in 1983–84, this one goes back to the mid-1960s, when *Time* magazine were reporting on the 'gospel night club' phenomenon that happened in several American cities.

Joe Scandore was the New York entrepreneur behind the idea, inveigling the unfortunate Nat Lewis Singers from one of the largest Pentecostal churches on the East coast, and the Ellison family gospel group – the Golden Chords, to take part in his ill-conceived venture. The Chords were led by Lorraine Ellison (later to achieve brief but spectacular acclaim for her soul music classic *Stay With Me Baby*) who brought in the Philadelphia All Stars to become the Sweet Chariot Singers; Joe took over the lease on the Peppermint Lounge, turning the former campaign headquarters of the Twist into *The Sensational New Pop Gospel Night Club With 'Soul'*.

The Sweet Chariot opened in May 1963 and drew big crowds for an experience that was bizarre almost beyond belief. The club hostesses were clad in choir robes that reached only to the thigh, where they met opera length stockings. Attached to the back of the robe were a pair of small angel wings and the ensemble was crowned with a wire halo. While the 'angels' served liquor, the singers croo-

109

*Al Green Ministers at the Royal Albert Hall*

ned *What Do You Know About Jesus?* The smart money, as they say, went for it in a big way. Customers (including Barbra Streisand, Neil Sedaka and Diana Dors among hordes of other minor celebrities and socialites) collected their tambourines at the door and relieved themselves in toilets labelled 'Brothers' and 'Sisters'. Kapralik hardly needed to point out that 'these people are not here for a religious catharsis, they are here for entertainment.' It wasn't gospel's most edifying moment.

Mercifully, the fad passed within a year but not before Columbia Records had milked three live albums out of the Sweet Chariot groups, all uniformly repellent – affectations of frenzy and parodies of black religious music. There's an unconscious irony in the cover photo of one album showing the singers holding tambourines clearly, but unconvincingly, marked 'Not For Sale'. Another album carries the barely less plausible claim that 'this album may well serve to mark a turning point in America's musical history: a time when gospel music, of and by itself, is reaching the wide audience it deserves.'

After that little episode it's surprising that gospel was able to command any audience at all, outside of the churches, and indeed six years passed before the music next reached the mass market. Then it was to be in the form of an old black Baptist hymn re-arranged by a young Holiness pianist and singer from California – Edwin Hawkins.

In the meantime the church just got on with the business of being the church and the gospel singers just got on with the business of speading the gospel, perhaps even relieved that white marketing corporations had once again failed them. Despite all the bribes and seductions of the music industry, gospel has survived as the only remaining slice of Afro-American culture that is relatively inviolate. It's often discreetly suggested that this is a function of inverted racism – a black religious exclusivity – when it's simply the defence mechanisms of a culture under attack. Black churches and black gospel singers aren't hostile to white people, only to the secular presumptions and ambitions that they invariably bring with them.

Rev James Cleveland personifies the cultural defender, resolutely defying every attempt to draw him into the mainstream of American entertainment. 'I will not perform for the white man for the purpose of financial profit . . . I don't feel I can do much good in a club. I don't feel that the atmosphere is conducive, and I don't feel that the reason for bringing me there is the reason for which I'm singing. I feel that if they want religious music in the clubs, in the casinos where folks are ten feet away and drinking and gambling, then they should get white singers . . . But they would not insult the intelligence of white singers by asking them to sing in a club.'

Cleveland isn't a political radical by any means, but he is an extremely astute and commanding figure-head, for gospel music at its most uncompromising. Where others will twist and turn and accommodate the curious and usually insensitive outsiders, he has acquired over many long years the right to demand acceptance on his own terms and his own terms only. He's especially scathing about those who seek merely a vicarious musical diversion in the gospel experience: 'You'll find that most white folks, when they do come to a Black concert, all they want to hear is your up-tempo stuff. They're not concerned about the message you're trying to give. They just want a funky beat, something they can clap their hands to, and they enjoy it because it's fun to them.'

Now in his mid-fifties, James Cleveland is the heavyweight champion of gospel music and inevitably he gets dubbed 'The Godfather' by friends and enemies alike. He seems to have been everywhere and always in black gospel, his booming gravel voice on a hundred albums, his name linked to all the great names from the first to the last, his imposing barrel frame fronting dozens of choirs from East coast to West. His six gold albums, his countless production and publishing credits and his massive personal appearance fees have all served to accord him superstar status in Beverley Hills, surrounded by all the trappings of success – a hundred suits, fifty pairs of shoes, a Persian lamb overcoat ('made by the best furrier in Chicago') and a veritable truckload of trophies and awards. Not for Rev Cleveland, the vow of poverty.

It wasn't always so for James. He was born slap bang into the Depression in Chicago and raised in the strict traditions of the gospel church. 'My folks

*Rev James Cleveland growls his praises*

being just plain everyday people, we couldn't afford a piano. So I used to practice each night right there on the window-sill. I took those wedges and crevices and made me black and white keys. And baby . . . by the time I was in high school, I was some jazz pianist.'

By incredible good fortune, his first minister at Pilgrim Baptist Church was the grand old man himself – Thomas A. Dorsey, so the young James had the very best of training as a singer and pianist. When I talked to him recently, he remembered Dorsey with great affection. 'Thomas was, like . . . *magic*, you know. I would go to choir rehearsals with my grandfather and I'd be just electrified by him. He was just about the only exponent of gospel music in those days – he was teaching it and putting choirs together before anyone else. I still keep in touch with him – he's nearly 90 now!'

By the time he was sixteen he was writing songs and selling them to the pioneer gospel singer and publisher Roberta Martin at $40 a time. Two years later he cut his first records for the Apollo label as part of the Gospelaires – not the major quartet from Dayton, Ohio, but a short-lived spin off from the old Roberta Martin Singers.

The 1950s saw him in various guises, none especially satisfactory, but he spent time with the Caravans and featured on their two big hits *The Solid Rock* and *Old Time Religion*. At the end of the decade, James began his famous association with choirs, working first with the Voices of Tabernacle from Detroit and taking them to national fame with a gospel ballad borrowed from Johnnie Taylor and the Soul Stirrers – *The Love Of God*.

Discovering that James wasn't, in fact, under contract at that point, the sagacious Herman Lubinsky moved in and snapped him up for his Savoy label against some stiff competition. 'I didn't want to go with him because I wanted to go to Vee Jay which was a big successful company then.' Lubinsky out-manoeuvred Vee Jay though and the Cleveland signature inaugurated a recording partnership that endures even to this day.

His first choir album for Savoy was devised by Fred Mendelsohn, the new A&R man on the label and now the overall boss of Savoy. He set Cleveland up with the Angelic Choir of Nutley, New Jersey to make the album *Christ Is The Answer*. 'It was recorded under very tough circumstances. We were in the cellar of this very old church, before the Angelic Choir and Rev Lawrence Roberts rebuilt their church in the 1960s, and it was one of the most exciting afternoons I can remember. We were in the cellar, we ran the equipment down there. It wasn't of the best kind. In fact I think we recorded monaural. But we could hear the excitement mounting through the walls and floor when the choir was singing, and when James was singing, and especially when the choir was really getting the Spirit. That was very successful. Now when I say successful, we sold over 100,000 of that album, and in those days it was an unheard of figure in the gospel field.'

It was the second album with the Angelic Choir however that really established him as the hottest property in gospel and earned him his first title as 'Crown Prince of Gospel'. Fred Mendelsohn remembers that session with undisguised pleasure too. '*Peace Be Still* was also live, but Rev Roberts had razed his church and was building another one. So were recorded it in a Seventh Day Adventist Church as that was the only church not already in use on a Sunday. We got the crowds and it was a piece of magic. There too, you could feel the excitement running high and that's what makes an album. The inspiration was there.' It stands as Cleveland's greatest work, selling over a million copies to make it the best selling gospel record of all time.

Gospel was now, finally, big business. Although James Cleveland is the very last person one would ever imagine connected to an enterprise like the

Sweet Chariot, he nevertheless must be considered as one of the first major figures to become involved in the mass marketing of gospel. The essential difference between the two – apart from the financial motives and results – is that Cleveland's market is almost totally confined to the black community. Since he has never been concerned to dilute or package the product for white consumption, his contribution to the internal and organisational strength of modern black gospel has been pre-eminent. Whatever he may have taken out of the black church, he has always re-invested massively in its people, its groups and its choirs.

Nothing illustrates this more completely than the long nurtured ambition he fulfilled in 1968 when he convened the first of what was to become the annual Gospel Music Workshop of America. 'We have tried,' he explains, 'to put our hands out to the many young people who have a desire to better themselves in gospel. We put together these classes where they could learn everything they wanted to know.' The influence of the Workshops – working in local chapters and in national convention – was phenomenal, spawning mass and community choirs right across the country. Cleveland's own project, the Southern California Community Choir, is fittingly the most renowned, due in great part to the patronage of his former protégé Aretha Franklin, who recorded the most impassioned performances of her career with the choir on her double album *Amazing Grace*.

In business he is gruff and calculating, but on stage he is the flamboyant showman of gospel, a silk-suited catalyst growling his praises before massed ranks of be-robed gospel shouters. Whether appearing alongside Jesse Jackson at PUSH concerts or as pastor of his Cornerstone Institutional Baptist Church in Los Angeles, he is always a towering *presence* amongst his people. He's never crossed over to the wide, white market and he probably never will, but his popularity with black church audiences – on both sides of the Atlantic – has never been greater.

'James always did love the music,' says one of his fellow Chicago singers, 'But I can remember when folks paid him no mind. He'd just go to everybody, begging them to let him sing on their programs. Remember, we had some singers back then. The folks weren't particular about that boy. Hmmm, he was so skinny then, he'd go begging us all for food off our plate. It wasn't nothing to see James anywhere, out there hustling. But it paid off, didn't it?'

The long years of service and the indefatigable commitment have indeed paid off, earning for James Cleveland universal respect from all the regular church folks who embrace gospel music simply as the ordinary mode of their worship. It's they who bestow on him the title 'King of Gospel' and it's evident he takes his majesterial responsibilities very seriously, descending without pomp to his subjects, ministering continually to all the choirs who look to him for guidance and support. His is a benevolent patronage, as close to the grass roots of modern church-based gospel as it is to the pervasive traditions of the art. He was, for instance, just as eager to introduce me to the awesome vocal triumph of Vanessa Bell Armstrong's debut album as he was to talk over old times.

True men and women of the people are less rare in gospel than in other musics, but even within the select band of saints and survivors who dominate the modern scene, James Cleveland has perhaps the greatest ability to express the plain faith and exercise the common touch. He's just the big man of gospel and they all love him.

\*   \*   \*

Cleveland's regal counterpart of course is Shirley Caesar, the reigning Queen of evangelistic gospel singing, whose personal calling card still bears the legend 'Down-To-Earth Singing For An Up-To-Date God'. It's an apt description of what Shirley does for a living but it demonstrates equally her delight in the snappy turn of phrase. Her conversation and her singing is peppered all the time with churchy clichés, gospel jargon and stock phrases – 'We're out to reach the lost, at any cost, for Pentecost.' Her audiences roar their appreciation. When she testifies to her Jesus, as she does most of the time, she unleashes a torrent of standard praises – 'He's my Rose of Sharon, my bright and morning star, my lily of the valley, my mountain mover . . .' For a lot of singers this would just be a routine they fall back on when things are getting slack and the folks are getting restless. Shirley's particular genius lies in her ability to take a cliché and infuse it with an original power. It doesn't always quite work but, at her best, she's able to take just about any old truism and turn it into a pearl of wisdom.

It's something she couldn't pull off without that voice of hers. There's a rough kind of urgency in the way Shirley sings that leaves you in no doubt whatsoever that she's in deadly earnest. A lesser singer will sometimes coast along for effect, content to be applauded for being on stage and staying in tune, whereas Shirley gives the impression that she could never sing two notes without hinting that the third might be her last. She's what you might call an eschatalogical singer – nobody sits comfortable, or immortal, while she's on.

She was born to be this kind of evangelist. Myrrh Records put the start of her career at the age of seventeen, but by that time she was already a hardened professional. At only ten years old she was singing with her sisters Anne and Joyce, and a cousin Esther, as the Caesar Sisters, appearing at school and at her church, The Love Calvary Holy Church. She first toured and recorded as Baby Shirley (she cut three sides for Federal in 1951 when she was only twelve) and later in the fifties as a duo with Leroy Johnson. 'Leroy was originally from Suffolk in Virginia and he has only one leg. When I met him he was a gospel radio announcer as well as a singer. I went to the station one Sunday with my Pastor for a radio service and he invited me to come back the following Sunday to sing on his programme. From there we started to sing as a duet and that's really how I first came to meet up with a lot of the top gospel singers.'

The city of Durham in North Carolina is her home base. She was born there, one of twelve children, and she still lives there today, refusing to be drawn as so many gospel singers are to the big recording centres of Los Angeles, Chicago or New York. Durham by contrast is in the heart of southern gospel territory and Shirley is about as down-home as you can get. The death of her father, Big Jim Caesar (a minister and the regular lead of the Just Come Four) dealt a disastrous blow to the family and Shirley was out singing to raise the rent before she entered her teens. The experience has forged an unusually deep and extremely public bond between Shirley and her mother Hallie – celebrated often in her songs and in live appearances. After Jesus, her mother is her favourite topic of conversation, to the extent that she nominated the sickly-sweet *No Charge* to me as her favourite recording of all. It's a maudlin country music epic written by noted country writer Harlan Howard and Shirley recorded her version using an all-white session band for the first time. The sentimental song contrasts the materialism of a modern child with the unselfish devotion of an idealised mother. Shirley is the child – but repentant. 'I felt that if I went out and sang as a child, why should I bring my Mum back all the money? Why should I have to take a nickel to school to buy a carton of milk and a biscuit? Why can't I buy hot lunches like everybody else? Back then my mother explained it; she said it was because she needed the money and because we were way down on the totem pole when it came to prosperity. See, I owed her everything but I didn't appreciate that fact. So I say that for all you may give to your mothers you still owe them something and when you add it all up the cost of real love is no charge.'

The recorded version of *No Charge* originally included Shirley's addition to the secular lyrics: '. . . when I think about that, I think about the day that Jesus went out on Calvary and gave his life as a ransom for me. I think about the words: If any man be in Christ, he is a new creature. I like to think that the very minute that he shed his blood, my debt was paid in full.' Scepter Records edited all this out and went for a non-gospel market, though they shrewdly tacked the full version on the B side, thus generating huge sales across the board. There were suggestions at that point that Shirley might take up a secular career, but she countered them in her inimitable way. 'Everybody knows that Shirley's hooked, an addict on gospel, and that I'm an evangelist. The USA doesn't have enough money to make me sing rock 'n' roll!'

Like James Cleveland, Albertina Walker, Inez Andrews, Dorothy Norwood, Bessie Griffin et al, Shirley Caesar is a graduate of the famous Caravans. 'The Caravans came to our area to sing in July 1958,' she told me. 'And I remember there was three of them – Albertina, Inez and Sarah McKissick. I was out of school and I didn't have any money to go back. I went to see them first in Raleigh, then when they left there that Sunday afternoon to go on to a little town called Kingston in North Carolina, I followed them. Sitting in the audience during their programme I wrote a request on a piece of paper and sent it up to them "Please call Shirley Caesar to sing a solo". And they did. I used the song *The Lord Will Make A Way Somehow* and Albertina Walker, who managed the Caravans, said "I want that little girl". After the programme she came up to me and said "ask your Mama if you can go with us". My Mum said yes, so I sold my biology book and I met them the following Thursday in Washington, DC.'

She spent eight glorious years with them, first as the opening act in their programme but quickly establishing her own reputation with fiery solos and blistering sermonettes. 'The Lord used the Caravans as a bridge to bring me to where I am today and I praise Him for that. They were happy days. I was the youngest and enjoyed the good and the bad.' The super-abundance of talent in the Caravans took them into the very front rank of gospel groups in the early sixties but it also generated an impossible pressure within the group itself. Eventually the constraints of the group proved too frustrating and Shirley broke out. 'I felt they weren't letting me use everything. I wanted to do something broader than just singing lead on my numbers. I wanted to go on and say something else, as God and the Spirit took me.'

Shirley Caesar, without the Caravans, took on the mission of evangelist, holding revivals all over the country, preaching every bit as hard as she sang. The people – young and old – flocked to hear her and 'then I came further in two years than in the previous eight'. She began recording in her own name for Hob Records and produced a superb debut album for them called *I'll Go*, recorded with the Young People's Choir of the Institutional Church of God in Christ in Brooklyn. She scored a massive gospel hit with *Stranger On The Road* (duetting with sister Anne). Both records achieved gold

*Evangelist Shirley Caesar – 'Down-to-earth singing for an up-to-date God'*

status. Her 1969 sermonette, *Don't Drive Your Mama Away* took up the matriarchal theme Shirley is so attached to and turned herself into the heroine of every under-appreciated mother. (Another recent hymn of mother devotion appears on her Myrhh album *Rejoice* . . . 'I just stood at the mike, closed my eyes, visualised my mother sitting there, and I talked to her . . . *I Love You Mama*').

From Hob she went to Road Show Records, where they gave her the title 'First Lady of Gospel Music' but it was a difficult period. Though she wouldn't admit it publicly, she told me something of the hiatus they created in her career. 'When I got to the studio to record *Shirley Ceasar – First Lady*, I found that they'd already laid the tracks and it was really rock music. Now here I am the same type of traditional gospel singer and never ever in my life had I sung to that kind of music. Now that's more the kind fo stuff they're doing but then the church wouldn't accept it and so consequently it made my career be sort of at a standstill for a while. I was just singing gospel but the music was too far out for the churchgoers. I never had any control over it.'

In a curious way it may have eventually worked to her advantage. As she joined the Christian label, Word Records, in 1979 she took with her the unearned reputation of an artist far ahead of her time. Coupled with her more proper identity as the ferocious queen of down-home country gospel, she was able to extend her appeal to the widest audience. Almost like one of her own clichés, Shirley Caesar today combines the best of the old with the best of the new.

In the hands of a lesser personality, that combination would end up as a very soft option – old time schmaltz mixed with tepid funk. Shirley's special qualities, transforming the most mundane and corny of songs, are to be found in her unique voice and her evangelistic commitment to a 'deliverance' ministry. 'I teach. I preach. I have a praying ministry. I have an altar in my home where I pray for hundreds and hundreds of people. I have a radio ministry every Sunday morning, 10–10.45 am on WSRC in Durham. God is doing his thing right from Durham, N.C. I don't have to move to a big city, big attorneys and this and that. The Lord chose this little spot where I'm home with my invalid mother and family.'

'My ministry is more geared to the lowly . . . to those really going through something, who are broke, busted, downtrodden and destitute . . . really out of it. For some reason the Lord always gives me an answer for them. A girl came by my office the other day who was on her way to kill somebody and the Lord gave me a message for her. She was saved right then and there. Another girl last week in St Louis was getting ready to commit suicide. God gave me a word for her. Now she wants to live and live for Jesus.

'I have a person-to-person ministry. I'm not a

star. You spell star backwards and it spells rats. I'll take time out and witness until they turn the lights out on me backstage. Our mightiest place should be at the feet of Jesus. The minute we get too high, the Lord brings us down.'

Shirley Caesar came up from grinding poverty and retains an intimate relationship with the ordinary poor in the black community, though she is herself now extremely wealthy. At her wedding a couple of years ago, when she married Bishop Harold Ivory Williams of the Mount Calvary Holy Church, 2,500 fans turned up to the lavish and spectacular event and many of them stayed for a slice of the eight foot long wedding cake. The bride and groom sang their vows to each other, George Scott of the Original Blind Boys sang *One In A Million* and the Durham Youth Orchestra played Pachelbel's Canon. Not counting three officiating ministers, there were no less than 140 people in the wedding party, including three best men, 23 bridesmaids, 14 junior bridesmaids, 14 junior groomsmen, a complement of flower girls, train-bearers and candle-bearers, and two preschoolers acting the part of miniature bride and groom. Only the fog-machine, hired to provide a mist effect during the ceremony, refused to play its part in the Hollywood-style production. 'This wedding's costing me something like twenty-five thousand dollars,' said Shirley, adding with a mischievous chuckle, 'But I've never been married before and I felt like this was a chance for me to feed the hungry and clothe the naked.' Hallie Caesar, the bride's mother and object of Shirley's undying devotion, sat fanning herself centre stage and fended off the man from the Washington Post. 'Don't you think she's entitled to it?', she demanded.

Shirley Caesar would be a bizarre anachronism were it not for the fact that she is supremely able to communicate great truths through her music. Hers is a populist gospel – the simple, unsophisticated faith of working men and women told in a raw, uncomplicated fashion. To those who don't know her, she might be taken for the kind of boot-legging evangelist who sells religion by the pound, but she's utterly genuine and the regal razzmatazz is just a side-show – her way of knowing how far up the rough side of the mountain she has come. 'Those that have come up the smooth side of the mountain will slip because they have nothing to hold on to. But because the Lord has taken me the slow and sure way I've learnt to use something special that you can't buy anywhere else. Any group that climbs to the top overnight, if they should fall there is no rock or twig, no branch, no nothing that they can hold onto.'

Shirley is unique in modern gospel music, seemingly able to draw upon all the strongest elements of the gospel tradition and weld them into a thoroughly contemporary and thrilling ministry. 'I can sing for any audience, whether they are young or old. I think it's a shame that many talented singers put themselves into a box. I'll sing for anybody who needs to hear the message I have to share.'

\*       \*       \*

In terms of white understanding of black gospel, no-one has more actively crossed over in recent years than Andrae Crouch. Out of the self-proclaimed Jesus Movement of dis-inherited evangelicals arose a demand for an overtly Christian counter-culture which manifested itself largely as music with a message. At open-air festivals and in Christian coffee bars, through radio and records, a whole generation of young white Christians seized upon Andrae Crouch as a synonym for black gospel. It was something at which he worked consciously, toning down the emotional excesses of the gospel performance and absorbing the smooth pop sophistication of the West Coast session singers.

Unlike James Cleveland, Andrae was happy enough to adapt to the white market as he made clear in an interview he did with the influential NBC programme *Today*. 'Sometimes you sing for white audiences and you know they're thinking "Oh, these guys are going to be swinging from the chandeliers." So I start out with something nice and easy (demonstrating on the piano), and after I get them warmed up, I can move to something like this . . .' Which would be fine if he were simply offering a starter to a substantial main meal, providing a point of access to the uninitiated. The problem so often with Andrae is that he has wandered ever deeper into territory that delights in bland and superficial music, so much so that after his nice and easy intro he'll usually follow in with an equally nice and easy snack. Middle America in the seventies went overboard for it, just as they did exactly a century before with the Fisk Singers – and for exactly the same sort of reasons.

In view of what he's said elsewhere on the subject, we ought to ask whether James Cleveland is merely being diplomatic when he tells the (white) Gospel Music Association, 'Andrae Crouch has bridged the gap between black and white audiences . . . The white artists are very interested in the more soulful type of gospel music . . . In the contemporary sound of gospel music, many black musicians are now embracing the contemporary sound. There is a great upsurge of white choirs that sing like black choirs, and the blacks have always tried to excel and perfect performances relating to sound, arrangement and instrumentation. Orchestrations and the like bring us closer to what the white man has been doing all the time . . . So they're coming our way and we're going their way. Somewhere in the middle of the road we're bound to run into one another!'

Andrae occupies that middle ground like nobody else, with the result that a lot of his recordings sound like a test-card soundtrack, but his roots go much deeper. His father, Rev Benjamin Crouch, ran a family cleaning business in East Los Angeles, conducting a spare-time ministry as a 'boot-leggin' street Preacher' before setting up the Emmanuel Church of God in Christ with Andrae's great-uncle Samuel M. Crouch. With his twin sister Sandra – currently beginning to rival him as a gospel artist – he remembers 'playing Church' at the age of eight, using a pie tin for a tambourine and a commode for a pulpit. At nine he got saved for real, through his father's preaching. 'I sat there in the audience listening. When he gave the invitation I went forward. I just felt so close to the Lord. I cried and cried. When everybody started singing, I was so happy jumping around that I split my new shoes!'

Several months later his father had to decide whether or not to accept a pastorate at a church with no music director. 'One day in the service dad

*Andrae Crouch – Singer, songwriter and salesman*

called me up front, laid hands on me and prayed "Lord I don't know what you want me to do, but if you want me to be a pastor full-time, really give Andrae the gift of music." He asked me, "Andrae, if the Lord gives you the gift of music, will you use it?"'

Within two weeks the nine year old was sat at the piano bench and playing his first hymns. 'Dad kept his promise and took the pastorate. I played for all the services and later started a choir. At district meetings and youth rallies, I'd play the piano when I could.' It was a commitment made under duress though and privately he was looking for ways out. 'I never had any intention of going into the ministry because my folks were pastors and I knew the hassles. I never wanted to live by "faith" – that is, having to live on the support of people for everything.'

Instead he toyed with teaching as his first career but dropped out to join 'Teen Challenge' – the fundamentalist organisation set up by Dave Wilkerson, author of *The Cross and The Switchblade*. At their Los Angeles rehabilitation centre for drug addicts, Andrae began to develop his songwriting skills. 'There the Lord really put a burden on my heart for people. I saw the effects of my music on people that didn't know the Lord and I began to write songs like *A Broken Vessel* and *I Find No Fault In Him* because there were a lot of troubles around at the time. I was spiritually moved and impressed because I could see the work of God . . . miracles happened right before my eyes . . . and how God used me!'

He formed a choir with a group of ex-drug addicts and started performing with them around the Southern California churches. Although he'd already made some tentative stabs at gospel music in a group with sister Sandra and brother Benjamin Crouch Jr, this was the first time he'd really thought of a career as a gospel singer. 'We saw thousands come to the Lord, so that really launched it. I really had *no* intentions of full-time ministry but it just happened!'

His first taste of recording was with the local COGIC Singers (who were also featuring Billy Preston) but it wasn't until he left 'Teen Challenge' and formed his first touring group that he began to issue records under his own name. *Take The Message Everywhere* was the first album issued in 1969 by Andrae Crouch and The Disciples and it sold well enough to establish them on the professional circuit. A successful second album eighteen months later *(Keep On Singing)* kept them in business and a prime spot on the Johnny Carson Tonight show brought them national fame overnight. By the time of their third album *Soulfully*, Andrae was already developing his persona as the acceptable face of progressive black gospel. In came the slick production techniques and publicists talking about 'a unique fusion of rhythm and blues, country, jazz and Latin rock.' Two huge radio hits resulted – *Everything Changed* and the neo-gospel *Satisfied* – firing Andrae with an ambition to cross over in all directions. 'I want to reach as many people as I can with my ministry and music. I want to take my music to people that have *never* heard the gospel. They have a right to hear it. A lot of times we don't promote our music like the secular field and I don't think that's fair.'

1974 saw him on stage at New York's Carnegie Hall in front of ten thousand devotees and though he was declaring 'we couldn't care less about recording a concert . . . we had church', the subsequent live album proved to be his biggest promotional triumph so far. As gospel music itself began to be recognised in some quarters as a legitimate and viable form of modern show-business, so Andrae came to greater and greater prominence. A succession of best-selling albums followed, each more refined and lavish than the last, until the production techniques came to rival anything that LA session funk could offer. On *This Is Another Day* he went the whole way, drafting in people like Joe Sample from the Crusaders and Leon Russell so that, lyrics apart, there began to be little to differentiate Andrae's style of gospel music from the predominently bland sounds of West Coast pop.

His songwriting redeems him. While he cannot really be considered as having added greatly to the sum of gospel music as a performing art – he's more of a musical chameleon than an innovator – he has certainly written some great and memorable songs. *Soon and Very Soon* and *Start All Over Again* are already beginning to enter into common congregational usage and *Jesus Is The Answer* became universally known through Paul Simon, who featured it heavily for years, earning for Andrae his first gold disc. 'I have one question when I write a new song: Does it reach you? I feel the feedback from an audience if the song is working. I know what is real – that's what I get being raised in the church, before those congregations,' he says.

In 1981 he disbanded the Disciples after losing mainstay Danniebelle Hall and founder member Billi Thedford and all future albums were credited solely to him. He still put together loose aggregations of singers for tours and for special occasions but the gruelling round of live shows was giving way rapidly to studio recording. With his long time drummer and co-producer Bill Maxwell he made a determined bid for commercial breakthrough to the national charts with *Don't Give Up* – a studio extravaganza involving just about every top LA session musician. Despite the backing of the giant Warner Brothers corporation, the album failed to impress pop fans and left Andrae with only the murmers of church critics for having attempted it. To them he replied 'I believe the lyric of a song and the actual feel of the music are two different things. For example, by taking the infectious beat of Motown, the well-produced, innovative Philadelphia Sound, the simplicity of Nashville or Muscle Shoals, and attaching it to the Lord's message, a lot of people are going to listen.'

If this was controversy, nothing could prepare the church for the thunderbolt which struck one cold night in December 1982. While his parents were away at a Church of God in Christ convention in Atlanta, one of the church deacons met up with Andrae at his Marina del Ray apartment. The intention was to go out for a meal but they never made it to the restaurant. 'When we got ready to leave, we were pulling out and I saw these police cars. In Marina del Ray they're always pulling people over. I'm a very cautious driver. I was getting ready to make a turn. I see this police officer on the side of me. Before I knew it their lights were on, I thought, "What is this guy doing? I'm not speeding". I was just totally blown away. So I pulled over. He said, "You're Andrae Crouch aren't you?" The deacon pulls out a new album I'd just given him and says, "Yeah, this is really him". So it was just like a joke.'

The joke was over though when they searched the singer, found an empty vial and arrested him for possession of cocaine. They held him for nearly ten hours until the deacon could arrange for the $2,500 bail. 'I kept going to sleep and waking up every 10 minutes,' Andrae remembered. 'I thought it was possibly a dream, but I couldn't snap out of it. One of the other prisoners told me that God would pull me through. "Just listen to your songs, man" he told me.'

Within a few days the district attorney dropped the charges for lack of sufficient evidence but the damage was already done. Sadly, it's not at all unusual for gospel singers to dabble in drugs – especially on the West Coast, where dope is as much an accepted stimulant as whisky – and there were many who shrugged their shoulders and presumed him guilty. Andrae's own explanation and detailed rebuttal of the claims were set out in a lengthy interview with the magazine Contemporary Christian Music. It allows for only two possible conclusions. Either he was the innocent victim of a chain of unfortunate circumstances or he was repeatedly lying through his teeth. Surprisingly perhaps, in the light of their frequent criticisms of Andrae's worldly ways, the church gave him the benefit of the doubt. 'I got over 4,000 phone calls, thousands of letters and telegrams from around the world. If I had any fears that the church, the precious body of Christ, would come to me and say "I told you so", those fears were blown away from the first day. "Andrae is just like us," it seemed like they were saying. "He hurts like we hurt. He's a criminal . . . we love him." Suddenly, all the differences I'd ever had with the church just faded away. People who'd criticised my music the most were loving me!'

It was a measure of the church's capacity for trust, even in extreme circumstances, but it doesn't (and shouldn't) preclude critical appraisal. The pursuit of opulent life-styles by a handful of top gospel singers sits as uneasily with the tenets of the Christian faith as any other vice. Andrae's empire has grown to become a massive global operation through his Crouch Ministries, run by the former head of the South African based 'Invisible Church'. His several palatial homes in California and Hawaii bear witness to the vast financial gains he has made from gospel music. Where people like Shirley Caesar and James Cleveland seem to have retained a simplicity of faith *as performers*, despite all the trappings of fame, the same cannot be said for Andrae Crouch. There is a complacency in his music that is more a reflection of casual Californian values than the righteous fire of the black churches. He himself describes his studio base as the 'laid-back laboratory of the Lord' and he's far more likely these days to be found alongside Pat Boone and Billy Graham than with fellow COGIC singers like the Clark Sisters. Whether it's God or mammon that leads him into the middle of the road isn't really the issue – the motives of an artist are hardly ours to pass judgement on – what is of legitimate concern is the end result. Gospel music is but a *representation* of eternal Christian truths. Insofar as faith is a light in temporal darkness, so gospel music must stand in shining contrast to the superficial trivia of popular culture. All too often, Andrae Crouch sounds like a pale imitation thereof.

There have been times when the same could have been said of Jessy Dixon. Like Andrae, he crossed over to the more lucrative white audiences – largely thanks to Paul Simon, who regularly featured the Jessy Dixon Singers in all his performances and recordings and even films – he acted and sang in Simon's feature film *One Trick Pony*. For a while, he became every pop singer's favourite gospel novelty and he turned out regularly for Phoebe Snow, Leo Sayer, Diana Ross, Natalie Cole and Cher. The word was, that if you needed a bit of discreet gospel vocalising to liven up your act, Jessy was your man. It helped that he wasn't a Christian. Like many singers who earn a living singing gospel, Jessy Dixon sang without believing, which meant he could be relied upon to provide the facsimile without waving the original around in an embarrassing manner.

His origins are authentic enough. He was discovered in his native Texas by the Pilgrim Travellers, whose manager J. W. Alexander (also Sam Cooke's manager) set him up as accompanist to Brother Joe May – the 'Thunderbolt of the Mid-West'. His parents were less than delighted. 'My father was a Methodist and doing pretty good in business. My mother was Sanctified but she didn't approve of gospel – she wanted me to go to college and be a proper musician.' For a while he was dutiful, enrol-

*Jessy Dixon, the crown prince*

ling as a music major in his local San Antonio college, but James Cleveland passed through and offered him a job with the Gospel Chimes.

Chicago was his first stop but New York saw his debut. "My first professional engagement was at the Apollo Theater and James Cleveland had me to work hard. He was headlining and he had some local acts – I think the Caravans were on that bill. I remember that James took me there from Chicago and I didn't know he was going to have me sing. I was so nervous I almost fainted! I sang *There's a Brighter Day Ahead*, a song which he had written.' Cleveland took over where the San Antonio college was obliged to leave off and Jessy talks with great affection about his basic training. 'I was like an apprentice – I played the piano and Billy Preston played the organ. James would teach us and talk to us like a father. He'd tell us how to stand at the microphone and how to enunciate. He used to say, if I was in college I'd have to pay for this but he'd taken me on *and* was giving me money to sing. I thought I was rich, making twenty-five dollars a week!

'Then he took me to New Jersey, out to Savoy Records which was owned by this Jewish guy, Herman Lubinsky. He'd recorded the Davis Sisters and all these people and they liked my organ playing, so I played on the Roberta Martin Singers' albums. I was about eighteen then and much younger than them. One day Herman Lubinsky was in his office and heard me singing a song called *There Is No Failure In God* – this was from the studio two doors down – and he came out with his big cigar and asked who was singing. I was afraid to say it was me, I thought I'd done something wrong, but he said "I'll record you on your own", and that's how I got started.'

It was the era of the big choirs and Savoy had already had their first smash hits with James Cleveland and the Voices of Tabernacle *(Love of God)* and the record breaking Angelic Choir *(Peace Be Still)*. Where Cleveland led, his pupil Jessy Dixon was still bound to follow and he began a long association with the Chicago Community Choir. 'This was a choir which had something like a hundred voices – school teachers, nurses and people who didn't have anything to do at night, who wanted to sing in hospitals and jails and places like that.

This wasn't for money, it was just as a hobby. Lubinsky asked me to use them on a record, which was a hit and we were asked to come to Carnegie Hall to sing gospel with James and Shirley Caesar.'

In many ways it's surprising that Jessy Dixon stayed with gospel. The pop attraction was ever present and he was keenly aware of the opportunity. 'I remember meeting Dionne Warwick in New York. We were both fans of gospel singers, though neither one of us was saved at that time. So we'd go around and listen to people like Marion Williams with the Ward Singers and Alex Bradford. These people made an impression on me and when the opportunity came for us to sing, Dionne chose secular music because she was doing background vocals. I was doing the same thing, I was playing on secular records but I didn't want to sing it.' Even the way he dresses now – cream-suited like an Ebony sales director – is something he got from Sam Cooke. 'Sam was with the Soul Stirrers when I was a little boy. He had such a manner about him, he was always very calm. He always had a suit on and he was always immaculate. I think I dress like him!' Mahalia Jackson would have laughed at that – she used to say that she always thought of Jessy Dixon as the little boy with the runny nose.

For a man who's got three gold albums to his credit. Jessy's recording career has been patchy in the extreme. Not that he's lacked the wherewithal, just that he seems never to have shaken off the 'young James Cleveland' tag. This, together with his lack of Christian conviction, has made for some half-hearted performances. It should by rights, have all changed in 1972 when he underwent a dramatic conversion. 'I was making a living singing,' he says, 'It was all I knew how to do because it was all I had ever done. My singing was anointed, but I wasn't.' He'd put on a pretty good act over the years and was known to get happy in the spirit with little provocation, but the shouting and the fervour were a sham and some of the other singers were beginning to spot it. Not that they were all entirely blameless in this respect and it's to Jessy's credit that he at least came clean.

The immediate consequences of his conversion were a new record label and a testimonial album with the re-assuring title of *It's All Right Now*. Unfortunately, it wasn't. Jessy's soul may have been saved but his music continued to be losing to the suffocating confines of his adopted pop culture. Whatever may have happened to him spiritually, he *sounded* lazy, smug and self-satisfied and this album stands out as such a low point that I was tempted to think it was actually an earlier recording. That suspicion grew with his second post-conversion album – *You Bring The Sun Out* which is probably his finest recording in every respect.

These days, like Andrae Crouch, he'll sing more often for white audiences than black and he accepts the limitations that are attached to the bigger paydays. It's a subtle thing, but in return for a mass market he tacitly agrees to deliver a high quality acceptable product. This is relatively new for gospel music. The distinctly low-tech, and discomforting traditions have kept all of its best art outside of the entertainment mainstream, but things are changing. Now someone like Jessy Dixon gets the best arrangers, studios, musicians and producers that money can buy. He jets around the world, stays at the Hilton and enjoys all the orgainisational back-up of a big record company. His part of the bargain is to write and sing songs that will sell and he's a conspicuous professional at the job. He'll stroll into a TV studio looking like a man on holiday and execute a demanding song like *Through The Blood Of Jesus* in one take – with feeling but without excess. Even so, white audiences still get uneasy. At Greenbelt Festival in Britain, after a particularly committed performance by Jessy Dixon, he was dismissed by more than a few for being 'all very over-emotional'.

\*   \*   \*

There's a kind of triumvirate of superstars who work this circuit, reap its rewards and accept its occasional indignities: Andrae, Jessy and the Hawkins family. To them, and particularly to Edwin Hawkins, must go the credit for opening up a world constituency for black gospel.

It happened by chance back in 1969, when the teenage Edwin got involved with the community choir based at his Ephesian Church of God in Christ. Calling themselves the Northern California State Youth Choir, they began preparations to represent northern California at the Youth Congress in Washington DC. To raise funds for the church they cut an album and included the old Baptist hymn *Oh Happy Day*. Edwin was a student of interior design and totally unprepared for what happened next. 'I'd almost completed the curriculum when my whole life turned in a new direction.' Out of nowhere the record began to assume the proportions of a hit. 'We cut it privately by a local recording enterprise who turned out 500 records the first order. The next order for 1,000 also sold quickly. Then things began to happen. A young man who worked in the warehouse used by the non-commercial recorder (Century Records) took the record to the underground rock station KSAN in San Francisco. Shortly afterward, the record hit in 'Frisco – then New York. This was God's blessing on our ministry.'

By Easter, the Hawkins family were being inundated with offers from every major record company in America. The choir went professional, the record got repackaged and the re-named Edwin

*Rev Walter Hawkins*

Hawkins Singers found themselves with a No. 1 worldwide smash hit. Completely bewildered by it all, the Oakland church choir – 56 singers plus 22 chaperones – were flown to New York for their first national concert, at the gigantic Madison Square Gardens. Yankee Stadium was next, for the Isley Brothers' anniversary celebration, but the pressure was too great for some and by the end of the year the choir was down to 22 rapidly hardening professionals.

'Then we began doing lots of rock concerts and festivals. Coming from our Christian background, we weren't sure rock festivals were right to be involved with. We'd been taught not to associate with that part of the world. To see if it was God's will to perform at festivals, we started gathering daily for prayer.' It's doubtful if the Lord's mandate extended quite as far as a tour of the Playboy circuit or the Las Vegas casinos but that was where they went. The folks back home in the church were up in arms but Tramaine Hawkins still feels it did more good than harm and rejects the obvious criticisms. 'Although scripture says that the Gospel should be taken to the highways and hedges, they didn't really consider clubs as highways and hedges,' she says. 'A lot of times I felt the people in clubs were there to party and tuned us out, but a lot of people come to clubs or bars to find some kind of companionship or empty their problems out, and we were up there ministering and singing the same songs we would in church. Nothing new, nothing different. It was the same gospel and I know a lot of people were touched.'

Tramaine met and married Edwin's brother Walter in the group and the three of them are all valuable recording property. The album *Tramaine* for instance sold 75,000 in 60 days. Tramaine Hawkins started singing in her grandfather's church at four and joined the Heavenly Tones three years later. With them she recorded a Savoy album *(I Love The Lord)* and travelled up and down the West Coast until she was fifteen. Sly Stone made them a handsome offer and they crossed over to become his backing group Little Sister but Tramaine bowed out saying 'I knew this wasn't for me'. She joined Walter Hawkins' first group, Praisers of

God, when she was sixteen and also organised the Progressive Three with Walter's sister Lynette and Gail Smith. She's done two stints with the Edwin Hawkins Singers and one with Andrae Crouch and the Disciples. She got engaged to Walter during an appearance by the choir at Caesar's Palace in Las Vegas and married him in March 1971.

Both Tramaine and Walter spent time in Los Angeles attempting secular recording careers for a while but it didn't work out. 'I just really couldn't get into it. There was no feeling there like I can get in gospel . . .' is Tramaine's brief comment but Walter is more forthcoming about it. 'I grew up in church and got to the point where I started rebelling against some of the set-up,' he says. 'I started my own group from the Edwin Hawkins Singers and started doing night clubs because I wanted to do secular music for a while, but I couldn't break the ties because everything I was writing was really Christian orientated as far as lyrics were concerned. And even the people I was meeting in night clubs, we'd sit down and start to converse and we'd end up talking about God.'

*Tramaine Hawkins and brother-in-law Edwin*

The same year he married Tramaine, Walter Hawkins took a Master of Divinity degree and a year later became an ordained minister in the Church of God in Christ. Mrs Mamie Hawkins was beside herself with joy. Like a good COGIC mother, she'd kept her children off the Oakland streets by immersing them in church and she'd always wanted to see one of them ordained. Walter reciprocates with his tribute to her memory – at the back of his church is a shiny wooden chest full of books that carries the plaque 'Mamie Hawkins Memorial Library'.

By 1976, Rev Walter Hawkins was emerging as the new star of the family and his *Love Alive* album released that year stayed at the top of the Billboard gospel chart for over forty consecutive weeks, selling more than 300,000 copies for Word Records. He did almost as well with the two follow-ups, *Jesus Christ Is The Way* and *Love Alive II* and he used the money to set up his own Love Centre Church in East Oakland. His friends were sceptical of his new-style store front ministry: 'They thought it was just a passing phase. All they could see was me

singing all the time. But God has blessed our work. To be a minister is much more rewarding and more fruitful than music alone. We see people of all denominations responding to the message of our church. I look to God to mesh the talents of my music with my calling to preach.'

On the road they're billed as 'Walter and Edwin Hawkins and the Family', but they all give high priority to the Love Centre Church and its musical ministry. It's a non-denominational, charismatic outreach and it roused up further criticism from traditional black denominations. 'We made our appeal to people who were probably normally rejected by other churches because they didn't look like they belonged or because others thought it would ruin their church's reputation . . . I don't think we have a reputation to protect . . . we're not dealing with ceremony, we're dealing with people's real feelings.' (In 1981, the whole family ran into massive controversy for performing at a Gay Rights rally in San Francisco. It was Walter's decision to allow the choir and family to perform, but Edwin backed him all the way: 'I felt it was necessary. Anywhere there's a door open to take the Message in gospel song, we should do it. We're ministers of the Gospel, we're in the music *ministry* . . . I still don't know why the Christian world makes a distinction between the *music* ministry and the *preaching* or *speaking* ministry. I think a *preacher* would or should go anywhere he had an opportunity to preach and reach souls. Why can't musicians do the same thing?') Walter Hawkins sums up his attitude with a prayer: 'Let us be spiritual dynamite, Lord, not just mediocre.'

In recent times, Edwin Hawkins has taken to working the opposite end of the economic spectrum with the very first attempt to mix gospel with classical orchestras. In September 1979 the family found themselves on stage with the National Symphony Orchestra at the John F. Kennedy Center for the Performing Arts and they continued the experiment with a *Gospel at the Symphony* album with the Oakland Symphony Orchestra. Edwin describes it as '. . . God's door to reach a totally different segment of society with the Good News. They're not a church-orientated crowd who ordinarily respond to gospel music. They're the symphony crowd, the sophisticates who would not darken the door of a church.'

The move up-market seems to have gone to the head of the Hawkins' family manager/sociologist (!) Dwight McKee, who came over all pompous at the Kennedy Center: 'Because Washington is the focal point of the world artistically and politically, it was only feasible to present and institutionalise this exciting concept before the White House, the National Black Caucus, the National Council of Arts and other cultural and religious leaders. We can now transcend cultures by presenting this new art form in concert everywhere we go.'

Fortunately, the music transcended the exciting concepts of Dwight McKee but it was a close run thing. Real musical fusions just don't happen at this level of high culture – if they happen at all it's always as an accident of cross-fertilisation, just as the first spirituals were themselves created. If a Committee for the Arts had been set up in the eighteenth century charged with the task of combining Isaac Watts' hymns with African ceremonial music, you can be pretty sure they would not have produced anything remotely like a negro spiritual.

The symphonic excursion of the Hawkins family is less of a deviance if you review the whole scope of their entertaining ministry. They present their Christian religion as great popular show-people would and one avenue of dramatic spectacle is just as useful as another. Edwin Hawkins will use hit records to evangelise and he'll use the National Symphony Orchestra to the same end. 'I think,' he says carefully, 'that many Christians fear some important words such as "concert", "performance", or "show". But we have to realise that this is a business too, and people are paying money to come and see a performance . . . to see a show. The result has to come from the artists on stage, from their motives and objectives, and ours is to minister. At the same time, we want people to be entertained . . . entertained by the Spirit.'

\*     \*     \*

Al Green is a singer who knows *all* about soulful entertainment. Like thousands of others he joined the one-way traffic out of the black churches and into the pop limelight. Then, right at the very peak of his commercial career when he was quite the biggest soul star of the 1970s, he did the most extraordinary thing and quit – to become minister of the Full Gospel Tabernacle in Memphis. It was the most sensational turn-around and it had a huge impact on modern gospel music. Not so much musically, though he *has* forced some important changes, more a kind of psychological boost for gospel morale. Al Green, the man they called The Last Soul Singer in America, the voice that stirred a million hearts, the hero of countless lesser singers, had finally decided that there was more to life than 'scooby-dooby-doo' and had packed up shop and gone on home to Jesus, just like the prodigal son.

He's not the first to have done it. Solomon Burke went from child preacher to soul star and back again and Little Richard's done the trip a few times, but the conversion of Al Green was a massive propaganda blow for gospel music. When he stands up in the pulpit and declares 'He took the rock 'n' roll and the twisting the night away from me, and gave me a new song, a song the angels can sing, and I want you to know his name is Jesus', he's turning the tide of the last forty years . . . all of his lifetime.

He grew up in Forrest City, Arkansas (an hour's drive from his current home) and got a staple diet of gospel music from his family. 'I was raised on it,' he remembered. 'It was put into my cornbread. I ate it. My mother and my father, they were Baptists. We were raised in church, and we sang at home. I started when I was a little peewee. I was just raised on the sound of Sam Cooke and the Soul Stirrers and the whole trip; yeah, that was in the house.'

Al joined up with his brothers as a family gospel group, the Green Brothers, and got his first taste of performing as their tenor lead. Sam Cooke had just switched to pop and Al Green couldn't wait to join him. Clandestine visits to the local record store to catch up on Sam's new style were fuel to his fire but when father found out, he was exiled from the house and the family. It's something that still hurts. If you ask him whether his family liked his pop

records, he'll get very tight-lipped and mutter 'No. They were gospel folks. No.'

Green had moved up to Grand Rapids Michigan, where he scored a local hit with *Back Up Train* in 1967, but it took a few more years of struggle and business rip-offs before he finally got his big break with veteran producer and bandleader Willie Mitchell. Mitchell took him back down to Memphis and they recorded his first million seller in 1971, *I'm So Tired Of Being Alone.* Over the next five years he emerged as the brightest star in black music, selling over thirty million records, picking up just about every award going and in every way taking over the mantle of the big 1960s soul names like Otis Redding, with classic cuts like *Let's Stay Together* and *Take Me To The River.*

The return of Al Green to his gospel roots didn't happen in a blinding flash, but was a gradual process that extended over a period of four or five years. There are conflicting accounts of what triggered the transformation, including the famous story that he was burned by hot grits thrown by a scorned lover, but he dismisses all this as fiction. 'I was born again in 1973,' he says, 'Yeah, transfigured, transformed. It wasn't an incident that did it. No. People are silly when they write that. Nothing happened to bring me to Christ except coming into the knowledge of Christ and being transformed in mind and spirit on a particular morning. Like the old singers sing, "There's one thing I know/That I've been born again". Right. That's all I can speak about, that it has happened to me. I'm a gospel singer now, and when it happened to me, I was singing rock 'n' roll.'

And he carried on singing rock 'n' roll for a good few more years. Not until 1977 did he begin to put his faith on record with the critically acclaimed *Belle Album,* a mystical tribute to the indivisibility of sensual and spiritual love. 'That was the kick-off, the initial thrust-off, the saying that I'm going to do it. I'm going to follow that. If you are really genuine, why don't you go for the real treasure? Now I know all about the financial treasure and that whole trip, but I ain't worried about that. I'm talking about the real treasure, Jesus.' Another time he said of the *Belle Album,* 'The religious naturally goes with art because they're both so *ancient.* I think Belle was the kind of record it was because it channelled both

– religion and rock 'n' roll – and it channelled them so well.'

His next record was *Truth & Time* and it took his pre-occupation with things spiritual to further lengths, but behind the scenes he was slowly being torn apart by all the demands being made on him. Not simply the excesses of super-stardom but all of that in fierce conflict with his growing Christian faith. The crunch came – literally – at what turned out to be his last ever concert as a pop singer. In Cincinnati in September of 1979, Green fell twelve feet off the stage onto a flight case. 'I spent fifteen days in the hospital and I realised I was being disobedient to my calling. I was moving towards God, but I wasn't moving fast enough. The fall was God's way of saying I had to hurry up.'

Now Al Green has learned how to relax, even though he's still under pressure. How, I asked, did he cope with the vastly different demands he faces as a pastor? 'These days,' he answered slowly, 'I have to divide my time between my singing and my church in Memphis and well, I do my best to *rightly* divide it. And I have to devote a sufficient amount of time to do a good job, which is kinda difficult sometimes. I preach every other Sunday in church and we have so many members – in the town, out of town, members everywhere. I have so much work to do in the tabernacle.'

Of his years as a soul hero, he confesses that it's mostly just a blur. 'The only thing I really remember is lights, plenty of lights, always lights, always *psssh, psssh* – singing songs and just lights. I don't remember which days, which nights – who came where in what car, I don't remember . . . just like waking up off a dream – this *flood* of lights. People screaming, the Apollo Theater, roses, this *hustle* and this *bustle*. So, so much going on.' But he doesn't reject it all out of hand as other converts would. 'No regrets,' he says firmly, 'It was wonderful. It was bringing you to where you can understand what you're doing now.' And of his old hits he says, 'They're good songs that won't drive people to war.'

The new Al Green goes much further than that in his music. With a renewed purpose and vision, he's singing better than ever, though his records are on the smaller gospel labels and consequently much harder to find. The first all gospel album for Myrrh came in 1980 *(The Lord Will Make A Way)* leading up through *Higher Plane* in 1981 to the peak of Green artistry that is *Precious Lord*. It won him a Grammy and at the award ceremony Al returned to face once again the cynical music business he'd spurned. He brought them all to their feet with a stunning live performance, as if to prove that now he was more of a soul singer, not less. Robert Hilburn of the *LA Times* wrote then that 'There's no question that he has the same potential to be one of the most successful artists ever in gospel music.'

He's the man who came full circle, the man who re-claimed soul music for the church but his earthy, insinuous way with a song doesn't always go down well with the more traditional folks. Some have even walked out on him in church. 'Yeah, it's different from other gospel music,' he concedes, 'But I think the message, the story is the same. Yeah, I believe so. You don't have to use the same format that has been used for the past fifty years. You can come up to the eighties to deliver the same message and do it with a bit of class and quality.' As a producer he brings the same sort of quality to the records of groups like the New York Community Choir and his close associates like Laura Lee – who began in gospel as Della Reese's replacement in the Meditation Singers, went on to become the deepest and most radical of women soul singers, then teamed up with Al Green in Memphis after her own Christian conversion.

Al Green's supreme ability was always to move the listener, to touch the heart deeply with joy or sorrow, and none of these very special qualities has in any way diminished in the man. Rather, his skill as a communicator harnessed to the new fire in his soul conspires to produce a fresh spiritual music that is awesome in its power and beauty. He's the great prodigal son of the church and he has indeed returned to where he belongs.

\*       \*       \*

Gospel music in the 1980s is a huge corporate business – part evangelism, part entertainment. In that sense, it is now what it has been since it began. The major figures who dominate the contemporary gospel scene have all had to learn how to 'take care of business', how to project an image, how to market a product, how to build a professional organisation. The fact that the product is a type of Christian music makes no difference. The God that gospel singers today sing about is the same God that brought deliverance to the captive slave, but today it seems, He needs a higher brand profile. Whether they're great survivors from a glorious past like Shirley Caesar, the Mighty Clouds and James Cleveland or cross-over artists like Andrae Crouch, Danniebelle and Jessy Dixon or returned prodigals like Al Green, Candi Staton and Barry White, they're all faced with the same dilemma: is it possible in the eighties to sing of Jesus without selling Him by the pound?

There are many who just concern themselves with the former, preferring to sing only at church functions and conventions without any attempt to sell product or advance a career. And they're by no means the minor talents. Vanessa Bell Armstrong went to middle age, brought up five children and served her church in Detroit without ever doing much more than guest vocals on a couple of records. Fortunately for us, she finally got to do an album of her own and took the opportunity to make what was probably the most important gospel record of 1984 – *Peace Be Still*. Now she too will have to cope with the dilemmas of the modern gospel business, but there are still dozens more like Vanessa who stand every Sunday in church choirs across the North American continent.

The relationship between religion, art and business is more crucial in gospel music now than it has ever been. Some gospel singers manage to get one or other of the elements right; more singers than might be imagined get two of them right; but there are precious few who can claim integrity and excellence in all three. Shirley Caesar gets pretty close. Her evangelistic commitment is beyond question and her music is as eloquent as it is stirring. She's also a very sharp (perhaps too sharp) businesswoman who proved it recently by taking a business studies degree at Shaw University and passing out with honours. 'As my businesses expanded, I knew that I was going to need some more business knowledge for my own publicity company, my booking agency, my outreach ministry and for our food programmes. When I was in high school they told me not to go to college, don't use up your mother's money they said. All those years when I was in the Caravans, I was riding in the car and I'd look out and see all those kids coming to and from school and my heart said, go back there. So now I have.'

*Vanessa Bell Armstrong – one of the most expressive gospel singers of modern times*

The singers themselves may see this differently, since they're the ones who've suffered the short-changing and the down-grading, but it's likely that the faith and the music will always need to take precedence over the business if the heart of gospel is to remain healthy. It's not just coincidence that the golden age of gospel music was accompanied by the greatest level of marketing ignorance. While there's no sense in wishing for a return to those difficult days, there are more than a few singers who have turned the whole thing on its head, who won't move a muscle or sing a note without a massive fee payable a third in advance. Competence and good order in business dealings is one thing, profiteering under the guise of Christianity is quite another. Perhaps it's time to reverse the process and begin insisting that the ministry of gospel music *should* be an unfavourable financial deal. Blessed are the poor in spirit.

A tough note on which to introduce the Clark Sisters, but they epitomise for me the very best of contemporary gospel in *all* of its diverse functions. Not that they're particularly poor (or particularly rich) but they seem to have struck exactly the right balance between their faith, their music and their organisation.

Back in June of 1983, these five well-fed sisters from the Detroit Church of God in Christ sneaked quietly into London with their mother Mattie, spent several days shouting up the black churches and flew out again. If you weren't already in on the British gospel circuit you wouldn't have known they'd been here. Yet they delivered the most electrifying slice of soul-scorching this side of the day of judgement. Now this family of christian singers ain't exactly meek and mild. In fact the two nights I saw them they sung so hard and preached so strong that they had to be helped, shaking in the spirit, from off the stage.

These were at the time America's premier female gospel act, weighing in at one thousand pounds of pure soul dynamite and two months later, the rest of the country woke up to them through the cross-over single *You Brought The Sunshine*. The song was already a big dance floor hit in America through the plugging of ace New York jock Frankie Crocker and in Britain it also notched up healthy sales and massive airplay. Soon the Clark Sisters were being hailed in the hip music press as 'the rootsiest, throatiest black music act of the year' and Twinkie Clark as 'nothing short of a musical genius of soul'.

Twinkie is Elbernita Clark, the powerhouse songwriter and musician behind the group, and I asked her about their breakthrough to a commercial market. Had the single made a lot of difference to them? 'Well, our singing is our ministry and having a hit just means we can minister to a wider audience. Now we're drawing secular crowds as well as church people and we play auditoriums as well as churches now. Quite a few of the people in our church were shaken up by the crossover because we were being played in the bars and the clubs and on the rock stations. There's been a lot of criticism but at the same time we know that young people have gotten saved by hearing the record in bars and clubs. I think the church is just going to

have to be more open minded, because these kids are the ones that need our ministry. These are the last days and the word has to get out before the return of Jesus Christ.'

The Clark Sisters – Karen, Jackie, Dorinda, Niecy and Twinkie – range in age from 24 to 36 and all learnt to sing at the knee of gospel legend Mother Mattie Moss Clark, the formidable but charming international music director of the Church of God in Christ. 'It all started with my mum,' said Twinkie. 'She's recorded about 28 albums since 1958 and is the recipient of three gold records. She drilled us, she trained us and raised us in the church. My father was the pastor and we started first singing in the choir and then later I began accompanying my mother – we're all a close family group.' Niecy puts it more bluntly, 'We're like the Jews, we like to keep it in the family.'

The Clarks believe in starting young. Mattie Moss was playing for COGIC at six years old and launched her daughters when they were even younger. 'The youngest was only 2½ . . . I used to stand them on a table to sing. If I had a song come to me in the middle of the night, I'd even get them all out of bed to try it out!'

Mattie Moss (sister of Bill Moss of The Celestials) claims to have been the very first to record a gospel choir – the Michigan State Community Choir – though there might be a few counter claims to that distinction. Her first self-penned song was *Going To Heaven To Meet The King* which appeared on her debut Savoy album. The punishing schedules and public commitments back then took their toll of her personal life and she's now parted from her minister husband. 'We've been divorced for fourteen years now. You see I practically raised these girls single-handed.' Niecy chips in, 'It comes from being on the road. Some men cannot adapt to the life we have, going where the Lord tells us to go . . . even though we are married to them, our lives are not our lives, our lives belong to Jesus Christ and he's the master.'

Niecy is just as keen to declare the family independence of the commercialised aspects of modern gospel. 'What we do is not like what everybody else does. They have their little songs that they sing, but we allow the Holy Ghost to totally take control. We project what God gives us, as the anointing falls on us, as the spirit falls on us, we act in that manner. Where a lot of people are very rehearsed, we are not rehearsed. I mean they come out and have a set thing to do and they will go through that set procedure. We don't work like that.'

After Mattie Moss, Twinkie Clark is the musical powerhouse behind the group. If she were in secular music she might quite easily come to be recognised as one of the greatest soul artists. She studied music at Harvard as well as in church, she is possibly the funkiest keyboard player around, she has a voice like distilled fire and she writes the kind of songs that would turn any sinner's head. *You Brought The Sunshine* got them to a mass audience but the real masterpieces are tracks like *Endow Me* ('I really felt the glory of the Lord come in the room as I wrote that song') or *My Soul Loves Jesus* from her stunning solo album *Power* – far and away the most important gospel record of 1983.

It's not *all* divine inspiration though. Twinkie has a thing about TV commercials and isn't above weaving jingle fragments into a song. 'You know that song we did called *Jesus Had A Lot To Give*? Well, there's a bit in that goes (sings) "the devil is trying to conquer you, he's been at you very long". Now that's from the Pepsi Cola advert,' says Niecy, laughing. 'And "Oh triumph . . ." is the Alka Seltzer tune. She's got the MacDonald's commercial in another song too if you listen hard!' They repaid the debt by doing one of their own for Sunny Delight Orange Juice. If they weren't so evidently genuine in their religious commitment, this might come over as a cheap shot for easy money. In their case, it's just a humorous throwaway, a tongue-in-cheek interlude.

There's certainly nothing coy or half-baked about Mother Mattie and her girls. They give of themselves in a way very few modern gospel groups care to, whether it's within the church – they run their own music school in Detroit and teaching workshops across the country – on record or live in front of an audience. At the heart of their operation stands the matriarchal figure of Mattie Moss, with a reputation for severity so great that many choir singers are terrified to work under her. 'Some people don't understand Mama,' Niecy counters

quickly. 'They say she's hard core, they say she could make a little dog creep . . . but she labours. She's a perfectionist – just doing it won't do. She spends most of her time reading scriptures. It's vital that we can pick up the same identical thing, because we are a blood family and we fill each other. We can rehearse with a band and do it her way and then the spirit comes upon her, it hits her and her hands become anointed. She has a saying, that Jesus is the baddest man in town and we just follow his footsteps.'

The significance of the Clarks lies in the full-blooded spirituality of their performances. While much of the rest of gospel music slips into lifeless production formulas, their divine vocal chorus regenerates the inspired, righteous, shouting tradition. Twinkie Clark especially has discovered how to be years ahead of her time by going right back to the biblical roots of the music. She can take a simple benediction like 'Now unto Him who is able to keep you from falling . . .' and transform it into a majestic opus of breathtaking musical dimensions. At the same time she's not above throwing a line like 'God's economics beats Reaganomics' into another song. With gospel now tending to imitate the drab predictability of contemporary soul and funk, Twinkie has wisely chosen to start her run from further back and has leap-frogged the lot of them. This is a prophetic act on her part because it places black gospel once again out in front of other music as being of infinitely greater significance – artistically as well as spiritually.

Surrounded as we are by joyless songs and heartless singers, the Clark Sisters diffuse a very special kind of sunshine.

Gospel today extends its varied traditions. Off to one side are those like jazz-funk keyboardist Donn Thomas and singer/songwriter Leon Patillo, re-casting the mould of Rance Allen's classy 'message' pop in the 1970s. That is, danceable music with lyrical integrity and cross-over potential but only barely within gospel's broad church.

Solidly in the middle stand the new community and mass choirs, the firm foundations – Florida, New York, Triboro, Sacramento, New Jersey, Southern California, Philadelphia, the many CO-

GIC choirs and groups like the Charles Fold Singers who feature the blistering lead voice of blind singer Rosetta Davis. The modern choir sound is more disciplined, more tightly arranged but still an exhilarating experience for singers and audience alike.

Soft focus gospel in the Crouch tradition survives and succeeds through protegé groups like The Winans – twins Marvin and Carvin and brothers Michael and Ronald. Out of Detroit's Shalom Temple Pentecostal Church, the Winans personify the new breed of quartet harmony, referring far less to the Nightingales than to the Commodores. 'Some people call our music contemporary gospel and others jazz gospel, but we don't try to put a label to it,' says Marvin. 'We do feature a tight vocal blend and a very strong lyric accompanied by a strong melodic line you can wake up to humming the next day.'

The Clark Sisters exemplify gospel's current front line, but the inspired tradition also continues through the young music of Bobby Jones' New Life, Teddy Huffam and The Gems, Keith Pringle and the immensely gifted Richard Smallwood Singers. As the studio production of gospel finally comes of age through people like Thomas Whitfield and Greg Nelson, the vocal priorities of the music once again come to the fore. Not since the 1960s, when gospel began to collapse under the weight of cheap R 'n' B, has the human voice and its uniquely personal expression of faith been accorded such a pre-eminent position in the recorded mix. The best of the new gospel records (particularly those from companies such as Onyx International) are superbly crafted and produced, bringing all the artistry of modern studio techniques to bear on the central vocal witness. Where in the recent past, engineers and producers (such as they were) would take a gospel group and attempt to reduce righteous fire to an unholy mess of third-rate pop, now there is evidence of gospel creating its own professional standards. There is a fresh recognition that everything matters – that for a singer to be heard and a message delivered, a proper context must be created. It's a simple lesson but a long time in the learning, that a great performance can be destroyed utterly by the circumstances of recording and marketing.

Gospel in the 1980s still works best as the Word of God delivered in the most fundamental way: as one heart speaking to another, as one soul to another. Everything else is just an adjunct to this, subverting or enhancing the process. Musicians can underpin or they can overbear, arrangers can channel a song to greater effect or they can deflect its impact, producers can elevate the witness or they can drown it in superfluity. Take the Richard Smallwood Singers' eponymous album or Vanessa Bell Armstrong's *Peace Be Still*, as proof that the job can be done. This is contemporary gospel that

*The fabulous Clark Sisters of Detroit with Mother Mattie Moss.*

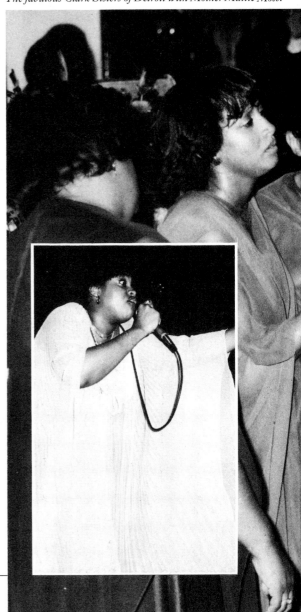

succeeds on all levels: spiritually, artistically, technically and, yes, commercially. For there is a hunger to hear gospel music as it *confronts*, rather than reflects, popular culture.

Yet, however advanced the music becomes, gospel tradition is never far away. Perhaps it's all part of the same hunger, but one of the biggest gospel successes in recent times has been the down-home country songs of a North Carolina couple, Rev F.C. Barnes and Rev Janice Brown. Their album 'Rough Side of The Mountain' sat at No. 1 in the gospel charts for the best part of 1984, proving that there'll always be plenty of room for unsophisticated saints singing unsophisticated songs.

For as much as it challenges, gospel still serves to comfort and strengthen when the burden gets too heavy. As Inez Andrews, now pushing 60 and still the high priestess of gospel song, observes: 'If you've never had an urge to read the Bible, maybe a song will inspire you to. Everybody don't go to church and some people don't want to be saved. But when trouble comes, they want to have something they can reach out to. And most times, if it's not the Bible, it's a song.'

*Insets: Karen* (left) *and Twinkie*

131

# 7

# ANOTHER DAY'S JOURNEY

## Gospel Music in Britain

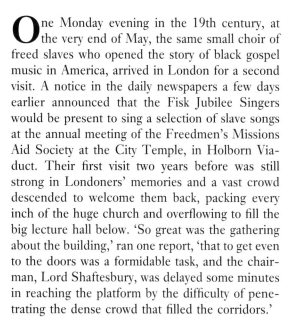

One Monday evening in the 19th century, at the very end of May, the same small choir of freed slaves who opened the story of black gospel music in America, arrived in London for a second visit. A notice in the daily newspapers a few days earlier announced that the Fisk Jubilee Singers would be present to sing a selection of slave songs at the annual meeting of the Freedmen's Missions Aid Society at the City Temple, in Holborn Viaduct. Their first visit two years before was still strong in Londoners' memories and a vast crowd descended to welcome them back, packing every inch of the huge church and overflowing to fill the big lecture hall below. 'So great was the gathering about the building,' ran one report, 'that to get even to the doors was a formidable task, and the chairman, Lord Shaftesbury, was delayed some minutes in reaching the platform by the difficulty of penetrating the dense crowd that filled the corridors.'

Shaftesbury, the great philanthropist and reformer, opened by saying, 'I am delighted to see so large a congregation of the citizens of London come to offer a renewal of their hospitality to these noble brethren and sisters of ours, who are here tonight to charm us with their sweet songs. They have returned here, not for anything in their own behalf, but to advance the coloured race in America . . .'

Dwight Moody and Ira Sankey, the barnstorming American evangelists, were at the height of their English campaign (their *Moody and Sankey Hymn Book*, published just two years earlier, was changing the face of Non-conformist music) and both men were quick to spot the advantage of such drawing power. 'The Singers had not been in the city an hour before a request came from Mr Moody, that they would take part in the service that afternoon at the Haymarket Opera house. The next day he desired them to sit on the platform, and sing . . . after the sermon. At its close the great congregation bowed, with tearful faces in silent prayer. Soon the soft, sweet strains of *Steal Away* rose from the platform, swelling finally into a volume of conquering song that seemed to carry the great audience heavenward as on angels' wings.'

The fame of the Fisk Jubilee Singers was growing so fast by that time in England, that when they appeared nightly a few weeks later at a series of meetings in the Bow Road Hall in London's East End, they were besieged by popular acclaim. 'The attendance was so large, that hundreds were sometimes turned away, *even after a congregation of ten or twelve thousand had crowded into the hall.*'*

All this happened more than a century ago, in 1875, and there is no evidence of any link – direct or indirect – between this early introduction of Afro-American spirituals and the present upsurge of black gospel in Britain. Slavery *did* exist in Britain from as early as the 16th century right up until 1834, though not on anywhere near the scale of its existence in the Americas. Estimates vary, but there were sufficient numbers in 1596 for Elizabeth I to advocate repatriation in extreme terms: '. . . there are of late divers blackamores brought into this realm, of which kind of people there are already here to manie, consideryng howe God hath blessed this land with great increase of people of our own nation . . . those kinde of people should be sente forth of the land . . .'

The royal complaint wasn't followed through however and black slaves continued to be brought into England as part of the 'Triangular Trade' between Africa, the American colonies and Britain. There was, therefore, by the middle of the 18th century when Dr Watts was writing his *Hymns and Spiritual Songs*, a definable black community in cities like London, Bristol and Liverpool, with a visible leadership in men like Ottobah Cugoano. Born in what is now Ghana, he was seized and taken to the West Indies where he was kept in 'dreadful captivity and horrible slavery'. After being brought to England and eventually freed, he published a book of his experiences and described his subjection to slavery in Grenada: '(Every day I saw) the most dreadful scenes of misery and cruelty . . . my miserable companions often cruelly lashed, and as it were cut to pieces, for the most trifling faults . . . I saw a slave receive twenty-four lashes of the whip for being seen in church on a Sunday instead of going to work.' He wrote with others to the Governor of Barbados protesting '. . . the horrid cruelties practised on the . . . people in the West Indies, to the disgrace of Christianity . . .'

*My italics

With a common African heritage and a common exposure to Christianity and its hymns, it might be thought likely that black people in Britain would create religious songs to compare with those that developed in America. If they did, there is certainly no proof of it and it is probable that other factors intervened to make it impossible – almost certainly the most important being the individual isolation of slaves in Britain as they were bought for household service compared with the communal toil of the American plantations.

Spiritual and gospel music, insofar as it was heard at all in Britain, was until very recently heard only as an imported American culture. The Fisks were the first – making a total of five trips from Nashville to sing throughout the length and breadth of Britain and Ireland. In the late 1920s, the Utica Jubilee Quartet made a successful three month European tour. The group were all students of the Utica Institute in central Mississippi, and were probably the very first black quartet to be regularly featured in a national radio programme in America. Their first visit here was so successful that they were brought back in January 1930 – this time for a tour that lasted eighteen months and took in all the major concert halls of twenty-two European countries.

These and other isolated visits by groups like the Golden Gate Quartet, were the only exposure that early gospel music gained in Britain. Not until Mahalia Jackson's first visit in November 1952, did black gospel begin to have any impact at all. Then it was purely as a musical phenomenon, severed from its religious source. Jazz collectors were the first in Britain to discover (in Mahalia, Sister Rosetta Tharpe and Clara Ward) a vocal music that was as clearly related to the forms of jazz as blues and ragtime. Veteran jazz critic Max Jones, who met and became close friends with Mahalia on that first visit, remembers the opening night at Oxford Town Hall: 'It was very cold and the place was half empty. Mahalia looked very ill, paler than when I'd first met her at the hotel. She was puzzled and dismayed at having been put on the same programme with Big Bill Broonzy – the whole thing was pretty incongruous. She came out in a flowing black dress with a huge sequinned cross on it and began to sing *Amazing Grace*. Irreligious as I am, the force of the words, the way she delivered her message in that awesome voice, made the maximum impact on me. We had tears streaming down our faces by the time she'd finished.'

Another British jazzman with a passionate love of gospel was Chris Barber who was responsible for bringing Brother John Sellers and Rosetta Tharpe here in 1957. 'I remember the first time she sang with us in November that year at Birmingham Town Hall. She was a frothy, bubbly person in a fur coat with her husband and her dog in tow – I often wondered later how she'd managed to get the dog in! She'd brought this 16 piece arrangement of *Everytime I Feel The Spirit* with her and was almost paralysed with shock when she discovered we knew how to play her music. She had no idea that anybody outside America, or even white people in America, would be able to play gospel. After that we got along fine and British audiences loved her.'

The ebullient Clara Ward followed in April 1959, having lost all her best singers the year before. English jazz critics, oblivious to the fact that they were getting a second-rate replica of the fa-

mous Ward Singers, were fulsome in praise of their vocal and rhythmic dexterity, which they said, '. . . make one forget even the awful words of the modern spirituals.' Having said that, Francis Newton announced in the *New Statesman*, 'Nobody can afford to miss the Ward Singers of Philadelphia, whom we fortunately have with us, supported by Humphrey Lyttleton's band: a group of ladies in flowing white robes and dramatic hair-dos, who retain their and our respect even when doing a maypole parade round the microphone, like a flock of large soft birds. (They can be seen on ITV this Sunday.)'

**B**ut the first big public breakthrough for gospel in Britain came with Langston Hughes' dramatic stage-play *Black Nativity*. Using Marion Williams and the Stars of Faith (the Ward Singers minus Clara) and the Alex Bradford Singers, Hughes had created a perfect vehicle that allowed gospel music to reach a mass audience without compromise – religious or musical. After a successful Broadway run, the show came to Britain in the summer of 1962 – originally just to film the performance for Associated Rediffusion. Madeleine Bell was in the show, singing with the Alex Bradford group, and recalls the sequence of events as the play turned into a box office phenomenon. 'Before we did the TV show we were told that an agent wanted to put us on for two weeks at the Criterion Theatre in Piccadilly and did we all want to stay. He couldn't afford to pay us much, so we got seventy-five dollars and Bradford and Marion Williams got 125 dollars *and* we had to pay our hotels out of that. For two weeks we did two shows a night and it was packed every night, so it got held over and we went from the Criterion to the Piccadilly and then to the Phoenix Theatre. In the end we stayed fifteen weeks. Then we took it up to Manchester and Liverpool and off round Europe – Scandinavia, Switzerland, Paris. We did a midnight show in Hambourg where we ran into Little Richard and Billy Preston who were about to tour England with Sam Cooke. So when *Black Nativity* came back to London, both Sam Cooke and Little Richard turned up at the Strand Theatre to see us.'

For the first time in England, the genuine gospel article was being heard and supported by mass audiences. There was something irresistible about *Black Nativity*, with its theatrical mixture of modern spirituals and joyful fervour drawing people back night after night. All the singers were in great voice – Marion Williams twisting her flawless, jubilant contralto round *When Was Jesus Born?* and *A Pity And A Shame*. Bradford booming like a super-charged fog horn on songs like *Come All Ye Faithful*. 'The quality of his voice was quite unbelievable,' said Chris Barber, who saw the show even more times than I did, 'At the Phoenix Theatre, which was a thousand-seater, Bradford and his singers would come on, carrying gold-painted crowns on purple cushions. He'd start singing from the wings behind the curtain, pointing across the stage, and he'd be extremely loud even at the back of the stalls, without a microphone! This was impossible we thought – but he had such an amazing voice.'

For a while it seemed as though gospel might take its place in the lexicon of English received cultures – as integral as Handel's *Messiah* or Gershwin's *Porgy and Bess* – but this was barren territory and nothing grew. British singers simply could not sing gospel convincingly – even if they wished

*Marion Williams and Alex Bradford on stage during 'Black Nativity'*

to – and the black churches in Britain were not yet making the sort of musical connections they're making now. In 1965 a bold attempt was made by two German promoters, Horst Lippman and Fritz Rau, to bring the very best of America's black gospel to Europe in the form of the first 'Spiritual and Gospel Festival'. The Five Blind Boys of Mississippi were joined by Inez Andrews and the Andrewettes, with Bishop Samuel Kelsey and the congregation of his Washington Temple Church of God in Christ, and all appeared on stages in Manchester, Sheffield, Liverpool, Birmingham, Leicester and London. The programme was a sensation – not even *Black Nativity* had prepared Britain for singing like this – but paying customers stayed away and the tour played to near empty houses. Elsewhere in Europe, they did sufficiently well to risk a second festival the following year, returning with Bishop Kelsey again and a line-up that included the Harmonizing Four, the Dorothy Norwood Singers and the amazing Gospelaires of Dayton, Ohio. This time the tour was cut to just one UK appearance – January 16th at the Fairfield Halls in Croydon – but the place was still half empty for one of the hardest gospel programmes Britain has ever witnessed. Small though it was, the audience (who included 1960s stars like Dusty Springfield and Eric Burdon) were forced beyond entertainment into catharsis, and I saw several people shouted into comas, lying slumped in their seats.

It was the stuff of legend; in different circumstances it would also have been the stuff of spiritual revival. Certainly, it was *not* the stuff of pop acclaim. Indeed, the Gospelaires even managed somehow to appear briefly on BBC television's *Top of the Pops* and a hundred bemused teenagers gaped disbelievingly at four guys screaming into a single microphone.

Nevertheless, as attempts to import black gospel into Britain for white consumption ultimately failed, an indigenous music was busy being born. Far removed from theatres, concert halls and TV studios, independent black churches were beginning to meet in private houses and rented halls to preach and pray and sing the gospel.

Black people from the Caribbean islands began to arrive in Britain soon after the Second World War – initially just a few hundred in 1948 on the returning troop-ship the *SS Empire Windrush*. Then during the 1950s, they came in greater numbers until, by 1961, a total of almost 172,000 West Indian settlers had arrived in Britain. Drawn by the prospect of a labour shortage, it resembled the great migrations northwards by black Americans in the late 1920s and, just as then, wherever the community went the church went too.

One Jamaican who made the journey in 1951 from the farming village of Claremont was Oliver Augustus Lyseight, a convert to pentecostalism from the Methodist Church. He was a brilliant young scholar then, rising rapidly to the pastorate of churches in the parish of St. Ann, before setting sail for England. Arriving on a cold, grey November day, he settled in Wolverhampton in the Midlands, where he founded what is now the largest black-led church in Britain – the New Testament Church of God. The black population of Wolverhampton in those days numbered just fifteen and the first meetings at the Waterloo Road YMCA had seven members.

As more West Indians arrived and met the shock waves of racism as it infected even the English churches, so the Church of God grew – from Wolverhampton into Birmingham, where the first all-group convention in 1954 drew fifty delegates to their temporary headquarters in Handsworth. A year later, the movement spread to Brixton and Willesden in London, thence to all the inner city areas with large black populations. Formally, the Church of God is governed by an American parent body in Cleveland, Tennessee who officially recognised the British developments later that year, conferring the office of National Overseer on Brother Oliver Lyseight. Today the New Testament Church of God has over 6,000 full members, 20,000 adult adherents and 6,000 Sunday School scholars.

The origins of the Church of God go back to 1906, to William Seymour's historic revivals in a derelict Methodist Church on Azusa Street in downtown Los Angeles. Though this is often given as the start of the black pentecostal movement world-wide, the other main black denomination that travelled via the West Indies to Britain was already in existence before the turn of the century. The Church of God in Christ (COGIC) was founded in Memphis in 1895 by Reverend Charles Mason, from Lexington, Mississippi and grew to become the largest independent black church in the world with some 3.5 million members. The impact of the Church of God in Christ on gospel music in America has always been tremendous, from Bessie Johnson in the late 1920s, through to the Clark Sisters today, and its influence is almost as great in Britain.

The church came to England in a small way with Mother McLachlan and her children in 1948. Two years later they began holding 'cottage meetings' in Navarino Road in Hackney, East London. 'I was about twelve or thirteen at the time,' remembers daughter Jean, who grew up to become 'Mum' to the current COGIC mass choirs. 'There were only about ten of us then. Bishop Charles Mason came over for the World Pentecostal Conference and we began to hold cottage meetings in different areas of London. Wherever there was a meeting there was always a group who sang. We used to sing out of the *Redemption Songbook* – songs like *Lord You Know I Feel The Spirit* and *Down By The Riverside*. There weren't really any choirs back then but we would go out as a group and just sing in the open air. At Hyde Park every Saturday afternoon and on 'the waste' in Kingsland Road, Dalston. We let them know about the happy church!'

COGIC in Dalston was based at the old Methodist church with Sister Georgianna Creary organising the first real choir there in the mid-1950s and later the Wings Over Jordan Gospel Singers, robed in blue and gold gowns, took their songs beyond the black church circuit and into the Methodist, Salvation Army and Elim churches, even making it onto the TV programme *Hallelujah*. Dalston was a hive of gospel music activity by this time and the best young women singers of the church teamed up as the Sacred Sisters and travelled all over the country. Jean Reynolds and Georgianna Creary were joined by Janet Edwards-Brown, Beverly Edwards-Scott, Norma Roberts and Ettis Ennis, often sup-

plemented by the cool tenor voice of Roderick Riley. The Sacred Sisters were known for their powerful ministry through preaching and a programme of gospel songs – some original, some re-written to suit the blend of their rich, melodious, spiritual voices. A record contract was even offered at one stage but they rejected it and the group's legacy is now only to be found as it continues in the music and ministry of today's COGIC.

Curiously though, some of the earliest fully-organised gospel groups in Britain emerged, not from any of the Pentecostal churches but from the Seventh Day Adventists, with their equally strong black membership and tradition of fine singing. In marked contrast to the American history of gospel, Adventists have a pioneering record in the music here through groups like the Singing Stewarts and the Golden Chords. The Stewarts – five brothers and three sisters – grew up singing spirituals and religious songs in Trinidad and Aruba. 'My mother taught us songs like *The Books Of The Bible We Know So Well* and we just carried on with them as a group when we came to England in 1960,' says Frank Stewart, who now broadcasts

*Church of God in Christ Convention at Camden Town in the early 1950s*

over Radio West Midlands. 'When we arrived in Handsworth we were helped by Lennox Edwards who put us in touch with Charles Parker, a BBC producer. He was looking for people to sing spirituals in films like *The Colony* and *Of One Blood*, so we went from that onto all kinds of TV and radio programmes.' The Singing Stewarts also have the distinction of being one of the first UK gospel groups to get on record, with a remake of *Oh Happy Day* and other spirituals as their first album for Pye Records and a second called *Here Is A Song*. Their folksy style of gospel has taken them to Germany, Belgium, Austria, France and the Netherlands, as well as extensive tours throughout Britain, singing at schools, in prisons, churches, concert halls and clubs. They're still out there too, though set against the younger choirs and singers it is evident that they're the product of an older and gentler culture, owing more to Caribbean folklore than Handsworth street-life.

The Golden Chords are similar holders of an older spiritual tradition being displaced by the new wave of gospel. They compare closely to early American quartets – especially the Harmonizing Four and the Soul Stirrers – though they claim inspiration first from SDA groups like the Kings Heralds and the Gospel Heralds, who were based in South London at their local church in Brixton. 'It was these groups that gave us the idea in January 1969 of promoting the gospel through music,' says founder member Alric Williams. 'During those early years we had to move people around to produce what we felt was the best sound. In those days, using instruments was unheard of, so the voice was used to produce all the music. For us then, getting the right sound and training the voices was very important.'

Trevor Brown, Alric Williams, Murray Fuller, Tommy Williams, Leonard Reid, Lennox Fuller, Clive Coke, Errol Lawrence and Hugo Kennedy were the nine original men of the Golden Chords but they've swapped around personnel amicably, with members moving on to become ministers or pursue other careers. 'It's given us a stability that's enabled us to survive for so long. The new members have brought new goals and new ideas and have helped us to vary our style while keeping to the basic four part harmony. It's meant we're not tied to the straight singing but are able to cope with all kinds of songs.'

The Chords have travelled some miles over the past sixteen years, singing gospel quartet in hospi-

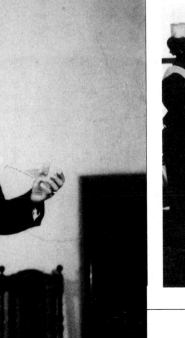

*Stanley Wright* (left) – *an early gospel soloist in Britain;* (right), *the only known photograph of the Sacred Sisters (with Kitty Parham)*

*The Singing Stewarts* (left) *and the Golden Chords*

*The Soul Seekers with the late Tony Mosop on vocals and
Barry Ford on drums,* opposite page.

tals, old people's homes, prisons and churches of
all faiths, both in the UK and on the continent of
Europe. They've recorded three albums of fine old
spirituals and jubilee songs, with some original material in similar style. It's difficult sometimes to
believe that these guys come from South London
and not South Virginia, so carefully created are
their harmonies. 'We've seen a lot of changes in
gospel music over the years,' says Alric. 'The demand for instruments has been more and more.
The young people especially want a bigger sound as
it were, so we've introduced guitar along with the
piano but we don't want to lose the delicate harmony that we've cultivated. People should be able to
hear the voices and appreciate the melody that can
be produced by the male voice. We feel that the
natural voice supported by the minimum of instruments is by far the most effective way of promoting
the gospel of Christ. This makes us very different

from the many gospel groups in the UK now . . .
there aren't many who use our style today.'

The Pentecostal churches meanwhile were
already into a second generation of gospel.
Pastor Latouche, who ran a little independent fellowship in Sussex Road, Brixton (later to affiliate to
COGIC) was the founder of one of the most
influential. The Harmonisers set out in the very
early 1960s featuring Sister Cameron on lead vocals, with Latouche bringing in daughters Blossom,
Hopelyn and Carol as they grew up. Touring
churches and conventions throughout the sixties,
the Harmonisers recorded a rare early album and
caused quite a stir as their sound nudged towards
pop. 'I remember first seeing them at a COGIC
convention,' says singer Juliet Fletcher. 'They had
all the equipment, they were the first organised
electric group. They had a big home-made sign

over the Hammond saying "The Travelling Har-monisers".' When Doug Wallace joined them as keyboard player in 1973 they still had Pastor La-touche on lead guitar but Angela Henriques was now leading the voices with Clive Allen on bass, Roy McCleod on rhythm and Lloyd Grosset on drums. Using this line-up they put out a single – *We Shall Overcome* – and began to go further afield throughout the 1970s, building a reputation now outside of the churches as well as in. With the young Lavine Hudson joining them in 1978, they were on the verge of breaking through with new songs like *Make Room For Jesus* and a soulful ver-sion of *Jesus Loves Me This I Know*, picking up a record contract with Pilgrim and a Granada TV appearance, as well as a much heavier schedule of live concerts and becoming incidentally in 1979, the first black gospel group to appear at the Green-belt Festival. But within a year they'd disbanded,

having laid the foundations throughout nearly two decades for much of the music that now dominates gospel in Britain.

Over those two decades, other groups came and went. During the 1960s the big names were The Heavenly Hopes from Battersea in South London, with an outstanding singer in Jean Williams, the Soul Seekers from nearby Camberwell (whose lead singer Tony Mosop became Tony Tribe and had a UK Top Fifty hit in 1969 with the original reggae version of *Red Red Wine and* whose drummer was Barry Ford, who became a major reggae star), the Overcomers, the Persuaders and the Heaven Bound Brothers; all had significant followings throughout the main Pentecostal denominations but almost all were ultimately forced to disband through lack of funds or organisation. British gos-pel groups only really began to come into their own during the 1970s.

My Soul Magnifies The Lord — GENE MARTIN

GOING HOME AFTER A WHILE
THE GREAT CORONATION
YOU'VE BEEN BLESSED

MY SOUL
HE NEVER HAS FAILED ME
COME ON JESUS

SINCE JESUS FIXED ME UP
TILL HE COMES
JESUS OF GALILEE

NOTHING TOO HARD
SET YOU FREE
TO THAT CITY · O

**B**azil Meade is best known now for his inspired leadership of the London Community Gospel Choir, but back then he was the mainstay of a number of groups and choirs. Converted at a New Testament Church of God summer school in 1967, he followed Rev Olive Parris as she split away to form the Latter Rain Outpouring Revival the following year. He'd been wavering, unsure of his direction and had stopped going to church but Rev Parris called him over to talk. 'I went over to her house and she just told me to follow her into the living room where she showed me a little electric organ. I'd never touched a keyboard before but she came back later with a songbook and I found I could accompany her. Two weeks later I was playing for her at her first big London crusade in the Co-operative Hall in Finsbury Park.'

Significantly perhaps, the American style of gospel was beginning to arrive and have its influence – not as an adjunct of the jazz circuit, but through the controversial revivals of the evangelist A. A. Allen. Allen was the dean of fast-talking evangelists from Miracle Valley in Arizona, a loud man with a shady past, a drink problem and an extremely healthy bank account – the original Elmer Gantry in fact. When his circus hit Britain in the 1960s there were scandals in the papers and riots at the meetings, but Allen knew a thing or two about old time religion and good time gospel . . . 'miracle music' he called it. The reporter from the South London newspaper the *Wimbledon News* noted that 'women fainted and went wildly hysterical at the Town Hall, Wimbledon on Tuesday. Men writhed, shuddered and shouted. All rejoiced . . .' Billy Preston, the keyboard prodigy who began with Sam Cooke and Mahalia Jackson, spent time in the Allen entourage and put his stamp on their gospel organists. Gene Martin was built up as the featured vocalist, his classic gospel voice supported in fine style by a rocking black choir.

It all had a profound effect on Bazil Meade, who was fascinated by Gene Martin especially. 'I went down to Allen's meetings at the Horticultural Hall in Westminster and down in Tooting he held one I remember. I was about twenty then and all we'd really had to work on up to that stage was the *Chuck Wagon Songbook*, stuff like that. This Gene Martin had such an amazing voice, he didn't need to use a mike at all. He was about six feet two inches tall and he wore the loudest suits you ever saw!' At the Central Hall in Westminster several years later, the two finally met and became such firm friends that Bazil was invited back to the USA for a five weeks tour. A. A. Allen had drunk himself to death by that time and the new head man was Don Stewart (who still holds crusades). Bazil went from city to city with Gene Martin and Don Stewart – New York, Atlanta, Carolina, Chicago, Ohio, Minneapolis – returning again for a second trip when he remembers a big gospel programme with the Pilgrim Jubilees, Dorothy Love Coates and the Mighty Gospel Giants.

The American experience rubbed off. Back in England, Bazil Meade was introducing the swirl and shout of Chicago gospel to the Latter Rain Outpouring Revival. 'About eight others had left the New Testament Church of God originally in 1968 to join the meetings with Rev Parris at her house in Alcester Crescent, Upper Clapton. Numbers just grew and grew and eventually I started my first choir there. We really broke out of the traditional style of church singing then but we were restricted for places to sing. Apart from the crusades twice a year, we weren't allowed to go off and do public concerts or anything, so it got a bit frustrating.'

Contemporary American gospel was booming by this time and records by Andrae Crouch and Edwin Hawkins were arriving in Britain by the early 1970s. Their effect was principally to fire the imagination of young musicians in the churches. Because it is only very recently that there have been gospel *voices* in Britain to match those of the Americans, the group emphasis has tended to be instrumental as much as vocal, and bands were the most popular British development during the 1970s. Ralph Weekes, now one of the three main gospel promoters, came to London in 1961 from Barbados when he was nine years old. As a schoolboy he met up with Bazil Meade and a young Carl Booth on the cricket field and from the Shiloh church in Dalston in East London which he joined in 1972, he began tentatively to form the Children of the Kingdom – later abbreviated to the CK Band. Playing at church weddings and special functions, they developed a style of gospel that absorbed Andrae Crouch with reggae and some pretty adventurous lyrics. A first 'outside' date in North London at Edmonton Baptist Church in 1976 set them off on a heavy schedule of gigs, and in 1978 they went fully professional for two years – mostly in Europe. 'It was very tough going,' says Ralph, sitting in the Finsbury Park office of his freight and shipping business, 'we were literally working for nothing; but we travelled all over the place, opening up new avenues for gospel. We even played a gospel set in an Amsterdam disco once.' The experiences and the contacts made, served Ralph in good stead and though the CK band are still active, his main mission is as a promoter. He was one of the first to directly import gospel from America to the British churches – bringing Danniebelle Hall to the UK in 1979 (and three times since) and the Edwin Hawkins Singers in 1981.

Bazil Meade and Carl Booth meanwhile were putting together the influential outfit known as Kainos. With Joe Pitt from the Heavenly Hopes on piano, Joel Edwards on guitar, Bazil's brother Errol on drums, plus a bass and rhythm guitarist and Bazil's Hammond organ, the sound of Kainos was modern, full and exciting. The focal point however was the big lead voice and stage presence of Carl Booth. 'I remember going to see them and being amazed by Carl,' says singer Paul Johnson. 'He was a really muscular guy, athletic and extrovert. He would jump down into the aisle, jump back on stage, jump on the piano, he was jumping everywhere!' They made their public debut in North West London at a legendary concert one Saturday night in the winter of 1978 at the New Testament Church of God in Willesden High Road, sharing the bill with Bazil's Latter Rain Outpouring Revival Choir. They were an immediate hit with songs like *Put A Little Love In Your Heart* and Joe Pitt's own *Father Of Mankind*. Kainos was then the most progressive of gospel groups and provided the now ordained Rev Meade with a second outlet for his prodigious musical talents. Though even this couldn't contain him for very long . . .

Amongst the other male groups who pursued their elliptical careers throughout the decade, one of the most interesting were the Doyley Brothers from South London. Originally just a duo with Errol and Dennis when they were both under ten years old, the boys were known in churches all over London for their precocious rendition of *The Lord's My Shepherd*. Older brother Freddie joined, likewise young Trevor Doyley and the quartet looked all set to be the first UK gospel group to cross-over to pop success when they won the TV talent show *Opportunity Knocks* outright in 1973. The young teenagers were being hailed, improbably, as a British Jackson Five and some pretty lucrative recording contracts were waved around but they either couldn't or wouldn't go through the necessary changes and though they did put out three singles, the Doyley Brothers remained solidly with gospel and its own peculiar rewards.

However, the immediate result for the Doyleys was a backlash of hostility and suspicion from the church, who had presumed them to be flirting with secular entertainment and selling gospel cheap. Still in their early teens, the brothers took this criticism hard and stopped singing altogether for four years. 'We got very, very depressed by all that,' said Errol. 'We couldn't believe they'd take that attitude. We didn't even feel like rehearsing but eventually our Mum persuaded us to try again.' They became one of the very first groups to take gospel back to the USA, when they toured the northern cities with gospel star Rev Cleophus Robinson in 1982, performing in Chicago for Rev Jesse Jackson at his PUSH headquarters. For Dennis, who has always had a strange fixation with the singer Michael Jackson even to the extent of mirroring his dress, hairstyle, mannerisms and voice, America was a dream come true and he stayed behind for two years, returning only recently to rejoin the Doyley Brothers. Sporting a white tuxedo and Jackson's current wet-look hairstyle he even attracted a posse of screaming girl admirers to their gospel concerts; to the uninitiated it can all seem somewhat bizarre. But the seven brothers (Jeffrey, Gene and twelve year old Chevron having subsequently all joined the front line of harmony vocals) are sincere and committed – as active in their New Testament Assembly Church in Deptford on a Sunday morning as they are on a Saturday night punching *Reach Out And Touch* in the spotlight to a big gospel crowd. With a wealth of experience visibly lacking in some other groups, and their intuitive fraternal harmonies, the Doyley Brothers may well emerge as the foremost British male gospel group of the 1980s.

I t could and should have been the title bestowed on Paradise, at one time the most accomplished and brilliant of young Christian bands who walked the precarious line between gospel and secular, eventually to the satisfaction of nobody. Where the Doyleys took their musical cue from the Jackson Five and Motown, Paradise were looking via Andrae Crouch to the giants of 1970s black instrumental music – the Crusaders, the Commodores, Earth, Wind and Fire. For a while it was a potent mix of gospel and funk that generated a huge following among young black Christians and Paradise were the top group on the gospel circuit. Paul Johnson became their number one fan, following them from gig to gig, eventually to join them as lead singer in 1980. 'I'd heard a lot of rumours about them – people in the churches said they played the devil's music, but I was really impressed with the

*The Doyley Brothers* (below) *nearly crossed over in 1973 but are still with gospel today* (bottom). *Paradise* (right) *with their most fruitful line-up*

Robin Luke

way they prepared themselves through prayer before every gig – that's what got to me. I started doing two or three songs in their set and the one that launched me in pentecostal circles was Walter Hawkins' *Be Grateful.* Everybody knew me for that. After a break, the band reformed and by March there was talk of a tour with Andrae Crouch and they asked me to join them.' It was the highpoint of the band's career, but they were firmly relegated by the Crouch management to a second-class supporting role, even to the extent of being thrown off the main coach. 'We'd been travelling packed in a mini-bus with all our equipment and on the last night one of Andrae's musicians invited us onto the coach. When the manager saw us he just said, "Bad idea" and turned us out. When Andrae found out he made the guy apologise, but it was still like a superstar thing ... Andrae himself travelled in a limousine. We had a great time though, playing all over the country and ending up with two nights at the Hammersmith Odeon. Sandra Crouch was great – a born preacher. When the girls came up after the show and tried to kiss Andrae, she would whip out her Bible and say, "Don't you know it says here ..."'

Paradise became a unique attraction for both black and white audiences. In 1981 making their second visit to the big Greenbelt Festival on the one hand, and a memorable date at Brixton Town Hall on the other. 'It was slap bang in the middle of the riots and the place was surrounded by riot police. We were on with the Doyleys and Lavine Hudson. The PA guy left us cold – decided he had an urgent prior commitment – and the concert started two-and-a-half hours late. It was incredibly tense that day but the place was packed – people were so glad for us to come.'

In March the following year, Pilgrim Records gave them the biggest budget so far for a UK gospel album – £7,000 to record the influential *World's Midnight.* 'It was the second Paradise album and it set a precedent for the group. We went for something that would be very street-wise but Pilgrim had no idea how to promote it.' With hot music press reviews and airplay on soul stations, a group strategy emerged to reach a mass youth audience through secular channels, leading them finally to sign an important deal with Priority Records. Ha-

black churches, left last year to follow a solo career and (despite the energetic commitment of similar outfit Clarity) the likelihood of a successful gospel/funk hybrid seems remote.

The real movement in Britain in the 1980s belongs to the choirs. It's they who have attracted the massive media attention and the record deals but, like everything in gospel, they've been a long time in the making. Essentially a product of the main congregations and their youth departments, they've grown slowly from loose ensemble chorus singing to highly disciplined spectaculars, overflowing with musical and vocal talents.

Juliet Fletcher is a COGIC sister and a gospel singer who has seen all the choirs develop. Born in Stepney Green in East London, she was baptised at eleven into the New Testament Church of God by Rev Maxwell and transferred with him when he went over to the Church of God in Christ. 'All the choirs were combined back then and it was only at conventions that special youth choirs started. At Leytonstone we had one of the first young gospel choirs. We just started out as the thirteen children of the church, doing songs from the church hymnal, with me banging out chords on the piano. Then we began picking up on the American gospel records – we did just about every song off of Aretha Franklin's *Amazing Grace* album. When our pastor went to the COGIC convention in Memphis he

ving reduced their lyrics to ambiguous statements of praise that could equally be taken as secular love songs, the group began to get national airplay for *One Mind, Two Hearts*, putting it into the lower reaches of the UK pop charts. Now they were caught in the great dichotomy – the pop world wanted them for Paul Johnson's heavenly soprano and the band's tight danceability while the church wanted them back into line as a straight ahead gospel group. When their follow-up singles (including a classy but distinctly secular version of the Beatles' *We Can Work It Out*) failed to hit and a big church audience gave them the thumbs down at the Gospel Poll Winners concert, the writing was on the wall for Paradise. Paul Johnson, certainly the most soulful male singer to come out of Britain's

brought back a singer called Brenda who taught us all kinds of stuff – *Deep Down In My Heart* and *You Don't Know*. There was also a group from the American Air Force bases called the Gospelaires who influenced us. We became known then as the New Jerusalem Choir from a song we did off a Caravan's album called *In The New Jerusalem*. So we were doing all this great American gospel singing and it went down a storm in the churches.'

When the progressive Pastor Wallace took over in the mid-1970s, Leytonstone COGIC was growing fast and he was quick to give permission for the choir to hold the first joint public concert with Bazil Meade's Latter Rain Outpouring Revival Choir in the local British Legion Hall. Six hundred people turned out that night in East London and a whole new movement in British gospel was launched through these two pioneering choirs, both of them heavy with afro-americanisms, but nonetheless representing an incredibly exciting development for British black church audiences.

The transatlantic connection was also being made through the main COGIC mass choir who had regular visits from Kitty Parham of the Stars of Faith and before that the Ward Singers. As a leading COGIC singer, Juliet Fletcher was also a prominent voice in the COGIC Youth Choir and remembers Kitty Parham's training sessions at the church headquarters in Tottenham. 'She picked me out to be the soloist on a song called *Send It On Down* and I was just terrified. But we sang it at the next youth convention which was called *Pentecost At Any Cost* and it was truly a blessing.' Becoming increasingly involved in the organisation of choirs and groups, Juliet made some tentative contacts with white Christian agencies who might be willing to lend some support. Her first call was to Norman Miller of Word UK, the biggest of the British Christian record companies with an impressive ros-

ta of Americans like the Mighty Clouds of Joy and Shirley Caesar. Miller's response was less than encouraging. 'He told me straight that he wouldn't invest in black gospel for years and years because he had no confidence in its stability. He said it didn't have what it takes to be a marketable success.' With major secular record companies now moving in on black gospel in a big way, Norman Miller (better known as Mr Sheila Walsh) must be eating his words.

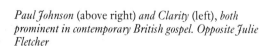

*Paul Johnson* (above right) *and Clarity* (left), *both prominent in contemporary British gospel. Opposite Julie Fletcher*

With the initiative remaining firmly within the black church circuit, Juliet formed one of the first promotion companies and launched it with a major public concert in North London at Islington

Town Hall in 1979, featuring Kainos and the Lakenheath Gospel Choir. 'The churches tried to stop it because it was a paying concert and they considered it to be selling the gospel. Young people were told that if they attended they'd be in jeopardy of being suspended.' Despite this, a big crowd turned out and the church leaders, sensing an incipient rebellion, attempted to nip it in the bud. 'We were summoned to a tribunal before Bishop Bell, Pastor Reynolds and Superintendent Anderson and threatened with excommunication from COGIC. You might find this difficult to believe but Anderson even laid his hands on my head and started praying the demons out of me!' Times have changed and the COGIC Choir themselves can now be found at paying concerts, but the question of *control* in gospel music is still as thorny as ever and the youth of the churches are still warned away from independent ventures.

Recognising the growing importance of gospel singing to their young people, the churches began to actively encourage youth choirs within their own denominations. The Merrybells Gospel Choir originated back in the 1960s when evangelist Eileen Hendricks of the Church of God (Seventh Day) recognised the need for a youth group to promote Christian fellowship through music. The first group was formed in 1966 and given the name Merrybells Faithful Youth Challengers, and soon there were other groups forming around the country fulfilling the same need at local level. From time to time, all the groups joined together for large concerts and in 1979 they made a first album themselves, called *Get It On*.

In 1980, twelve members were selected from the various groups to form The Challengers, with a special commission to spear-head the singing ministry. The Thomas family from Manchester – especially Tyndale and Jean – are the leading lights in the Challengers, blazing a trail for gospel music with their powerful voices, and they are both deeply involved in the choir. The Challengers followed up a first EP *God Always Answers* with successful concerts at places like the Free Trade Hall, Manchester and the Digbeth Hall, Birmingham. They were one of the first groups to appear in secular venues – at the Ace Cinema and the Fridge nightclub in Brixton – where the excellence of their singing quickly won over a sceptical audience.

The Merrybells Gospel Choir itself was formed in early 1983, with fifty singers drawn from the various local groups. Since then they've appeared on BBC Radio One's *Walter's Weekly*, on London's Capital Radio and on BBC television. Their first album was released in 1984 and featured some of the oldest gospel songs of all, *His Eye Is On The Sparrow* and *Worship The Lord*.

Within the main New Testament Church of God, the Midlands roots of the denomination are reflected in the two major choirs associated with the area. The Handsworth district of Birmingham, home of the Majestic Singers as well as the Singing Stewarts, has a thriving branch of the New Testament Church of God and the energetic services of their erstwhile District Youth Leader, Justin Lewis. Taking twenty-six of the best voices he put them together as the Majestic Singers and presented them in March 1976 to the rest of the local church. Nearly one and a half thousand people showed up on the night, enthralled especially by the dramatic lead voice of Maxine Simpson. Maxine and the Majestics they became known as, touring and recording under this name until November 1982, when Maxine married and went to live in the USA. In the early years they used an ad hoc backing band (with the exception of pianist Stephen Thompson, who started out with them when he was just eleven years old) but a huge turnover of both choir and band members has brought them to a present state of readiness and discipline famed throughout the West Midlands and further afield.

They were guests of the Church of God European Youth Convention twice – in Germany and the Netherlands in May 1979 and August 1981, respectively. They took on a spectacular 1982 US tour, appearing in front of 39,000 people at the Church of God General Assemblies in Kansas City as well as touring through North Carolina, Cleveland, Tennessee, Georgia, New York and Florida over a five-week period.

Out of the original twenty-six, only three remain, including Paulette Harley who directs the group. With membership now drawn from many New

*Birmingham's Majestic Singers*

Testament churches in the Midlands (and one or two from outside the denomination) the Majestics have a decade of gospel singing behind them and manager Justin Lewis confidently expects 'to continue in this same groove for as long as the Lord allows.'

The reputation of Birmingham's Highgate Choir is for great vocal strength out of comparatively few voices. Originally called the Balsall Heath District Youth Group, they were only fifteen strong when they moved with the New Testament Church of God to new premises in Oughton Road, Highgate about five years ago. Pam MacIntyre, director of the choir, is the daughter of the church's national overseer, Rev Jeremiah MacIntyre. 'My family are all very musical. My Dad plays saxophone, trumpet, piano and guitar and I worked with my first choir in Clapton when I was 14.' The first concert for the Highgate Choir was in March 1979 at the Friends Meeting House on Moseley Road in Birmingham and they've slowly risen to national prominence among gospel choirs for songs like *What A Mighty God* and their adaptations of *Calvary* and *Glory To His Name* out of the New Testament Church of God hymnal.

Strictly denominational gospel choirs like the Highgate, the Majestics, COGIC and the Merrybells have been the rule for so long that maybe it was only right that this traditional style beat the newer model into the media spotlight by a whisker. Outside the black churches, the very first inkling for most people that a gospel explosion was primed and ready to blow, came with the extravagantly named Inspirational Choir of the Pentecostal First Born Church of the Living God...

John Francis, choir director/organist/singer/evangelist is short on years as well as inches, but makes up for it with a wealth of talent and experience. His father is the Bishop of the church and he's been immersed in its musical culture right from birth. In his early teens he made an important trip to the USA where he was greatly influenced by Douglas Miller – a leading COGIC choir trainer, evangelistic singer and close associate of Mattie Moss Clark. Bringing Miller's thunderous brand of traditional gospel back to the North London church in Islington's White Lion Street, John Francis was all fired up to make it happen here. 'When I was in America, I was really inspired by a lot of things. It made me sick of England and the way it was: England's churches, England's choirs. We were not striving for the same things as the Americans. I felt within myself that I could change that. So I came home determined to start a choir. So we got going, we sang, but nothing compared to what we do nowadays because this time, I've got a goal, an aim. When we first started . . . it really came initially as a branch of a united choir. The united choir became difficult to cope with because some of us couldn't make it. Those of us who could, eventually formed this inspirational choir. We began to do a few concerts and it began to come together.'

The tale has often been told of how they came to enter the pop arena in 1982 by the back door, appearing first on the Channel Four TV programme *Black on Black*. 'They had a gospel competition going,' explained John. 'We came second and thought that was it. But one day I came home and my sister said, "Guess who telephoned?" It was a guy from the pop group Madness. They wanted us to back them on a song. I said "no" straight away! I was really against it, at first. But my sister persuaded me that I should wait until I heard the song.' When the demo of *Wings Of A Dove* arrived, John found no offence in the lyrics and gave the go-ahead. 'The next thing I knew, we were in a studio starting a recording and the song got to number two in the national charts. From there we went and asked the record company whether they'd be interested in signing us up to do something on our own . . . and before we knew it, we were back in the studio.'

Stiff Records, characteristically, spotted a novelty with enormous media potential and they exploited it for all they were worth. A five-track mini-album of traditional gospel, including a boisterous version of *Do Not Pass Me By*, was expertly crafted by pop producers Alan Winstanley and Clive Langer out of the choir's enthusiastic but ragged ensemble singing. *Clean Heart* won't finally go down as one of the great artistic triumphs of gospel music, but it was quite perfect for the time, picking up massive radio airplay and prime TV exposure, and putting British gospel in front of a mass audience for the very first time.

The effect of the pop liaisons on the little church in Islington was devastating. 'The deejays kept going on about the choir. So what happened then, Sunday, when we came to church, we had a big discussion and our own church wasn't too happy about it. People were saying it was a disgrace to gospel. The criticism, I tell you, was getting deep . . . The phone calls and letters that I had and anonymous callers all claiming that we were a disgrace to the church and that kind of thing.'

The 'most important development in the black community at the moment' was well and truly under way – and so was the backlash to it.

*The present COGIC Mass Choir* (left) *and the Inspirational Choir*

Patrick Friday

Hot on the heels of the Inspirational Choir – in fact some way ahead of it in a strict chronological sense – came the most revolutionary collection of singers ever to emerge from Britain's black churches. The vision of a choir drawn, not from one denomination, but from churches right across the pentecostal spectrum, had been received by more than a few key figures in the gospel movement. With Rev Bazil Meade parted from Kainos and restricted to the Latter Rain choir, he had become the man many were looking to for a kind of leadership. When his Latter Rain choir met up with Delroy Powell and the New Testament Assembly choir at a programme in St Matthew's Church in Brixton, the spiritual sparks flew and the flame was lit. 'Both choirs happened to be singing there and spontaneously joined together for one song. Afterwards we met up and discussed the idea of a mass choir with young people from all the churches in London,' says Bazil, with Delroy adding, 'We'd had the idea for some time really but what we were lacking was someone mature and experienced enough to co-ordinate it and that was where Rev Meade came in.'

The first meeting of the London Community Gospel Choir took place in August 1982 and plans were laid for a debut concert in December, postpo-

ned eventually to May 14th of the next year. However, an impromptu show of the merger had already been forced through the *Black on Black* TV programme when they appeared in form, but not in name, on the Christmas edition. The debut proper, at Kensington Temple, was a spectacular affair. A queue of people who couldn't get in stretched down the road and inside it was standing room only. The atmosphere was electric as the sixty-five members of the choir – women in powder blue suits, men in navy blue – filed on stage and proved from the very first note of *Have Thine Own Way Lord*, that history was being made. With members drawn from thirty-two different churches around London, this was as much an ecumenical venture as a musical one and the massed young voices in kaleidoscopic harmony were also witnessing to a radical Christian unity – as they put it in their slogan 'Out of Many, One Voice'.

It was an unprecedented challenge thrown out by the youth to the leadership and predictably, it was not universally welcomed by certain pastors, concerned more with sectarian empire-building than the movement of God's people. 'It seemed to me,' said Bazil, 'that some ministers had the attitude that if anything was going to happen, it had to come directly from their church or they wouldn't back it. It's very negative and narrow and it just isn't a Christian attitude. It doesn't matter how much a minister may preach fire and brimstone from the pulpit, if he doesn't set a Christian example of conduct and behaviour then it's a waste of time. We're not trying to form a separate church and we're not trying to take young people away from other churches. In fact what we're trying to do is help train them musically . . . In the end it will enrich the churches – not empty them.'

Even Rev Meade's own church – the Latter Rain Outpouring Revival – was drawing back from the implications of the choir, perceiving it as a threat rather than an opportunity. Since they were at the same time providing a rehearsal base for LCGC, a crisis point was soon reached and the whole operation (Bazil Meade and Lawrence Johnson included) was put out in the cold. It was a symbolism of sorts: 'The time has come,' declared Bazil Meade, 'to take the music out of church buildings. This is a music of faith. We want to make people reflect on the better part of their nature, and promote a positive image of black youth and show that we are making a practical and purposeful contribution to the community.'

With a new base at Caribbean House, the community centre run by Ashton Gibson, the London Community Gospel Choir began to organise in earnest. 'Our initial members were handpicked,' explains choirmaster Lawrence Johnson. 'Now we needed a sifting out process. We devised a recruitment procedure that included an application form with details such as reasons for wanting to join LCGC and with references from their pastors or youth leaders; an age limit of sixteen years; an audition for voice quality, range and ability to harmonise. After all that, the new recruit is on probation for eight weeks. Recently we have introduced an interview by our Spiritual Advisor who notes the recruit's depth of commitment to Christ. Of course we cannot forget the membership fee of £5.00 per annum. This is no joke choir. It wasn't created to start a new trend of community mass choirs. LCGC is a ministry. We are out here to preach the good news of Jesus Christ wherever it is needed – in the youth clubs, prisons, concert halls, churches, hospitals.'

With a membership of more than a hundred singers and musicians by 1984, LCGC evolved strict codes of behaviour to prevent disputes from within and allay suspicions from without. 'We do not encourage any of the young people to turn away from their churches,' said their spiritual advisor Dennis Scotland. 'LCGC has the policy of "Church first, LCGC second". What we do encourage is a healthy questioning of the Christian commitment because we are on serious business. We cannot have weak Christians or hangers-on here. LCGC are here to help weak Christians grow, but not to harbour them.'

Dress is modest but stylish, in the manner of most young black churchgoers, and with the minimum of adornment. Internecine disputes are frowned upon. 'The choir members do not squabble over the differences in their local church doctrine but rather we concentrate on exalting the one person we agree on, Jesus Christ, as Redeemer and Saviour,' says Bazil. They have non-singing members who have formed themselves into the PRAY (Prayer, Rehabilitation and Action for Youth) Team, which goes into prisons and borstals every month. PRAY leader Primrose Bartley: 'Our aim is not just to sing to the inmates but we are developing a programme whereby we can help them find accommodation and jobs when they start afresh.' Gospel song never had so great a vision of spiritual resurgence, outreaching beyond the musical moment to address the whole human condition and the caring functions are just as evident within the choir. As one member, Veronica Joseph, put it: 'We are one big family and Rev is our Dad. There are arguments as well as times of joy. LCGC is more than a choir; Wednesday nights are the climax to our week. After rehearsals the members could stand outside for another hour, late though it may be, just chatting.'

The purpose and the message are deadly serious, but the music of LCGC is all joy. In making the point that they exist for reasons apart from music, it's worth remembering that they are also the most progressive and talented outfit so far in Britain. Their many TV appearances have not really done them justice, nor it must be said, have their recordings which seem to pander to prevailing mass tastes rather than communicate the essence of the choir. But live, when the sound is right and the spirit descends on them, LCGC are an unforgettable experience. The mass of young voices have been welded into a wall of harmony that punches at you like a multi-tracked brass section. The band, led by Wayne Wilson and Howard Francis, are quietly and solidly brilliant – the elite of gospel musicians, serving the whole with a minimum of

*Rev Bazil Meade* (above) – *founder and leader of the London Community Gospel Choir* (below)

individual glory. And the seemingly endless stream of remarkable soloists – Lavine Hudson, Patricia Knight, Paul Johnson, Pearl Sinclair, Donna Johnson, David Daniel, Lawrence Johnson, Judith Bennett and the gritty voice of Rev Bazil Meade himself, holding it all together on a wing and a prayer. This is a highly disciplined piece of human machinery that is nevertheless divinely inspired and therefore enjoys nothing better than getting just a little bit out of control. In this sense it is, quite properly, a congregation unto itself – caring, committed, transcendent, organised and open to the movement of the Holy Spirit.

As a role model, LCGC quickly inspired a second, independent confederation of gospel singers. The Angelical Voice Choir was formed by leading COGIC choir member Simon Wallace early in 1984, bursting into an already burgeoning London gospel scene with an even greater urgency and drama. Similarly based in East London and drawing its members from many different denominations, the Angelical Voice Choir professed a more dynamic approach to gospel. 'We sing under the anointing,' said Simon, 'and we meditate as we sing so that it's like God singing through us.' The COGIC influences are evident – particularly those imparted by Mattie Moss Clark during her visits – but they are given greater scope in the new context. Anointed singers make for a compelling and dramatic live intensity but they are elevated still further by the sheer discipline of the choir under Simon's witty and manic direction. In rehearsal, as on stage, he works them with boundless energy until they follow every flailing gesture instantly. He delights in holding the sixty-five singers to long drawn-out notes while he storms up and down the stage hurling both hands at them unexpectedly for a quick, stabbing response. As he builds the drama with double stabs, then triple, then quadruple, he forces the whole thing over into double-time clapping and the place is in uproar.

But like LCGC, the Angelics (as they soon became known) match their public excitement with private commitments which dissolve any suspicions that this might be happening for frivolous motives. They pray intensively, they fast before they sing (even before rehearsals) and they often include an altar call in their programme. Sadly, they also share with LCGC the opprobrium of the more conservative elements in the churches – simply for crossing the boundaries between talk and action. Black church leaders have a great deal to say about unity, but are slower to applaud it in practice, especially when it springs from below and is no longer under their direct control. There are definite signs however that this new order is irreversible. Despite pastoral opposition that cut their number from forty to twenty-nine, the interdenominational Choir Light in the Birmingham area has been established by singer Dalton Kerr (formerly of the Remission Gospel Choir) who is 'praying that the Lord in his own time will draw others to the choir and give wisdom to the Pastors.'

As gospel music in Britain now enters into full recognition as its own category of both music and witness, one of its most interesting features is the extraordinary proliferation of exceptionally gifted female soloists. Quite why there should be so few men in comparison – Paul Johnson, John Francis, Trevor Minto, Bazil Meade, Lawrence Johnson and Tyndale Thomas are the handful who spring to mind – is a bit of a mystery, but there is little doubt that the great future lead voices in UK gospel are all likely to be female. Shirley Fenty who solos for the COGIC Youth Choir and the Angelical Voice Choir has enormous potential, as has Donna Johnson from LCGC who easily held her own, duetting with Al Green at the Albert Hall. Patricia Knight, Pearl Sinclair and Judith Bennett are other LCGC soloists with great range and control; and then there's Sarah Brown and Hilda Campbell – two of the most moving gospel vocalists who both sing with the Inspirational Choir; and Joy Grant, who suddenly appeared from among the ranks of the Angelical Voice Choir to astound with a powerful and mature delivery. Not to mention Carol Wilson's superb solo work with the Majestics and Jean Thomas, who carries the Merrybells before her like a veteran; or Sarah Jackson from the Highgate Choir; or Carol Smith, whose storming performance of *Forgiven* is legend within the COGIC Choir. Any of these, and a dozen more, could emerge as a gospel star in the American mould, and to the same kind of musical standard.

The best young voice is already more than halfway there. Sister Lavine Hudson came up through the Harmonisers and the COGIC Choir to become a jewel in LCGC's crown and a very special soloist. Blessed with a voice that mixes Randy Crawford, Deneice Williams and the young Aretha in equal measure, she nevertheless has an innocent quality that is all her own and which is, in the context of British gospel, utterly breathtaking. I first heard her in Brixton at a poorly attended concert with the New Testament Assembly Choir and was instantly hooked on the way she treated the Leon Patillo song *Flesh Of My Flesh* – infusing it with a poignancy and spiritual power that belied her shy youthfulness. Visiting Lavine a few days later to interview her for *The Voice*, it wasn't difficult to tell which of the terraced Streatham houses she lived in. She was practising in the front room, putting down piano chords and allowing her sweetly soulful voice to shimmer out over their simple progressions. Even from behind closed windows you could hear her halfway down the street.

She's one of six children of Rev Austin Hudson, a Church of God in Christ minister at their big Vauxhall branch in South London, but she was eager even then to go beyond the church limits. 'See, I was brought up in the Pentecostal church and I've been surrounded by gospel singing all my life, ever since I could hold a tambourine at the age of two. I've soaked it all up and it's my roots, but now I want to take gospel music and make it really big in England, not just in the churches.' To do it she's been working to a plan. Having won a scholarship to the prestigious Berkeley School of Music in Boston, she's spent two years away from London (ironically during the period of gospel's greatest public growth) specifically to train formally (and informally) as a gospel artist. A week or two before leaving amidst emotional farewells, Lavine was saying, 'It's very important to me that I go, so that I can really develop my voice. Here there's no one to really inspire me but in America I'll have to push myself much harder because there are just so many great singers there. But I *am* coming back – I'll be ready for England then!'

At the halfway point we brought her back for a

*Clockwise from right: Shirly Fenty with the Angelical Voice Choir; The Trumpets of Zion; Sister Lavine Hudson; The Echoes of Joy.*

four day gospel festival at the Riverside Studios and she was already transformed. The clear, resonant soprano voice was fuller, more controlled, more emotional; where she once would have stood nervously still, left fist involuntarily clenched, now she displayed a stage confidence and a professional maturity that underlined her potential to be among the very best of gospel singers. In America the churches went crazy for her, especially in Detroit where she worked closely with the Clark Sisters. People just couldn't get over this slip of a girl who talked with a London accent and sang like a Chicago veteran, and inevitably the pressure is on her to remain on that side of the Atlantic. Some big offers have been made – to sing commercial – but she turns all those down flat: 'I tell you this, I'll always stay with gospel – it's harder, it's stronger and it's more important. You need real soul to sing gospel.' The speculation over here has been that she will end up as part of the contemporary American gospel scene with all the massive opportunities it offers her, rather than return to the rigours and problems of her original mission in England. She won't find it an easy decision to make, but deep down I have a strong feeling that Lavine Hudson will be back where she's most needed.

But it's not just solo voices that are coming under heavy female domination. The pick of the vocal groups in Britain are all fronted by women too. The Echoes of Joy from the Bibleway Church in Lewisham started out as the Voices Supreme in 1977, and have been steadily building a reputation with their powerful front line of Yvonne White, Faithlyn Wallen, Monica Knight and Elaine and Mary Bent. The Escoffery Sisters from Streatham – Sharon, Sandra and Marcia – are a second generation Adventist group (father George was a bass voice for the Golden Chords) who are following their own path into a kind of gospel/jazz vocal fusion, which could well blossom into something very special. All eyes in recent years however have been on an amazing quartet of young women called the Trumpets of Zion, all four possessing voices of incredible power especially considering their range of ages from fifteen to twenty-one. Originally they came together at the Church of God (Pentecostal)

in Southall, where Rev Lemuel Crossfield is the founder and general overseer. Rev Crossfield's daughter Monica and her cousin Winsome Thomas, from the Slough branch of the church (pastored by Rev U. T. Thomas), teamed up as a duet first of all, performing hymns at church services. Later, the two girls decided to form a proper gospel group, enlisting the aid of Winsome's sister Dawn and her two brothers Tony and Ken. Not to be outdone, Monica Crossfield persuaded *her* sister Pauline and brother Lloyd to come in and make it a real two-family affair . . . the sisters out front with their tremendous vocal power, the brothers supporting with keyboards, bass and drums.

Together they make a great and joyful sound that has sometimes been compared to the Clark Sisters, and in fact all seven Trumpets of Zion got involved in the unique gospel music workshop run by the Sisters at the Tooting NTA. It was clearly a great influence on them, both musically – they do several of the best Clarks' songs in their programme – and spiritually, with the formidable Mother Mattie Moss Clark hammering home the message that gospel singing must be spiritually grounded or it will have no substance. 'It's something that we knew before, but Mother Mattie really encouraged us further with the ministry of our singing,' says Monica Crossfield, 'but please, we're not trying to copy the Clark Sisters at all and though we do some of their songs, we have started writing our own.'

Monica has very clear ideas on the purpose of gospel music and the upsurge of interest in it: 'We'd like to see gospel spread in the right and proper way. Already the ministry of gospel music in this country is being mis-interpreted as something to dance to, just like ordinary dance music, and the message of Jesus Christ in gospel is not being presented fully. What's really important to us is that the spirit of God is manifested through what we do. As gospel singers we can't really predict what this means in a performance. We don't pre-plan what we do. Sometimes we might give our testimony, other times according to how the Spirit leads us, so that our communication with the people may be blessed.'

The Trumpets of Zion (Monica chose the name because 'I think of our voices being powerful like trumpets') are now in the forefront of the new generation of UK gospel artists, taking inspiration from the great American names but turning it into a thoroughly British style of ministry. Using the major secular record companies to reach a mass audience (the Trumpets, like LCGC, were snapped up by Island Records) a decisive breakthrough seems inevitable for gospel in Britain. It's been predicted before of course but there is an upsurge now that is entirely new and, amongst the women singers at least, there are now the vocal resources to carry it through. Even more importantly, there is now an outpouring of pentecostal fervour among black British youth that is finding its expression through gospel music. It may still be an obscure phenomenon but so was Rastafarianism before Bob Marley. As Ken Johnson, an indefatigable promoter of gospel through his Miracle Music business, puts it, 'Gospel music is firmly established in the community. The standard of music is now so high that secular companies cannot fail to see its appeal to all audiences, both Christian and non-Christian alike.' Of the ever multiplying number of new groups and singers he says, 'It isn't easy for them, but with conscientious leadership they will not go astray.'

Gospel music in Britain is only now just starting to come into its own as a popular culture in the true sense. The phenomenon of gospel as a media spectacle however shouldn't obscure the fact of it as a huge liturgical revival within the black churches, creating an entirely new body of religious song. The influence of American gospel is self-evident, but the new British sound springs from congregational worship and draws just as much upon the cultural diversity of the ordinary worshipper. 'If you go to a church in Dalston,' says Bazil Meade, 'where a lot of the people come from Montserrat and Barbados, you'll hear a definite calypso feel to the way they sing. Another church will have a ska or reggae feel. There's a church in Lewisham where the congregation is incredibly *rootsy*. Now that to me – the culture of the people – is what is going to bring about a British gospel sound.'

As this groundswell of cultural power grows, we shall not be hearing only the sound of music, however moving and thrilling it may be. Coming up from the bottom rung, this is a generation of black Christians who are uniquely placed to be a living witness to all the sorrow, brutality and corruption in the wider society. When gospel singers open their mouths to 'make a joyful noise unto the Lord' they sing out of an experience of salvation but they also sing out of an experience of being cheated and downgraded as all black people have been. White Christians tend to sing and speak from the other side of the fence, with their vision impaired. White churches have for so long been in a state of compromise with the sin of privilege, of violence, of misogyny, of racism, that they are unable to perform the works of prophecy.

The black churches are chosen now to be that prophetic witness. Whether or not the world cares to listen, they speak a righteous word and they sing a hopeful song. It's still good news in bad times.

# Index